U.S.–Taiwan Relations

U.S.–Taiwan Relations

Will China's Challenge Lead to a Crisis?

Ryan Hass, Bonnie Glaser, and Richard Bush

BROOKINGS INSTITUTION PRESS
Washington, D.C.

Published by Brookings Institution Press
1775 Massachusetts Avenue, NW
Washington, DC 20036
www.brookings.edu/bipress

Co-published by Rowman & Littlefield
An imprint of The Rowman & Littlefield Publishing Group, Inc.
4501 Forbes Boulevard, Suite 200, Lanham, Maryland 20706
www.rowman.com

86-90 Paul Street, London EC2A 4NE

The Brookings Institution is a nonprofit organization devoted to research, education, and
publication on important issues of domestic and foreign policy. Its principal purpose is to
bring the highest quality independent research and analysis to bear on current and emerging
policy problems.

British Library Cataloguing in Publication Information Available

Library of Congress Cataloging-in-Publication Data Available

ISBN 978-0-8157-4034-6 (cloth)
ISBN 978-0-8157-3999-9 (paperback)
ISBN 978-1-8157-4000-1 (electronic)

∞™ The paper used in this publication meets the minimum requirements of American
National Standard for Information Sciences—Permanence of Paper for Printed Library
Materials, ANSI/NISO Z39.48-1992.

Contents

Introduction

The U.S. relationship with Taiwan is unlike any other relationship in the world. Officials in Washington and Taipei are in constant communication. They coordinate on virtually every issue. The United States is acutely sensitive to threats to Taiwan's security, given Washington's determination both to protect the people of Taiwan from forceful annexation and to demonstrate the credibility of America's security commitments. America trades more with Taiwan on an annual basis than it does with France or India. Washington also recognizes the critical role Taiwan occupies in global supply chains. When U.S. automakers struggle to source components to build cars, senior officials in the White House call their friends in Taiwan to seek help ramping up production of key components. In other words, the U.S.–Taiwan relationship is deep, close, and consequential.

It also is unofficial.

Neither side has an ambassador or an embassy in the other's capital. Taiwan's diplomatic facilities in the United States are not permitted to fly Taiwan's flag. U.S. policy precludes Taiwan's top elected officials from visiting Washington, D.C., just as it also limits the level of American officials who visit Taiwan. There is no alliance or mutual defense treaty between both sides. And when U.S. officials misspeak and refer to Taiwan as a "country," it creates diplomatic tremors in Asia.

For the past four decades, the United States has maintained official relations with the People's Republic of China (PRC) and unofficial relations with Taiwan. This has required U.S. officials to maintain Talmudic precision in how they conduct relations to preserve cross-Strait stability, productive unofficial relations with Taipei, and functional official relations with Beijing.

Since its founding in 1949, the PRC has claimed Taiwan as a part of China's sovereign territory. Chinese leaders have faulted the PRC's weakness at the time of its founding as the cause for Taiwan's continuing separation from the mainland. As

China has gained strength on the world stage, many in Beijing expect that it also must make progress toward achieving unification of Taiwan with the mainland. President Xi Jinping refers to unification of Taiwan as a historic mission. The Chinese state is investing in military and other capabilities to put weight behind Xi's words.

For many years, a small group of U.S. officials and outside experts bore responsibility for ensuring America's approach to Taiwan was properly calibrated to serve U.S. interests. As time has passed and the stakes of U.S.-Taiwan relations have grown, policy decisions increasingly are being made by higher-level officials who do not have subject-matter expertise. This elevation in the level of policy attention on Taiwan has increased risk of consequential errors, as decisions increasingly are being made by officials who have less time to master the subtleties of Taiwan policy and are less aware of how departures from past practices for managing issues can create unintended international incidents.

At the same time, as Taiwan has become a consolidated democracy under threat from an increasingly assertive China, Taiwan policy has become more politically salient in Congress and with the public. Outside of government, the circle of commentators on Taiwan has broadened considerably. Now, discussions over how America should support Taiwan are a common feature of public debates about America's role in the world.

This book is designed to meet the moment by offering insight into several foundational questions of U.S.-Taiwan relations, including:

- How did the U.S.-Taiwan relationship arrive at its current point?
- How is China's growing national power and its determination to unify Taiwan with China impacting U.S.-Taiwan relations?
- Has the U.S.-Taiwan relationship outgrown its former framework for managing unofficial relations?
- What interests should guide America's approach to Taiwan?
- Where is the U.S.-Taiwan relationship headed?
- Is war between the United States and China over Taiwan inevitable?

EVALUATING THE CHALLENGE

Viewed comprehensively, the history of U.S.-Taiwan relations, and of the U.S.-China-Taiwan triangle, has been marked by a series of ebbs and flows. These relationships have not developed along a linear path. Actions by one side have prompted adjustments by the other sides.

In recent decades, several broad trend lines have emerged. First, U.S.-Taiwan relations have become deeper and broader in scope. This trend has persisted through periods of cross-Strait tension and cooperation, and also through ups and downs in U.S.-China relations. This trend has been driven foremost by Washington's and

Taipei's judgment that deeper, broader, stronger ties serve each side's respective interests. There has been an argument in Washington for some time that Taiwan could be a useful card for the United States to play against China by, for example, strengthening relations with Taiwan to impose costs on China for problematic behavior elsewhere (e.g., Hong Kong, South China Sea). Except for the 2017–2020 time frame, this view has been relegated to the fringes of foreign policy thinking, appeared occasionally in nonbinding congressional legislation, and has not guided official policy. Rather, U.S. decisions on deepening relations with Taiwan were driven primarily by the affirmative logic of pursuing benefits for the American people and remaining true to American values.

Second, China's national power has risen considerably, enabling Beijing both to sharpen its military tools and to expand its nonmilitary options for intensifying pressure on Taiwan. China's rise has also been accompanied by surging nationalism inside China and a more forceful pursuit of its interests outside of China. Changes in China have not stimulated a comparable response in Taipei to ramp up defense spending and sharpen doctrine for protecting Taiwan.

Third, China's entreaties to the Taiwan people[1] to unify with the mainland have experienced diminishing purchase. Taiwan's transition to democracy in the early 1990s gave Taiwan's people a say in the conduct of cross-Strait relations. Beijing's demolition of the "one country, two systems" model in Hong Kong in 2019 poisoned public attitudes in Taiwan toward applying a similar model to govern cross-Strait relations.

This confluence of trends has led many analysts in Washington, Beijing, and Taipei to ask if the current stalemate in the Taiwan Strait is sustainable, and if not, whether the PRC might use military force to break it. Many experts and senior U.S. military officials have concluded that the drumbeats of war are growing louder. Such arguments about the inevitability of conflict often are grounded in one or more of the following assumptions: China's leaders have growing confidence in their capacity to prevail in a cross-Strait conflict; China's leaders sense a narrowing window to annex Taiwan before China begins to decline; President Xi's ambition and impatience will cause China to wage war for control of Taiwan before he leaves office; and capabilities equal intent—that is, as China's military capabilities grow, so too will Beijing's appetite to employ them to unify Taiwan. Some non-Taiwan experts also occasionally postulate that China may annex Taiwan to gain control over Taiwan's world-leading semiconductor fabrication plants, given China's own limitations in producing cutting-edge chips. All these arguments have gained urgency following Russia's February 2022 invasion of Ukraine. Putin's war has prompted questions of whether Ukraine's plight today represents Taiwan's fate tomorrow.

At the time of sending this manuscript to publication in February 2023, the outcome of the war in Ukraine is uncertain. Russian forces appear to have curtailed their original ambitions of forcible annexation of Ukraine to limited seizure of territory in eastern Ukraine. Ukrainian and Russian forces are engaged in a ground war of attrition. The war has underscored the unpredictability of conflict; paper comparisons of force capabilities do not determine outcomes of violent conflict. It remains too soon to determine what lessons can be drawn from the conflict for Taiwan.

It is not too soon, however, to conclude that the war in Ukraine offers a stark reminder of the real risk of conflict in the twenty-first century. Beijing's militarized reaction to then-Speaker Pelosi's August 2022 visit to Taiwan only reinforced this conclusion. The risk is further heightened when decision-making power on war-and-peace matters rests in the hands of an authoritarian leader who faces few checks and balances. At a minimum, the conflict in Ukraine should induce sobriety about the possibility of conflict in the Taiwan Strait, and about the need for the United States, Taiwan, and other partners to bolster deterrence.

Events in Ukraine also have refocused attention on the role of nuclear weapons. One of the reasons cited for America's reticence to become directly engaged in fighting in Ukraine was Russia's nuclear arsenal and concerns about Putin's willingness to contemplate employment of nuclear force. China, which currently is in a rapid nuclear buildup, certainly has taken note of the deterrent value Putin has gained from his nuclear arsenal.

The conflict in Ukraine should focus efforts in Taiwan on the need to preposition critical supplies of fuel, food, and munitions, should it ever become necessary for them to draw upon such reserves. Other lessons Taiwan's leaders usefully could draw from Ukraine's experience include the benefits of developing a robust reserve force and establishing a territorial defense force to protect assigned geographic regions in event of an attack.

At the same time, there could be risks of overlearning the lessons of Ukraine in Taiwan. Taiwan and Ukraine are both located next to a large authoritarian country that covets their territory. Beyond this, comparison between Taiwan and Ukraine quickly becomes an apples versus oranges exercise. Whereas Ukraine is geographically contiguous to Russia, Taiwan is separated from the mainland by a one-hundred-mile moat. To put this in context, the Taiwan Strait is roughly three times wider than the English Channel, which itself proved to be a formidable body of water for Allied forces to cross for D-Day during World War II. Taiwan is a thriving democracy and a beacon of liberal values in a notoriously hard neighborhood, while Ukraine is an aspiring democracy struggling with an endemic corruption challenge. Taiwan sits at the heart of global value chains and is critical to the health of the global economy in ways that Ukraine is not. The United States also maintains a policy, codified through the Taiwan Relations Act, to maintain the capacity to "resist any resort to force or other forms of coercion that would jeopardize the security, or the social or economic system, of the people on Taiwan." No similar legal or policy instrument exists for Ukraine to guide America's response to threats to peace there.

In other words, while Russia's invasion of Ukraine is tragic and reprehensible, it needs to be measured on its own merits and not as a foreshadowing of Taiwan's future fate. There is no way to prove or disprove future scenarios.

From our perspective, many of the arguments about the inevitability of conflict in the Taiwan Strait underweight the indivisible risks that China would face if it ever attempts to annex Taiwan by force. For example, the People's Liberation Army (PLA) could fail to assert control over Taiwan, which could imperil the Chinese Communist Party's (CCP) legitimacy at home. China's use of force could compel an anti-China coalition of countries to emerge in Asia to hedge against risk of China's further use of force in pursuit of other objectives. China also could face a generational loss of economic growth if its links to the global economy become limited as a consequence of conflict.

Assumptions about the inevitability of conflict also ignore the broad continuities in China's cross-Strait policies over recent Chinese administrations. While China's tactics toward Taiwan have evolved in recent years, its goals and strategies have not. Assumptions about the inevitability of conflict fail to account for China's nonmilitary strategies for achieving its ambitions. They also overlook the fact that Beijing still judges time on its side as its power continues to grow relative to Taiwan.

This book does not discount the serious risk of cross-Strait conflict. Rather, it seeks to right-size the risk by situating the potential for conflict within a spectrum of future plausible scenarios. As U.S. Director of National Intelligence Avril Haines testified to Congress in April 2022, China would prefer to take over Taiwan without requiring use of military force, but it also is developing capabilities to enable its military to prevail if it judges that other avenues toward achieving unification are unavailable.[2] In other words, there is a real risk of conflict in the Taiwan Strait, but there is no inevitability of conflict.

Taiwan's security is important to the United States. There is broad public support in the United States for standing up for Taiwan. This support is reflected both in bipartisan congressional sentiment and in public opinion polling, such as the Chicago Council's 2021 survey, which found that over half of Americans favor using U.S. troops to defend Taiwan if it is attacked by China.[3] Many Americans view support for Taiwan as demonstrative of America's commitment to upholding values on the world stage, including democracy and individual liberties, given that the United States and Taiwan both seek to uphold these values in the face of China's authoritarian challenges to them.

There also is broad recognition in the American strategic community that Taiwan's security is critical for peace and stability in the Indo-Pacific. Taiwan is one of the few issues that could spark a great-power conflict between the United States and China. The steadfastness of American support for Taiwan's security in the face of the threat from China serves as a source of confidence for American security partners around the world that the United States remains unflinching in support for its allies and partners.

Taiwan's security also matters greatly for America's economic competitiveness. Taiwan is central to global value chains for advanced information and communications technologies. Many of America's leading firms rely upon inputs from Taiwan manufacturers to sustain their edge at the innovation frontier.

Taiwan's security is a strategic challenge for the United States. This challenge has a military component, but it is not exclusively a military problem. At the same time as China is developing military capabilities for cross-Strait contingencies, it also is employing a strategy of coercion without violence to seek to wear down the will of the Taiwan people. This is not a hypothetical future campaign, like a military assault on Taiwan. Rather, it is an ongoing everyday reality. China is employing diplomatic, military, and economic pressure; cyber and disinformation campaigns; political interference; and united front tactics to chip away at the confidence of the people of Taiwan in their future. In many respects, the will of Taiwan's people to resist Beijing's pressure and preserve their political autonomy and democratic way of life is the center of gravity.

American policy has not yet caught up to this reality. Washington's predominant focus is on the military dimension of the challenge. There has been an explosion of op-eds, reports, and books on the mounting military crisis confronting Taiwan. Many of these pieces treat conflict in the Taiwan Strait as an inescapable future destination. Some recent writings on Taiwan argue that the aim of American strategy must be to keep Taiwan firmly situated in the American camp and to deny China from pulling Taiwan closer to its own orbit, asserting that it would be a disaster for America's strategic posture if Taiwan ever becomes integrated into China under any circumstances, peaceful or otherwise. Others assert that the United States must shift its policy to one of clarity on its intent to intervene militarily in any future conflict in the Taiwan Strait, partly to strengthen signals of resolve at a time when America's military edge vis-à-vis China is eroding. There have been calls for the United States to significantly bolster military assistance to Taiwan. Former and aspiring U.S. politicians have suggested that the United States should normalize its relationship with Taiwan and treat Taiwan as an independent country. There also has been a debate over whether the United States should pursue a strategy of deterrence by denial or deterrence by punishment to prevent China from imposing its will on Taiwan.

This book stands apart from the avalanche of recent writing that treats Taiwan as a military problem with a military solution. It argues instead that U.S. policymakers and the U.S. public whom they represent must develop a deeper understanding of the sharpest stresses on Taiwan's future and the best tools for countering them. For the United States, sustaining military deterrence is the minimum threshold, not the measure of success. China already is embarked on an aggressive, multidimensional campaign that seeks to annex Taiwan without use of force, even as Beijing continues to build up its military capabilities to preserve the option of use of force if all other approaches fail. To fixate on a future military scenario without also focusing on the campaign of coercion without violence that already is underway against Taiwan would be to do a tremendous disservice to America's interests in Asia.

The proximate goal of American strategy is not to deny Taiwan to China or to treat Taiwan as an instrument for inflicting strategic pain on China. In addition to denying agency to the Taiwan people, such approaches would only accelerate the United States and China toward a conflict that would do immeasurable harm to American interests and to the lives of Taiwan's people. Rather, the goal of American strategy is to seek to slow the spiral of escalating tensions and to keep America's strategy and policy centered on its abiding interests in preserving peace and stability in the Taiwan Strait. Doing so requires properly diagnosing the threats facing Taiwan and the range of military and nonmilitary tools available to the United States, Taiwan, and others to counter them. It also requires steady, disciplined, purposeful American statecraft.

RECOMMENDATIONS GOING FORWARD

The maintenance of peace and stability in the Taiwan Strait and the prevention of conflict have been the bedrock objectives of U.S. policy since World War II. These goals should continue to guide U.S. policy in the future. America's strategy is designed to preserve Taiwan's political autonomy, its cultural and economic dynamism, and its dignity on the world stage, without triggering conflict.

U.S. policy has not been—and should not become—an exercise in seeking to define an outcome to cross-Strait differences. Those decisions rest in Taipei and Beijing, not Washington. But America has an indispensable role to play in protecting time and space for an eventual peaceful solution to emerge that is acceptable to Taiwan's people, who are capable of expressing their preferences through democratic processes.

To keep open time and space for an eventual peaceful solution, the United States and Taiwan will need to reach a common diagnosis of China's strategy and a coordinated plan for countering it. Beijing is working along two parallel tracks in pursuit of its goal of unifying Taiwan. The first is military and the second is political. The destination of both tracks is the same—to compel Taiwan's leaders and its people that resistance is futile and that they must accept unification on Beijing's terms to avoid catastrophe.

Leaders in Washington and Taipei cannot afford to fixate on one threat at the expense of the other. While it is unknowable when—or if—Beijing ever would launch a military assault on Taiwan, Beijing already has begun moving down the political track by pursuing a campaign of coercion without violence to pressure the Taiwan people into concluding that they have no alternative to capitulating to Chinese pressure. Chinese leaders accept that such a strategy would take longer to achieve its goal, but they view this approach as holding several advantages: first, it carries less cost and risk; second, it reflects Beijing's view that people on both sides of the Strait are compatriots who share common cultural lineage; and third, it aligns with their stated goal of "peaceful unification."

Washington and Taipei must act urgently to shore up defenses against threats on both tracks. Strengthening military deterrence is necessary but insufficient to the challenges at hand. Right now, the will of the Taiwan people to protect their democratic system and political autonomy is the center of gravity for determining the future of the Taiwan Strait.

It will be a challenge for the United States to formulate an effective counter to China's persistent pressure on the people of Taiwan. There is no single agency or organization inside the U.S. government that is responsible for countering gray-zone pressure on American partners overseas. There also is no policy playbook on the shelf for supporting Taiwan against Chinese pressure. As such, the United States will need to develop a disciplined and integrated policy approach that is organized around a unifying principle—the more confident the people of Taiwan become in their future, the less vulnerable Taiwan will be to Chinese coercion.

The United States is at its best in supporting Taiwan when it is resolute, disciplined, self-assured, and steady. Such a posture instills confidence that Washington has a theory of the case for what it is doing and understands how its actions augment broader strategic objectives. Projecting such a posture requires America's top leaders to demonstrate command of long-standing policy and strategy. This attribute has been lacking to varying degrees in the Trump and Biden administrations, both of which have sent inconsistent and mixed public messages on fundamental issues with potential war and peace implications, such as whether the United States has a treaty commitment to defend Taiwan, whether the United States considers Taiwan an independent country, and whether the United States would accept a peaceful resolution of cross-Strait differences between Beijing and Taipei. This is not to suggest a false equivalence between the Trump and Biden administrations on Taiwan; the Trump administration was uniquely disruptive in its approach to cross-Strait relations. Rather, it is to observe that both administrations have been imprecise and inconsistent in their articulation of the purposes of American policy toward Taiwan.

To dampen escalatory pressure while protecting peace and stability, America's support for the people of Taiwan will need to remain within the parameters of its "one-China policy." The broad boundaries of this policy are that the United States will not reestablish diplomatic relations or a defense treaty with Taiwan. Operating within these boundaries opens space for the United States to take meaningful actions to support the top priorities of Taiwan's 23.5 million people. These include helping Taiwan enjoy dignity and respect on the world stage, remain at the cutting edge of innovation, maintain economic competitiveness, deter war, and protect the health of its people.

Washington can and must deliver visible support to Taiwan in all these priority areas. Doing so will dilute Beijing's psychological pressure on the people of Taiwan, showing that Taiwan is not isolated and vulnerable, but rather is capable of thriving and deepening its relations with the United States and other advanced societies around the world so long as it does not take measures that could precipitate conflict, such as pursuing formal independence.

Within its support for the people of Taiwan, perhaps the area calling out for the most urgent remediation is the economic and trade relationship. A glaring failure of current U.S. policy is that its economic policy is not integrated with its overall strategy of support for Taiwan. Despite the significant volume of two-way trade and the strategic stakes for the United States of Taiwan's success, the U.S. Trade Representative (USTR) Office has been institutionally opposed to negotiating greater market access for Taiwan, although there are signs of potential progress toward strengthening trade ties under the Biden administration through the U.S.-Taiwan Initiative on 21st Century Trade. Given its statutory independence, the only remedy for increasing USTR's ambition to meaningfully strengthen trade ties with Taiwan likely will be presidential and congressional pressure on USTR with Taiwan.

The contrast in American policy between strategic prioritization and economic neglect of Taiwan was brought into focus on May 23, 2022, when President Biden vowed publicly while visiting Tokyo to defend Taiwan militarily if it is attacked on the same day he announced the launch of the Indo-Pacific Economic Framework without Taiwan's participation. Given its statutory independence, the only remedy to USTR's nonstrategic orientation toward Taiwan likely will be presidential and congressional pressure on USTR to strengthen trade ties with Taiwan.

An economically strong Taiwan is foundational to national security and to reducing vulnerability to Chinese coercion. Unless the United States leads the way in committing to liberalize its trade and investment with Taiwan, it will be difficult for others to do so. Typically, other countries draft off American efforts to strengthen economic and other relations with Taiwan, rather than front-run the United States and attract Chinese punishments for setting new international precedents for Taiwan. The only two countries that have established trade agreements with Taiwan in the past decade are Singapore and New Zealand. They are the exceptions that prove the rule. They both negotiated a trade agreement with Taipei after having already done so with Beijing, and they negotiated with Taiwan with the consent of Beijing. As Asian economic integration deepens through the adoption of regional trade pacts such as the Regional Comprehensive Economic Partnership and the Comprehensive and Progressive Trans-Pacific Partnership and initiatives such as the Indo-Pacific Economic Framework, and as Taiwan finds itself on the outside of these regional initiatives, the importance for Taiwan of making progress in strengthening trade ties with partners only grows.

From a military standpoint, the United States will need to adjust its doctrine and posture in the Western Pacific to respond to China's military advances. Major surface and air platforms will continue to play a key role in visibly demonstrating American presence and resolve to deter conflict in the Taiwan Strait. In the event of conflict, however, American forces will not be able to establish air superiority or local dominance as they have in recent wars in Iraq, Afghanistan, and elsewhere, given China's overwhelming missile capabilities. As a consequence, U.S. military planners likely will need to develop innovative new ways to wage war in a highly contested environment. As an example, this contested environment may cause the United States to field large numbers of dispersed and autonomous sensors and munitions that would be difficult and costly for Chinese forces to track or counter.

There also is work that needs to be done to support Taiwan's development of doctrine and capabilities to allow it to maximize its geographic advantages. Taiwan's national security establishment has yet to coalesce around a common concept of national defense. This failure of consensus has heightened Taiwan's vulnerability, both by highlighting divisions within Taiwan and by producing inconsistent decision-making regarding what military capabilities are needed. Taiwan's scattershot approach to weapons procurement has squandered scarce resources on expensive military platforms that would add little value in conflict with China, when what is needed most is large numbers of small, affordable, highly mobile capabilities that can hold Chinese forces at risk at their point of greatest vulnerability, in Taiwan's littoral.

Beijing needs to be disabused of any belief that it could prevail quickly and easily in a cross-Strait conflict. This will require Taipei to field agile, dispersed capabilities that would allow Taiwan to wage a prolonged denial campaign against invading forces. Part of this effort will require greater judiciousness on the part of the United States in what military capabilities it makes available to Taiwan. Another element of this effort will be for Taiwan's political parties to stop seeing each other as the existential threat to the future of Taiwan and instead focus together on the looming threat one hundred miles to their west. Washington also will need to demonstrate tangibly that it is refocusing its military, diplomatic, and economic weight toward Asia and is prepared to accept risk in relations with China to resolutely defend the security of its allies and Taiwan.

At the same time, it also will be essential for Washington and its partners around the world to develop a political-economic campaign plan for responding to Chinese aggression, should it ever become necessary. While some American allies might have the capacity and willingness to contribute militarily to a cross-Strait conflict, most allies and partners likely would be reluctant to become engaged in conflict and would instead contribute economically to raising the risk and costs to China of escalating to war. The organizing focus for developing such a campaign plan would be to remind Beijing of its vulnerabilities that would be put at risk in event of conflict, in hopes that doing so would sober China's leaders to the societal disruption that a conflict would cause inside China. Beijing would need to face a credible risk to access the global financial system, the global internet, global energy flows, access to food imports, and war-critical commodities and technologies if they attack Taiwan. Beijing's going-in assumption likely would be that China has far more capacity and leverage to resist external economic pressure than Russia did, given that Russia's economy is roughly the size of Guangdong province. Having witnessed the biting international sanctions on Russia, China likely will accelerate efforts to insulate its economy from similar vulnerabilities to dependence on the outside world for the functioning of its economy and the well-being of its people. China's leaders will need to be convinced that in spite of their aggregate economic size and their efforts to reduce external dependencies, they still face real risks that likely would be systematically exploited if they ever attempted to annex Taiwan by threat or use of force.

For such deterrence to be credible, it must also be paired with an acknowledgment that the United States remains open to any peaceful resolution of cross-Strait differences that the people of Taiwan support. Absent implicit American acceptance of such a scenario, the United States and China will find themselves accelerating into an unavoidable collision. If the United States signals that it would not countenance unification under any circumstances, it likely would generate pressure on China's leaders to intensify efforts to compel unification, including potentially through use of force, to demonstrate active opposition to American efforts to keep Taiwan in its corner and apart from China. If China's leaders failed to react robustly to American efforts to dictate the range of possible outcomes for cross-Strait relations, they could face internal challenges over whether they were worthy custodians of the CCP's founding mission to reunify the Chinese nation.

This posture of American openness to a peaceful outcome puts the onus on China's leaders to appeal to the interests of Taiwan's people. If China's leaders are committed to peacefully resolving cross-Strait differences, then it is incumbent upon them to develop proposals that attract broad public support in Taiwan.

America will be capable of exercising the greatest influence over events in the Taiwan Strait if it maintains the initiative and resists fatalistic assumptions about the inevitability of conflict. There is no preset path for the future of the Taiwan Strait. Assuming current trend lines lead inextricably to war requires willful ignorance of recent history. Relations between the United States and Taiwan have constantly adapted to changing circumstances, just as cross-Strait relations have ebbed and flowed.

The U.S. government recognizes that PRC coercion of Taiwan is a threat even when it falls below the threshold of conflict. Because China's campaign of coercion without violence targets the confidence of the Taiwan people, the United States has taken countermeasures to bolster the Taiwan public's confidence in Taiwan's capacity to maintain political autonomy and prevent war. For how much longer Beijing pursues policies that drive the United States to elevate the visibility of its support for Taiwan remains an open question.

Beijing is much stronger and more capable of projecting force now than it was during previous periods of heightened cross-Strait tensions, such as in 1995–1996. At the same time, Beijing still is not immune from significant vulnerabilities, including its access to energy, technology, food, and global financial markets. Beijing still has its incentives to avoid war.

Washington, Taipei, and others will need to strengthen their deterrent against China seeking to annex Taiwan by force. But they also will need to keep an eye focused on the larger strategic picture. The prospect of war is not the only threat confronting Taiwan. The people of Taiwan also face an unyielding campaign of coercion without violence. American policy and strategy must concentrate on countering both Chinese paths in pursuit of unification to sustain stability and prevent conflict in the Taiwan Strait.

NOTES

1. The term "Taiwan people" is used in this book to describe residents of Taiwan. "Taiwanese" is a term often limited to native inhabitants of Taiwan whose ancestors came to the island before the twentieth century. They often are contrasted with "mainlanders," whose families came to Taiwan after 1945 when the Kuomintang fled to Taiwan. The historical tensions between "Taiwanese" and "mainlanders" have mellowed with time, but the distinction is still prevalent. Therefore, when discussing the population residing in Taiwan, this book will refer to "Taiwan people."

2. "China Wants to Take Taiwan Peacefully but Is Preparing Militarily—U.S. Intelligence Officials," *Reuters*, May 10, 2022, https://www.reuters.com/world/asia-pacific/china-wants-take-taiwan-peacefully-is-preparing-militarily-us-intelligence-2022-05-10/.

3. Dina Smeltz and Craig Kafura, "For First Time, Half of Americans Favor Defending Taiwan If China Invades," *The Chicago Council*, August 26, 2021, https://globalaffairs.org/research/public-opinion-survey/first-time-half-americans-favor-defending-taiwan-if-china-invades.

1

The Historical Background of the Current Conflict

Before the early 1940s, neither the United States, nor the government of the Republic of China (ROC), then led by the Chinese Nationalist Party (Kuomintang; KMT), nor the CCP, which in 1949 would establish the government of the PRC, regarded the island of Taiwan and the people who lived there as a policy priority. Since 1895, Taiwan had been a colony of the Empire of Japan. In the late 1930s, both Chiang Kai-shek, the leader of the KMT regime, and Mao Zedong, chairman of the CCP, regarded it only as a territory to be freed from Japanese colonial rule and nothing more. The American connection with the island had been tenuous at best. That would soon change, and Taiwan would become a key point of contention between the PRC and ROC governments, and the United States. Along the way, the people of Taiwan would gain agency as well. The issue would become so sensitive that in 2021, a leading subject of international media commentary would be whether and when the PRC would go to war over Taiwan.

FROM THE SEVENTEENTH CENTURY TO 1894

Taiwan is an island about one hundred miles off the southeast coast of Mainland China. Geologically, it is part of the "first island chain" of the Asia-Pacific that runs from Japan, through Taiwan, the Philippines, and south to Australia. Thus, some observers believe it is a strategically important piece of territory.[1]

For thousands of years, Taiwan was inhabited by indigenous peoples who engaged in hunting and gathering and some farming. Ethnic Chinese (ethnic Han people) from Fujian and Guangdong provinces in Mainland China began trading with people on the island in the sixteenth century. People from across the Taiwan Strait began settling on the island in the seventeenth century to engage in farming and trade. At that time, the Dutch and the Spanish had outposts in Taiwan, and a Chinese rebel group was mounting a last stand there against the new, Qing (Manchu) dynasty. But the Qing were victorious and gained control of the western side of the island, and then designated Taiwan as a prefecture of Fujian province.

Han settlement continued, and over time ethnic Chinese constituted the vast majority of the population, assimilating a good share of the indigenous peoples. Up through the eighteenth century, Taiwan society had a frontier character. Different Chinese groups fought each other and indigenous people regularly. By the nineteenth century, however, Taiwan came to look more and more like society on the mainland. Public order was gradually established. Wealthy landlords dominated their local areas, and they steered their smarter sons into the imperial examination system. Merchants in towns like Taipei, Lukang, and Tainan marketed agricultural products for export. Temples sprung up for the worship of the Chinese Buddhist, Taoist, and folk gods that the settlers had worshiped on the mainland. In the late 1800s, Qing officials tentatively began a program of modernization.

JAPAN ON TAIWAN AND CIVIL WAR IN CHINA: 1895–1941

All this changed in 1895. Japan defeated the Qing government in a war that was fought mainly over Korea. In negotiations over a peace treaty, the Meiji government demanded that China cede Taiwan and the adjacent Pescadores Islands to Japan in perpetuity. One of its motivations was to possess colonies, just like the Western powers. Taiwan thus became Japan's first colony. It happened that the lead Chinese negotiator had an American advisor, John Watson Foster, who would later become the grandfather of John Foster Dulles, the U.S. Secretary of State during most of the Eisenhower administration.

There was some resistance to the Japanese military takeover by Chinese militia units. There was even a group that declared that Taiwan should become an independent country. But Japanese troops soon ended the opposition. The Japanese military would maintain tight control over Taiwan and later deal harshly with indigenous tribes in the mountains that run down the center of the island.

Soon, however, the Japanese government undertook policies to foster social and economic development. Along with preserving public order, colonial officials introduced scientific farming, improved public health, and encouraged industries that processed agricultural goods. During the 1920s and 1930s, members of the Taiwan elite sought without much success to gain representation in the Japanese Diet (legislature) and secure greater autonomy for the governance of Taiwan. Later on, some Taiwan residents would remember with nostalgia the good parts of Japanese rule.

Meanwhile, in Mainland China, the Qing dynasty was overthrown after the 1911 Revolution and replaced by the government of the ROC in 1912. Until 1928, a series of warlords controlled that weak government, at which point the KMT took it over. Under the leadership of Generalissimo Chiang Kai-shek, the new regime undertook to strengthen political institutions and unify China. These tasks were so all-consuming that Chiang continued the policy of accommodating Japanese sovereignty over Taiwan. Trade across the Taiwan Strait resumed, and the ROC government established a consulate on the island. The United States had a limited presence in Taiwan up until World War II. American traders bought tea and camphor. Missionaries tried to convert the island's residents. The State Department established consulates in Taipei and Danshui in 1914. Generally, therefore, Taiwan was a backwater for the ROC, the United States, and the CCP (founded in 1921).

From the beginning, it should be noted, some policymakers in China and Japan believed that the island of Taiwan had strategic as well as economic value. Shi Lang, the admiral who had defeated the anti-Qing rebels in the 1680s, urged the government to bring the island under its rule, to deprive other powers of using it as a base to threaten China. One reason Japan acquired Taiwan, aside from wanting a colony, was to gain a defensive shield for southern Japan and a possible staging area for Japan's expansion.[2] This latter purpose would be demonstrated on December 8, 1941, when Japan began its attack on the Philippines, a colony of the United States, from air and naval bases in Taiwan.

In 1937, an all-out war between Japan and the ROC began on the mainland and changed the features of Japanese rule over Taiwan. There was a concerted effort by colonial officials to impose more of a Japanese identity on their Taiwanese subjects. Ethnic Chinese people were required to adopt Japanese names. Chinese folk temples were closed, and Shinto shrines took their place. Taiwanese men were drafted into the Japanese imperial army as soldiers and construction workers. Many of them would move down the Malay Peninsula on bicycles and play a major role in the capture of Singapore in February 1942. Young Taiwanese women would be enlisted and forced to be "comfort women" for Japanese troops in various places in East Asia.

PEARL HARBOR TO THE KOREAN WAR

With America's entry into the war after Pearl Harbor, the United States and the ROC became allies in the fight against Japan. To keep China in the war, Washington tried to support Chiang Kai-shek's regime as much as possible within the limits of its resources. Still, there were disagreements both within FDR's administration and between the United States and the ROC over military strategy and the level of supplies.

Taiwan did not figure militarily in the U.S. campaign to defeat Japan. Some officials had proposed seizing the island as a base from which to conduct air raids on Japan, but Roosevelt gave into Douglas MacArthur's preference for taking the Philippines instead. The U.S. Army Air Force did bomb militarily significant targets in Taiwan from late 1943 to the end of the war.

Taiwan was more salient in FDR's thinking on U.S. policy for preserving international peace and security after war's end. By late 1942, he saw a place for Taiwan in his grand design. He envisioned that the United States, United Kingdom, Union of

Soviet Socialist Republics, and China—the "four policemen"—would work together to keep the peace through threatening naval quarantines and bombing raids on countries whose arms procurements suggested preparation for aggression. He knew that Taiwan had good ports and airfields, which he thought the ROC could use to play this policing role, so it made sense to return Taiwan to China rather than establish a trusteeship under the United Nations. (Obviously, FDR greatly exaggerated the ROC's ability to play any international role after years of war.)

Roosevelt's decision, which he conveyed to his senior officials in February 1943, converged with the views of Chiang Kai-shek. In late 1942, Chiang published a manifesto titled *China's Destiny*. He argued Taiwan could serve as an "outer fortress" for the Chinese mainland, and therefore should be returned to China after the war.[3] Roosevelt's decision and Chiang's ambition were confirmed in the Cairo and Tehran Conferences of allied leaders in late 1943.

With the end of World War II, a civil war between Chiang's KMT regime and Mao's Communists for control of the country seemed imminent. President Harry Truman sought to forestall that outcome by appointing General George Marshall as a mediator between the two Chinese antagonists. Marshall made a good try but soon concluded that the mistrust between them was too great. Truman recalled him in early 1947 and civil war began in earnest. The United States provided economic and military aid to the ROC government.

Meanwhile, in Taiwan, it was the forces of the ROC that accepted the surrender of Japanese forces, since Washington anticipated that a postwar peace treaty would take Taiwan from Japan and transfer it to China. The island's new KMT rulers proceeded to seize property and goods, engage in corruption, and quickly wear out their welcome with the native Taiwanese (those whose ancestors had immigrated earlier). An island-wide rebellion broke out in late February 1947 and was harshly suppressed. Quietly, the United States counseled Chiang to improve KMT governance in Taiwan.

By the latter half of 1949, the Communists were victorious on the mainland and Mao declared the establishment of the PRC on October 1. Chiang moved his government and army to Taiwan, whose population increased to around eight million, 85 percent of which were native Taiwanese and 15 percent were so-called mainlanders. Chiang had already declared emergency rule and suspended democratic features of the ROC constitution, and the resulting authoritarian system lasted for the next four decades. This regime not only deprived citizens of their civil and political rights but also sought to instill a conservative Chinese consciousness to replace the effects of half a century of Japanese rule.

THE KOREAN WAR TO NORMALIZATION OF U.S.-PRC RELATIONS

In early 1950, the policy conundrum facing the Truman administration was whether to defend Taiwan against a PRC attack to seize Taiwan, which seemed imminent. Chiang Kai-shek's supporters in Congress urged Truman to fortify Taiwan, and the administration certainly understood the island's strategic value to the United States. But it lacked the military resources to help the ROC military fend off an attack, given the tense situation in Europe. Moreover, it believed that what the KMT regime lacked was not military resources but the ability and will to use them effectively.

After extensive policy debates, the Truman administration signaled in early 1950 that it would not defend Taiwan against a military attack. It also indicated that Taiwan was a part of the state the international community recognizes as China. But the United States quickly reversed itself when North Korea invaded South Korea in June. Immediately, Washington moved to block any PRC invasion of Taiwan. It also announced that "the future status of Formosa [Taiwan] must await the restoration of the security in the Pacific, a peace settlement with Japan, or consideration of the United Nations."[4] Legally speaking, the administration no longer regarded Taiwan as a part of China. Practically, it began to restore and increase military support to the ROC military.

At this point, the conflict between Chiang's KMT and Mao's CCP changed. Up until 1949, it had been first and foremost a military conflict. After Mao's victory, there was a shift to a part-military, part-political struggle.

As to the military aspect, Taiwan benefited from the containment strategy that the United States adopted to block the spread of communism in Asia. Washington's tools were alliances with the countries of the first island chain, including Taiwan, and the forward deployment of U.S. troops to its new allies in return for a pledge to defend them in the event of attack. Washington and Taipei negotiated their mutual defense treaty in late 1954, not long after the PRC had shelled Jinmen and Mazu, ROC-controlled islands off the coast of Fujian province. The Senate ratified the treaty in early 1955.

The U.S.-ROC alliance was not without problems. Chiang Kai-shek's declared goal was to "return to the Mainland," which the Eisenhower administration judged to be reckless and futile. It only agreed to the mutual defense treaty after Taipei agreed to consult before undertaking any major military action against the mainland. The PRC again tested U.S. resolve in August 1958, with extensive shelling of Jinmen. As it had in 1958, the U.S. Navy assisted Taiwan vessels in resupplying Jinmen, and the crisis soon passed. But, as in 1954, the Eisenhower administration worried that the crisis might escalate to the point of using nuclear weapons to prevent the fall of the ROC's offshore islands, which in turn would trigger a Soviet use of nuclear weapons to defend its PRC ally. Such an outcome was hardly commensurate with the minimal strategic value of those. Then, in 1962, the Kennedy administration had to rein in Chiang, who appeared to be mobilizing troops to take advantage of the economic and political disruptions on the mainland that Mao's Great Leap Forward campaign had created.

Meanwhile, with Washington's encouragement, Taiwan leaders were shifting their economic strategy. Up until around 1960, import-substitution had been the government's approach, which produced only sluggish growth. Economic technocrats argued successfully that export-led growth was more appropriate for a country with Taiwan's factor endowments. As the prospect of "Mainland recovery" became remote, strengthening Taiwan itself, especially economically, made more sense. Moreover, the United States and Japan were willing to support such a shift. So, the government changed its policies on foreign trade and built infrastructure to support the new policy (e.g., a good education system, export processing zones, and institutions to facilitate innovation, such as the Industrial Technology Research Institute and science parks). Both Taiwanese and mainlanders with an entrepreneurial spirit created countless small and medium enterprises to exploit product niches for markets in other countries, constantly shifting to new, higher-tech products as comparative advantage and product demand required. The result was growing prosperity and social stability. Politically, the KMT began in 1969 to modestly reduce the harsh character of its regime. The key steps at this time were to coopt loyal Taiwanese into the mainlander-dominated system; expand the number of legislators elected from Taiwan to take account of population growth; and use local-level elections as barometers to gauge how much voters approved the performance of their local officials.[5]

The political side of the Beijing-Taipei struggle concerned which government—the ROC or the PRC—would represent China in the international system and which would have diplomatic relations with third parties. The primary battleground was the United Nations, where successive U.S. administrations worked hard to block the PRC's claim on China's seat. They used procedural gambits and lobbied member-states not to seat the PRC in place of the ROC. That became more and more difficult as former European colonies became independent and tended to support the PRC's cause. The contest was paused during the worst years of Mao's Cultural Revolution but resumed thereafter and the PRC came closer to victory. As an alternative, the United States proposed dual representation of both the PRC and the ROC, but the idea came too late. In October 1971, the PRC became the sole representative of China in the United Nations. Simultaneously, a growing majority of countries established diplomatic relations with Beijing.

The most severe blow to Taiwan in its political battle with the PRC was the decision of Richard Nixon in the early 1970s to "play the China card" and begin a rapprochement with Beijing. One reason was to strengthen the U.S. position against Moscow, but Taiwan naturally feared that Washington would sacrifice its interests for the sake of a new relationship with the ROC's sworn enemy. And with good reason. During Nixon's historic visit to Beijing in February 1972, he told Chinese leaders that he intended to "normalize" relations with the PRC during his second term, shifting U.S. recognition and diplomatic relations from Taipei to Beijing.

The Watergate scandal and Nixon's resulting need to retain the support of Taiwan's closest friends in Congress forced him to put off normalization. But the Carter administration, which took power in 1977, finished what Nixon started. The anti-Soviet motivation was still at play. Also, there were aspirations that American business could benefit from Deng Xiaoping's policy initiative of economic reform and opening to the global economy (Deng in effect was copying the secret of Taiwan's economic success). Carter accepted Deng's three conditions for normalization: terminating diplomatic relations with the ROC, ending the mutual defense treaty, and withdrawing U.S. military installations and personnel from Taiwan.

In the Normalization Communiqué of December 15/16, 1978, the United States recognized the government of the PRC as the sole legal government of China and agreed to establish diplomatic relations on January 1, 1979.[6] Ambassadors would be exchanged on March 1, 1979. It announced that its relations with Taiwan would be on an unofficial basis. On the important question of Taiwan's legal status, the English version of the communiqué only "*acknowledged* the Chinese position that . . . Taiwan is a part of China." That is, it did not adopt that position as its own. The Chinese version used the word "recognized," but the Carter administration insisted that the English version was authoritative.[7]

The Carter administration had wanted to include within the text of the communiqué the principle that differences between the two sides of the Taiwan Strait should be resolved peacefully. Beijing rejected that, and so that principle was included in an official, unilateral U.S. statement released simultaneously with the communiqué. For its part, Beijing released its statement which reiterated its position that the Taiwan issue was an internal affair (the implication that how the matter was resolved was its own business).

At the time, it was also revealed that the Carter administration had insisted on continuing arms sales to Taiwan, to deter a military attack by China. The PRC took the position that it strenuously opposed such a policy and reserved the right to revisit the issue at a later time.

With the normalization of U.S.-China relations, and the conclusion of a China-Japan peace treaty two months before, Taiwan had lost its battle with Beijing for dominance within the international system. If the United States had apparently abandoned Taiwan, what hope did it have? Understandably, anxiety about the future spread throughout the island. Courageous Taiwanese opponents of the KMT regime, known as "people outside the [ruling] party" (*dangwai renshi*) began organizing to criticize its diplomatic failures. This mobilization would lead to a large rally in the southern port city of Kaohsiung in December 1979, at which *agents provocateurs* connected to the security services caused the protest to turn violent, which in turn gave the security services the excuse they needed to arrest the leaders of the *dangwai*.

With their diplomatic victory, PRC leaders hoped that Taiwan had been so weakened that the time had come to end the ROC's existence and bring about unification. So, they extended something of an olive branch to Taiwan. On January 1, 1979, the standing committee of the National People's Congress (NPC; the PRC legislature) conveyed a "letter to Taiwan compatriots." It emphasized what the two sides of the Strait had in common and appealed for rapid movement toward unification. It promised to "take current [Taiwan] realities into account" and to "respect the status quo and "respect the opinion of people of all walks of life." It also stressed that the PRC government and the KMT regime both opposed an independent Taiwan. But the key assertion was that time was on the PRC's side, and Taiwan leaders should accept that trend.

By its own logic, Beijing's hopes for rapid progress were not unreasonable. Taiwan's leaders were mainlanders who saw themselves as Chinese patriots. Their government's nominal goal was unification, and their dominance of an authoritarian system would allow them to impose whatever agreement they reached with the PRC. Chiang Ching-kuo (Chiang Kai-shek's son and successor since 1978) was in failing health and, in Beijing's eyes, might be convinced to make one last achievement for the Chinese nation. Moreover, Deng's economic reform policies created opportunities for Taiwan companies, if the ROC government would lift restrictions on doing business with the mainland. In line with the CCP's "united front" approach, those businessmen could become a pro-PRC force within the Taiwan political system. And it was a long-standing principle of Chinese statecraft that one way to subdue an adversary was to weaken or destroy its alliances.

Yet the power advantage that PRC leaders believed they had gained over Taiwan was gradually diluted. The first apparent reversal came quickly. It happened that the Carter administration required congressional legislation to establish an institutional mechanism to conduct future, substantive relations with Taipei in the absence of diplomatic relations. In the Taiwan Relations Act (TRA), Congress did approve the creation of the American Institute in Taiwan (AIT), whose Taipei office became America's de facto embassy. But it also chose to amend the administration's draft bill to include sections concerning Taiwan's security.

Among other things, the TRA declared that it was U.S. policy "to consider any effort to determine the future of Taiwan by other than peaceful means, including by boycotts or embargoes, a threat to the peace and security of the Western Pacific area and of grave concern to the United States," and that the Pentagon should "maintain the capacity of the United States to resist any resort to force or other forms of coercion that would jeopardize the security, or the social or economic system, of the people on Taiwan."[8]

More significantly, the TRA authorized the administration to continue providing Taiwan with "defense articles and services" to ensure that the island had a "sufficient self-defense capability." It directed the president to report to Congress any threat to Taiwan's security and decreed that the executive and the legislature should determine the appropriate response to that threat, "in accordance with constitutional processes."

The TRA, which President Carter signed in mid-April 1979, buoyed the hopes of Taiwan's leaders and the people of the island, as well as Taiwan's supporters in the United States. It angered the PRC government, which objected to the interference of Congress in "China's internal affairs" through domestic legislation. Yet neither the hopes nor the anger was entirely justified. Much of the TRA's language relevant to Taiwan's security did not contravene existing presidential authority. Even the seemingly exceptional powers granted to Congress in the clauses that spoke to arms sales and the U.S. response to PRC aggression against Taiwan were cleverly negated by subtle references to the president's existing legislative and constitutional powers. For example, Congress seemed to assert for itself a joint role in deciding which weapons systems Washington should transfer to the Taiwan military. But a clause at the end of the relevant provision ("in accordance with procedures established by law") was interpreted by administration lawyers to mean that, as before, Congress played its role only at the end of the decision process. What made the TRA truly important was the strong *political* support for Taiwan of Congress and, by extension, the American people. The question for the future was how future presidents would exercise their powers in light of that support.

DUELING OVER UNIFICATION AND INDEPENDENCE

Now that Beijing had cut Taiwan's official cord with the United States, the nature of the struggle between Beijing and Taipei changed again. The competition over which government—the PRC or the ROC—would represent China in the international system had been settled, even though it did not disappear. Instead, the primary duel was now over whether and how Beijing could induce Taiwan's KMT leaders to end cross-Strait division and dissolve the ROC. But it faced three obstacles in doing so, obstacles that continue to this day.

The first obstacle was that U.S. support for Taiwan continued, even in the absence of official ties or a defense treaty. Carter himself had made clear that arms sales would continue, despite PRC opposition. Also, PRC leaders feared that a new U.S. president would renege on the normalization bargain, with good reason. During the 1980 American presidential campaign, Ronald Reagan was the most pro-Taiwan Republican candidate in the field, born of his deep and abiding sympathy for Taiwan (or at least the KMT regime), and he made clear his unhappiness with what he saw as Carter's abandonment of the island. To the PRC's dismay, he easily defeated Carter for the presidency and Republicans gained control of the Senate. Quietly, the Reagan administration sought to bolster Taiwan's sense of security and its successors would continue to do so, each in its own way.

When it came to the conduct of Washington's substantive relations with Taipei, however, the Reagan administration did little to change strict "rules of engagement" that the Carter administration had laid down. For example, the "instrumentality" in Washington that the ROC government created to conduct those relations was called the Coordination Council for North American Affairs (CCNAA), a title that did not refer to Taiwan at all. Taiwan diplomats assigned to CCNAA were required to meet their American counterparts in restaurants and hotel conference rooms, not in U.S. government buildings. Ensuring compliance with these guidelines was the State Department, which was led in the first eighteen months by Alexander Haig, who had assisted Henry Kissinger in accomplishing Nixon's opening to the PRC, and who still believed that the PRC could strengthen the U.S. hand against the Soviet Union. The Taiwan side had no choice but to forebear and put up with what they regarded as humiliating treatment, because the United States was its only bulwark against Beijing's unification campaign. It continued to place its hope on its friends in Congress, not just strong anti-communist conservatives like Barry Goldwater but also moderates in both parties.

The second obstacle was the lack of a formula for unification that would be mutually acceptable to Deng Xiaoping in Beijing and Chiang Ching-kuo and his subordinates in Taiwan. The latter would no doubt reject any attempt to make Taiwan a regular province of the PRC, as would Taiwan's supporters in the United States. On the other hand, the PRC did not want a setup that would leave openings for a movement for *de jure* independence or for U.S interference, or both. As it happened, the British government was exerting pressure on the PRC to find a formula by which the United Kingdom could transfer sovereignty over Hong Kong to China but avoid alarming the people of the colony, most of whom were refugees from Mao Zedong's misrule. The motivation was probably parochial—improving British companies' competitive position in the opening China market—but Beijing's need to respond to London accelerated PRC thinking about Taiwan.

The third obstacle the PRC faced to accomplishing unification in the near term was the transformation of Taiwan's political system. The baseline was the strong anti-communism of the KMT regime, which was still dominated by mainlanders who had no desire to admit defeat to the regime that had defeated the ROC forces in the civil war. Yet this ideological resistance would soon become the lesser of Beijing's frustrations.

DEVISING A UNIFICATION FORMULA

In September–October 1981, Deng Xiaoping initiated a three-pronged operation to remove these obstacles and to advance the PRC's objectives. He sought first to demonstrate progress on a Taiwan unification formula; second, to exert pressure on the United States to end arms sales to the island; and third, to create political allies within Taiwan (a united front approach). The first two prongs were directly linked. Deng believed that Chiang Ching-kuo would be unwilling to negotiate on unification as long as the United States was arming Taiwan, and Washington would not reduce or end arms sales unless it believed that Taiwan was assured a peaceful future. The third would be useful in advancing the first.

The first prong was a presentation by NPC Chairman Ye Jianying on Beijing's formula for "striving for peaceful reunification" with Taiwan:[9]

- Representatives of the CCP and the KMT should meet on a reciprocal basis to discuss reunification (note that the two parties, not the two governments, were the bodies that were to meet).
- Steps should be taken to "facilitate the exchange of mail, trade, air and shipping services, and visits by relatives and tourists, as well as academic cultural and sports exchanges, and reach an agreement thereupon."
- After unification, Taiwan "can enjoy a high degree of autonomy as a special administrative region, and it can retain its armed forces. The "central government" (in Beijing) would not interfere with Taiwan local affairs.

- Taiwan's existing socioeconomic system, including its way of life and economic and cultural relations with other countries, would not change. There would be no encroachment upon property rights, inheritance, ownership of housing, land, enterprises, and foreign investments.
- "People in authority and representative personages" in Taiwan could take up leadership posts in "national political bodies."
- The central government would assist Taiwan if it experienced financial difficulties.
- Proper arrangements would be made for Taiwan residents who wished to move to the mainland, and they would not suffer discrimination.
- Taiwan industrialists and businessmen were welcome to invest and engage in economic undertakings on the mainland, with guarantees of their legal rights, interests, and profits.
- Taiwan residents in various circles could make proposals and suggestions about affairs of state after unification.[10]

These were the essential elements of what would become known as the one-country, two-systems formula for unification. Taiwan rejected the model out of hand, and instead advocated national unification based on the "three principles of the people" of KMT founder Sun Yat-sen: nationalism, democracy, and people's livelihood. With some differences, Deng also applied one country, two systems to Hong Kong, and translated its basic principles into detailed policies and institutions in anticipation of the planned transfer of Hong Kong back to China in 1997. For Taiwan, the two sides have never gotten very far beyond fruitless discussion of general concepts. But the details of the Hong Kong model and how it changed for the worse between 2014 and 2020 do serve as a useful—and cautionary—point of reference for Taiwan.

Revisiting Taiwan Arms Sales

The second prong of Deng's unification campaign was to revisit the issue of U.S. arms sales, which was not resolved at the time of normalization. This came in October 1981, soon after Ye's speech. The logic was, because Beijing has a policy of peace, Taiwan no longer needs American instruments of war. Therefore, in an October meeting with President Reagan in Cancun, Mexico, Premier Zhao Ziyang demanded that the United States set a date for the end of arms sales and that until that point the amount of arms sales would not exceed the level of the Carter years and would decline year by year until the amount reached zero. The United States rejected the specific demands but proposed talks on the issue. Before talks had even begun Haig agreed to a cap on both the value and quality of arms transferred to Taiwan.

There ensued ten months of negotiations, during which Haig was replaced by George Shultz, who believed that U.S.–Asia policy should emphasize its treaty allies more and China less, and therefore Washington did not need to accommodate

China so much on arms sales. U.S. negotiators refused to set a date for the end of arms sales but did agree to the principles of a cap on quality and quantity and gradual reduction, and in August 1982 the two countries released a communiqué to that effect.

The agreement created shock waves in Taiwan, which had been led to believe that Reagan would not accept such an agreement. It foreshadowed a decline in the ability of Taiwan's armed forces to deter an attack by the People's Liberation Army (PLA; the principal military force of the PRC) and again raised questions about the credibility of the U.S. commitment of support. The Reagan administration emphasized that what it pledged in the communiqué was conditional upon Beijing continuing a policy of peaceful unification, and Reagan issued secret instructions to Secretary of State Shultz and Secretary of State Casper Weinberger to reinforce the point.[11] But U.S. officials understood that Taiwan's leaders would have no reason to trust Beijing's word and thus saw the need to address Taipei's concerns. Even before the communiqué was released, Washington conveyed to Taipei what has become known as the "six assurances." Some of these stated what the United States *had not* done in the communiqué: set an end-date for arms sales, agreed to consult with Beijing on the weapons systems it would transfer, agreed to revise the TRA, or altered its view on sovereignty over Taiwan. It also said that in the future it would not mediate between Beijing and Taipei or pressure Taiwan to enter into negotiations.[12] (Regarding the issue of Taiwan's sovereignty, the Reagan administration later stated its legal position that it took no position on the matter (consistent with the relevant clause in the Normalization Communiqué) and that the matter should be determined by the "Chinese people on both sides of the Taiwan Strait.")

The U.S. government made an effort to carry out the agreement. Officials conceived the concept of "the bucket," or the number of arms sales that could be authorized in any one year. Each year, the amount in the bucket was to decline. But flexibility was exercised in defining and implementing the agreement's commitments.

Cross-Strait Economic Relations

The PRC was much more successful when it came to the incentives it offered to Taiwan businesses to trade with and invest in the mainland and its openness to some types of human contact. The Taipei government approved steps toward closer economic cooperation more slowly than either the companies or Beijing officials wanted, but approve them it did. The companies had good reasons to sell their products to mainland customers and, more significantly, to shift their operations there. Wages and land prices in Taiwan were rising, and, under pressure from Washington, Taipei adjusted the undervalued exchange rate of its currency vis-à-vis the U.S. dollar, which made exports to the American market more expensive. The mainland offered cheap land and labor, and its exchange rate was not a problem. It needed capital, technology, and management talent from outside to facilitate export-led growth, all of which Taiwan companies could provide. To sweeten the deal, the PRC government allowed Taiwan companies to set up wholly owned subsidiaries, not joint ventures, which allowed Taiwan managers to maintain greater control of their operations. The most significant exception to this cross-Strait migration was the semiconductor industry, which for reasons of industrial security has been consistently cautious and kept most of its plants in Taiwan, particularly those that make the most advanced chips.

Taiwan factories in China produced both for the mainland market but also for Taiwan's long-standing overseas customers: major retailers in the West who valued the ability of Taiwan firms to produce products to precise specifications and to respond quickly to changes in foreign demand. Taiwan companies were also a boon to local PRC leaders in the places where their operations were located. They employed local people and strong economic performance improved promotion chances for local officials. Facilitating this shift in operations has been the fact that Taiwan industry is not tightly integrated into large firms but networked, with a main firm that sources from a large number of small and medium enterprises, each providing high-quality parts and components. Thus, if the main firm moved to the mainland, the whole network moved.

The opening to the mainland market came along at just the right time for Taiwan. In the late 1980s and early 1990s, there was a danger that the rise in income and living standards would stall because of rising production costs and competition from less developed economies (the "middle-income trap"). But moving operations to China allowed Taiwan companies to grow, particularly in the information technology sector. By the twenty-first century, the PRC represented around 40 percent of Taiwan's total trade, much of which was trade within Taiwan firms. The business success of those companies meant that many Taiwan families became much wealthier than might otherwise have been the case. Using the measure of purchasing power parity, Taiwan's per capita GDP increased almost ten times from 1985 to 2018 (from US$5,834 to US$53,023).[13]

In 1987, the Taiwan government also no longer prohibited individuals who had come to Taiwan in 1949 to return to the mainland to see their hometowns and aging relatives. These visits had a political consequence since many of the Taiwan visitors took away the impression that their own society was in better shape than post–Cultural Revolution China.

As early as March 1987, the United States took note of the new trends in cross-Strait relations and specified what role it would play. Secretary of State George Shultz, speaking in Shanghai, stated that "we have welcomed developments, including indirect trade and increasing human interchange, which have contributed to a relaxation of tensions in the Taiwan Strait." Within Washington's "steadfast policy" of one China and peaceful resolution of the Taiwan issue, it would seek to "foster an environment within which such developments can continue to take place."[14]

Over time, it would become apparent that although Taiwan companies depended for their prosperity on access to the mainland market, their employees did not necessarily become Beijing's advocates within the Taiwan political system. Although the KMT would become a pro-business party that favored expanding economic engagement with China, and although companies preferred to have the KMT in power instead of the Democratic Progressive Party (DPP), there was only one occasion—the 2012 presidential election—that prominent business leaders publicly urged voters to support the party's candidates. Large Taiwan companies undoubtedly made campaign contributions to the KMT, but by hedging their bets, many probably gave to the DPP as well (in the absence of a transparent disclosure system, a definitive judgment is not possible).

Wild Card: Taiwan's Democratization

As noted, Taiwan had an authoritarian political system from the late 1940s into the 1980s. But in the early 1980s, President Chiang Ching-kuo made plans to reform and open up that system, with profound effects on cross-Strait relations and ties with the United States.

Chiang had good reasons to consider a political reform initiative:

- KMT founder Sun Yat-sen had laid out a three-stage process of political development back in the 1920s, with genuine democracy as the final stage.
- Progressive, younger members of the KMT such as Ma Ying-jeou began to argue that the time had come to begin a political transition.
- The *dangwai* opposition to KMT rule was pressing for a say in the island's political life.
- A small but articulate group of U.S. members of Congress began criticizing the KMT's authoritarian rule regularly, a contrast to Congress's traditional support of the KMT regime. The most prominent individuals were Senators Teddy Kennedy (D-MA) and Claiborne Pell (D-RI), and Representatives Stephen Solarz (D-NY) and Jim Leach (R-IA), who became known in Taiwan as the "gang of four." Solarz was in the best position to push actively for political reform because he was the chairman of the House Subcommittee on Asian and Pacific Affairs and so could convene hearings to publicize the situation in Taiwan and move or block legislation in the subcommittee's jurisdiction.
- Finally, by the early 1980s, moreover, a new wave of global democratization had begun.

In late 1981, Chiang Ching-kuo quietly informed American officials that he had four goals to move toward before he died: expand the presence of Taiwanese in the upper levels of the regime, democratize the political system, maintain the island's prosperity, and open up to China, at least economically. Now that China was pursuing economic policies similar to those of Taiwan, Chiang wanted Taiwan to stay ahead of the PRC by undertaking democratization.[15]

But Chiang faced a couple of obstacles in moving forward on the democracy part of his agenda. The first was institutional. The ROC adopted a new, liberal, and democratic constitution in 1946. However, because of the civil war, his father Chiang Kai-shek suspended the liberal provisions of the charter in 1948, including the holding of regular elections, and authoritarianism continued after the KMT regime decamped to Taiwan from the mainland. Regarding elections, the 1946 ROC constitution established two representative bodies: the Legislative Yuan (LY) and the National Assembly (NA, which selected the president and approved constitutional amendments). Because the ROC government still claimed to be the government of all of China after moving to Taiwan, it took the position that it could only hold nationwide elections for the LY and NA after the ROC regime achieved the goal of "mainland recovery" and restored control over electoral districts on the mainland. Consequently, the pro-KMT members of those bodies elected in the late 1940s who went to Taiwan were kept in their positions. The only exception to this suspension of elections was seats representing districts in Taiwan, and those increased gradually in number as Taiwan's population increased. In addition, elections continued to be held at the local level. The *dangwai* contested these vigorously and they served as a proxy for public opinion.

The second constraint was Chiang Ching-kuo's health. He had suffered a health crisis in 1981, and there were fears that an ad hoc body set up to formulate mainland policy was secretly preparing the succession to Chiang. Whether he would live to carry out his democratization program became an open question. But he soon recovered and regained control of power. One of his first steps toward a more inclusive political system was his nomination of Taiwanese Lee Teng-hui to be his vice presidential running mate for the presidential selection by the NA in the spring of 1984. Lee would not be the first Taiwanese person to serve as vice president, but Chiang's age (seventy-four in 1984) and the state of his health almost ensured that he would not live to the end of his new six-year term. Consequently, a Taiwanese person would become the island's president for the first time. In the event, Chiang died in January 1988, Lee became president, and PRC officials began to worry about the Taiwanization of the island's politics.

The third obstacle was the balance of forces within the regime. After the termination of U.S.-ROC diplomatic relations in late 1978 and the Kaohsiung Incident in late 1979, the security services had the upper hand over more progressive elements in the regime. Despite Chiang Ching-kuo's 1981 message to American officials, and despite the gradual release of some political prisoners, more systemic progress seemed unlikely. Representative Steve Solarz offered his view of the gridlock in an August 1983 speech in Taipei to a *dangwai* audience. He argued that the time had come for Taiwan to undertake a "political miracle" to match its economic miracle. He also suggested that a democratic Taiwan would have a stronger claim on American support than an authoritarian one.[16]

In early 1985, the balance of forces changed. The previous autumn, Taiwan gangsters in league with the intelligence bureau of the Ministry of National Defense assassinated journalist and vocal critic of the KMT Henry Liu Yiliang outside his house in Daly City, California. This apparently was punishment for books Liu had written about key individuals in Taiwan's political history, in which he had criticized Chiang Ching-kuo. The U.S. government quickly gained information that identified the authors of the plot and was furious that agents of the KMT regime would murder on U.S. soil, harming bilateral relations and putting U.S. arms sales at risk. Steve

Solarz soon held a hearing on the assassination and secured passage in the House of Representatives of a resolution that condemned the crime.

This episode provided Chiang Ching-kuo the reason he needed to break the deadlock in his own government between conservatives and progressives and begin a democratic transition. In September 1986, leaders of the *dangwai* formed the DPP, but even though the action was still illegal, the regime did nothing in response. Soon after, Chiang Ching-kuo told *Washington Post* owner Katherine Graham that he would lift martial law, which was accomplished in July 1987. As a result, and over time, political dissent would no longer be prosecuted as a crime. The mass media became more open on political subjects, and those elections that were held were more freewheeling. Chiang Ching-kuo passed away in 1988, and Lee Teng-hui, his Taiwanese vice president, smoothly succeeded him. In 1990, in the run-up to the regularly scheduled presidential selection by the NA, Lee deftly deflected an effort by conservatives to replace him with a mainlander. Once assured he would be president for another six years, Lee had the NA lift the suspension of the liberal provisions of the ROC constitution imposed in the late 1940s, engineered the passage of constitutional amendments to elect all the members of the LY and NA by voters in Taiwan, and secured passage of another amendment which shifted selection of the president from the NA to voters at large for up to two four-year terms. Lee was the first person so elected in 1996.

Several factors made this transition quite remarkable. First, it was basically peaceful. Second, it occurred gradually. Third, under Lee Teng-hui's leadership, an ad hoc, centrist coalition of moderates of the ruling party (the KMT) and the primary opposition party (the DPP) in effect negotiated the scope and pace of political change. Finally, all this occurred in an ethnic Chinese society, which belied the argument of many observers at that time that Chinese people could not govern themselves. Taiwan thus became the poster child of the "third wave" of democratization, and this transition was underway at the same time as the tragedy of Tiananmen Square and its repressive aftermath that was unfolding in the PRC.

Democratization had some important consequences. New actors appeared on the political scene: political parties, along with an increasingly wide-open discussion of policy issues and shifts in political identity. Among parties, the DPP had a big advantage over other new organizations because it was formed early and could rely on the networks formed by the *dangwai*. When it came to the issue of Taiwan's future, the DPP soon adopted a radical position by adopting a party charter in 1991 that called for the formation of a "Republic of Taiwan." Soon after, the first popular elections were held for the NA, and DPP candidates were badly defeated. It would struggle to find a position that was true to the party's values but did not alienate voters.

The lifting of political controls had a profound impact on citizens' sense of identity. It will be recalled that the KMT authoritarian regime sought to instill a conservative Chinese identity in 85 percent of the population that had been subjects of the Japanese Emperor from 1895 to 1945. There is no way of knowing how successful that effort was, but in 1992, the year of the first popular election for members of the LY, the Election Study Center of National Chengchi University began surveying attitudes on identity. In its first poll, the most startling result was that the share of people who said they were Chinese only was only 26 percent. This was after forty years of regime efforts to instill a Chinese identity, and many of those 26 percent were likely born on the mainland and came to Taiwan in the late 1940s. Perhaps out of fear, only 18 percent said they were Taiwanese only and 47 percent said they were both (the pollsters did not define these terms). But as people's fear of authority declined across the board, the share who said they were Taiwanese rose, so that by the late 1990s, those who said "Taiwanese" or "both" was about equal, around 40 percent each. With the beginning of the twenty-first century, the Taiwanese share became the largest, rising to 63 percent in 2021. Those who said they were Chinese fell to less than 5 percent.[17]

Democratization had a profound impact on the new, emerging framework of cross-Strait relations. Before the transition began, there was every reason to believe that in the unlikely event that the KMT regime decided to accept the PRC's unification offer, the Taiwan public would not have a say in the decision but would have to live permanently with the result. But democratization meant that any decision that a Taiwan government made regarding cross-Strait relations would have to meet the test of public approval. In effect, the Taiwan people had gained a seat at the negotiating table.

The United States welcomed Taiwan's gradual transition to democracy. At a minimum, this was welcome on historical grounds. There were a series of decisions that successive U.S. administrations had made regarding Taiwan but with apparent disregard for the interests of the island's people.[18] Now those people would be able to express their interests directly. Taiwan's democratization was also consistent with the Reagan administration's decision to emphasize democratization in its policy regarding the nondemocratic character of many countries and reduce the stress on respect for internationally protected human rights. This shift in emphasis continued into the George H. W. Bush administration, and Taiwan was a beneficiary. For at least some Americans, including many members of Congress, support for Taiwan strengthened because the KMT had changed the island's political system, particularly as the CCP regime suppressed the protests of 1989 on the mainland. For these people, the cross-Strait dispute had become a struggle between a democratic David and a communist Goliath, and the American impulse was to support David. What was not foreseen in the early 1990s, however, was that Taiwan's democratization could become a mixed blessing for U.S. interests.

Beginning Political Contacts with Beijing

As Lee Teng-hui was laying the foundation for Taiwan's democratic transition in the early 1990s, he was also working to improve cross-Strait relations, born partly out of practical necessity. As Taiwan companies expanded their presence on the mainland, there was an increasing need for understanding with the PRC government to facilitate this economic engagement. In a May 1990 speech, he asserted that Taiwan and the mainland were both parts of China and that unification should be their goal. He signaled a willingness for exchanges between the two sides but set excessively high conditions before they could happen. Lee recognized that his government needed to create agencies to interface with PRC counterparts when the time came. Hence in late 1990 and early 1991, there were established the National Unification Council to set high policy; the Mainland Affairs Council (MAC) to devise more operational policies; and the Straits Exchange Foundation (SEF) to be the actual, semi-official interface mechanism. Beijing soon set up its own parallel structure: the Leading Small Group on Taiwan Affairs; the Taiwan Affairs Office (TAO) of the Communist Party and State Council, and the Association for Relations Across the Taiwan Strait (ARATS). The heads of SEF and ARATS, Koo Chen-fu and Wang Daohan respectively, were older gentlemen who had the confidence of their senior leaders. Gradually, the Taipei government elaborated its position on improving cross-Strait relations and the principles for unification. In the spring of 1991, at the same time that the suspension of the liberal provisions of the constitution were lifted, Lee declared that Taipei no longer regarded the CCP regime as a rebel regime, the rationale for suspending political freedoms. In August 1992, the National Unification Council declared that the ROC government had jurisdiction over Taiwan and its associated islands only, and that the Beijing government had jurisdiction over the mainland. It was no longer deemed a "bandit regime."

Beijing and Taipei had been conducting lower-level communications and there were even secret meetings between representatives of the two leaders. But given the growing economic interactions between the two sides, each soon saw the need to conclude agreements on practical issues like the authentication of documents, smuggling, and piracy through a meeting between the leaders of ARATS and SEF.[19] Before such a meeting could happen, Beijing insisted that any agreements be based on Taipei's acknowledgment of the "one-China principle." (This was a common PRC negotiating tactic: pressure the interlocutor to accept a Beijing principle and then use that acceptance to its advantage in the talks that followed.) In the fall of 1992, the two sides devised a set of overlapping but not identical statements that made a meeting possible. The overlap was that each capital agreed that it upheld the one-China principle and would strive for unification (which was still Taipei's official position at the time). The difference between them was that Beijing took the position that it was not necessary to agree on the meaning of one China when holding consultations on "routine" matters, while Taipei said that each side has its own, substantive understanding of one China.[20] This partial-but-incomplete agreement would come to be known as the "1992 consensus" and get redefined in the process.

Arms Sales Again

With the end of the Cold War and the collapse of the Soviet Union, there emerged a buyer's market for advanced weaponry, since the threat those weapons were meant to deter no longer existed. China jumped at the opportunity to purchase from Russia fighters, bombers, surface ships, and other weaponry that were much more advanced than what it could produce on its own. Taiwan took advantage of the new situation as well, approaching both France and the United States to purchase advanced systems. The looming increase in PLA capabilities led the George H. W. Bush administration to reevaluate the prior, benign U.S. assessment of Beijing's intentions toward Taiwan and the implications for arms-sales policy. That, and presidential politics in Texas and other states where the F-16 was produced, led the administration to decide to make 150 F-16 fighter aircraft available to Taiwan.

As a result, the 1982 communiqué became a dead letter, and that was probably for the best. The fact that peaceful unification was the basic guideline of the PRC's Taiwan policy was certainly not trivial. Still, PRC leaders had reason to believe that they were gaining leverage necessary to persuade and pressure Taipei to cut a deal. It was telling that Beijing firmly rejected the U.S. and Taiwan demands that it formally renounce the use of force. Its stated rationale was that such a commitment would reduce Taipei's willingness to negotiate and, even worse, encourage movement toward Taiwan independence. In short, Beijing was neither willing to place limits on the enhancement of its capabilities (something Washington did not even try to secure) nor reassure Taiwan and the United States by changing its intentions through a formal renunciation of the use of force. At the same time, through the August 1982 communiqué, Washington agreed to limit its contributions to Taiwan's military capabilities in an acknowledgment to change its intentions to "striving for peaceful unification." Striving for something is not the same as a guarantee of a peaceful outcome. Moreover, Beijing could quickly change its intentions (its basic guideline on peaceful unification) while it would take the United States a long time to ramp up arms shipments to strengthen Taiwan's defenses commensurately.[21]

STEPS FORWARD, THEN STEPS BACK

As of 1991 or 1992, the trends looked better for Taiwan than they had in some time. Relations with the United States were improving after two decades of setbacks and uncertainty. The opening of business and humanitarian contacts with the mainland was going forward, and there was the real prospect of a meeting of Koo Chen-fu and Wang Daohan. Democratization was enhancing Taiwan's international reputation. At the same time, and for some of the same reasons, Beijing had reasons for optimism about unification. But then trends began to take a turn for the worse. One reason was growing disagreements between Beijing and Taipei regarding their political relationship. Another was the impact of democratization on Taiwan's external behavior.

The earliest indication was a growing demand in Taiwan for international dignity. After having been marginalized from the international system by Beijing, people in Taiwan and their leaders increasingly believed that Taiwan deserved recognition for their movement toward democracy. The moral contrast with how the CCP regime cracked down on Tiananmen could not have been starker. As early as the late 1980s, Lee Teng-hui sought to respond to this demand by paying informal visits to countries in Southeast Asia. In 1990, leaders of the DPP, taking note that both North and South Korea were to become members of the United Nations, proposed that the government seek to return Taiwan to the United Nations. The public supported the idea, and the Lee administration coopted it as its own in 1993 rather than be outflanked politically by the DPP.

In 1993, Taiwan's supporters in the U.S. Congress challenged the restrictive rules that previous American administrations had followed in the conduct of relations with Taipei, to maintain the façade of unofficiality. The Clinton administration undertook a "Taiwan Policy Review," which it released in the summer of 1994. The new policy significantly liberalized the guidelines. For example, senior Taiwan economic officials visiting Washington, even up to the ministerial level, could now meet their counterparts in their offices.

More significantly, the guidelines also stated a new approach to Taiwan's role in international governmental organizations (IGOs). On the one hand, it maintained past policy that the United States would not support membership for Taiwan in IGOs for which statehood was a prerequisite for membership since the United States did not recognize Taiwan as a state. However, the government would support Taiwan as a member in IGOs for which statehood was *not* a prerequisite for membership, such as the World Trade Organization (WTO). It also asserted that Taiwan's voice should be heard in statehood-based IGOs and meaningfully participate in the work of those organizations.

None of the parties concerned—Taiwan, China, and the U.S. Congress—were happy with the result of the review but it allowed greater flexibility in bilateral contacts, and further liberalizations would occur in the future without requiring a formal review. Yet Taipei made little progress in gaining "meaningful participation" in IGOs where Taiwan could contribute, such as the World Health Organization (WHO). The reality was that such organizations operated by consensus and if the PRC was already a member, it would adamantly oppose on purely political grounds allowing Taiwan to offer the benefit of its expertise.

Lee Teng-hui took the quest for dignity to a new level in 1995 through his desire to visit the United States and give a speech at Cornell University, his *alma mater*. This stemmed in part from how the Clinton administration had treated him during a transit through Hawaii in April 1994. For the April 1994 Hawaii transit, Lee wanted to stay at the hotel of a prominent Taiwan businessman and play golf there. The Clinton administration, in the middle of fraught negotiations with the PRC over the most-favored-nation issue, declined Lee's request. He felt deeply humiliated and undertook to get the Clinton administration to accept a Cornell *visit* (which, if it occurred, would help his chances in the 1996 elections).[22] Lee employed a prominent Washington lobbying firm to lobby Congress and the media. The campaign was effective and ultimately President Bill Clinton allowed the visit, which occurred in June 1995. The PRC believed this breached the U.S. pledge to conduct relations with Taiwan unofficially and that Washington was encouraging what it said were Lee's Taiwan independence tendencies. It withdrew its ambassador to the United States and suspended cross-Strait dialogue. For its part, the Clinton administration was unhappy that Lee had used Congress to get his way.

Lee's visit went ahead anyway, but Beijing concluded that Lee's efforts to expand Taiwan's international profile were tantamount to promoting an independent Taiwan. The PRC mounted a robust response to induce restraint on Lee's part and to deter other countries from allowing visits by him and other senior officials. It conducted a series of military exercises in the late summer and early fall of 1995 and then undertook even more aggressive exercises in the days before the Taiwan presidential elections in March 1996. These included firing ballistic missiles with dummy warheads in the waters near the port cities of Kaohsiung and Keelung, which created a degree of panic in Taiwan. The Clinton administration decided to mount displays of force of its own, deploying two aircraft carrier battle groups to the region, both to deter further PRC actions and to deflect domestic criticism that it was not responding strongly enough.

The danger of war during the 1995–1996 Taiwan Strait crisis was not high. Washington and Taipei understood that the PLA was engaged in displays of force, not its use. But it was still the closest that the United States and China had come to war since 1958, and the danger of an accidental clash between fighters of the PRC and Taiwan air force was not zero. Beijing's coercive diplomacy also alarmed countries in Asia, particularly Japan (one of the ballistic missiles had flown near a Japanese island not far from Taiwan). Operationally, it also became apparent during the crisis that the rules that Washington had set in 1979 regarding restricting interaction between the U.S. and Taiwan militaries were too strict to allow the kind of communication between them needed for effective crisis management.

In the wake of the crisis, the United States revised its policy regarding the maintenance of peace and security in the Taiwan Strait. Secretary of State Warren Christopher enunciated the new approach in a speech to the Council on Foreign Relations and The Asia Society, stating a revision of U.S. policy: "We have emphasized to both sides the importance of avoiding provocative actions or unilateral measures that would alter the status quo or pose a threat to peaceful resolution of outstanding issues."[23] Whereas previously, Washington assumed that only the actions of the PRC might lead to war, it now signaled that Taipei could take steps of its own that could cause conflict. Symmetry had replaced asymmetry. Washington warned the PRC not to use force, but it warned Taipei not to take actions that Beijing would perceive as so provocative that it would feel no choice but to respond by using force. Taiwan was still admired for its democratic system, but the policies of the island's elected leaders would be judged according to their impact on the U.S. interest in the maintenance of peace and stability.

Temporary Stabilization

In a fairly short period, the tensions of 1995–1996 receded, and some degree of stability was restored. The Clinton administration was able to resume positive movement in the U.S. relationship with the PRC, despite the persistence of various contentious policies. The high points were PRC President Jiang Zemin's visit to the United States in October 1997 and Bill Clinton's return visit to the PRC in June 1998.

More impressive in a way was the improvement in U.S.-Taiwan relations. Among the steps taken were:

- Changes in personnel on each side produced a consensus that the conduct of bilateral relations should be guided by the norm of steady consultation, transparency, and "no surprises."
- A continuation of periodic, unpublicized meetings of senior officials of each government who could speak for their respective presidents (the first of these meetings had occurred in January 1996).
- The beginning of the "Monterey Talks," occasional meetings of defense officials on each side who discussed the bilateral security relationship beyond arms sales. This type of dialogue had not existed since 1979, and difficulties of crisis communication during the 1995–1996 Taiwan Strait crisis had exposed the need for one.
- The initiative of the Clinton administration to accelerate discussions with Taipei on its accession to the WTO, partly to get the PRC to negotiate seriously about its own accession. U.S. and Taiwan trade officials worked to conclude a bilateral agreement to be the basis for Taiwan's WTO accession. Parallel negotiations resumed on a U.S.-PRC bilateral accession agreement. The Clinton administration signed its bilateral agreement with the "Special Customs Territory of Taiwan, Penghu, Jinmen, and Matsu" in February 1999 (WTO entry then came on January 1, 2002, three weeks after the PRC),
- In August 1998, Richard Bush, then chairman of the American Institute in Taiwan, was authorized to state in a public speech that cross-Strait differences should be resolved peacefully but also in a manner acceptable to the people of Taiwan. This addition to the lexicon of U.S. policy, which took note of the fact that Taiwan's democratization had changed the dynamics of cross-Strait relations, was affirmed by President Clinton in a speech on economic policy toward China in March 2000. He said that the United States should be "absolutely clear that the issues between Beijing and Taiwan must be resolved peacefully and with the assent of the people of Taiwan."[24]

President Clinton caused a flurry in Taiwan during his visit to China in June 1998, when he uttered the "three nos": that the United States did not support two Chinas (or one China, one Taiwan); Taiwan independence; and Taiwan's membership in international governmental organizations for which statehood is a prerequisite for membership. Yet each of these items was a long-standing element of U.S. policy, and Taipei was informed in advance that Clinton would reaffirm them.

Tensions Rise Again

By the summer of 1999, there was growing hope that cross-Strait relations were back on a positive track. Koo Chen-fu, chairman of Taiwan's SEF, visited the mainland in the fall of 1998 to meet with his counterpart, Wang Daohan, the chairman of ARATS. This was not billed as a resumption of dialogue, but it was a step in that direction. More significantly, Beijing and Taipei agreed that Wang would visit Taiwan in the fall of 1999 and that dialogue would resume. This would be the first time that a PRC person of Wang's stature would make a public visit to Taiwan. That Wang was regarded as Jiang Zemin's mentor on cross-Strait relations was probably more important than his position as ARATS chairman. In mid-summer, U.S. officials received encouraging briefings from the Taiwan side about the arrangements for the visit.

Then, the train went off the rails again. On July 9, Lee Teng-hui in an interview with the German television network *Deutsche Welle* asserted a new formulation on the character of cross-Strait relations, saying that they were "special state-to-state relations."[25] Lee's suggestion that Taiwan was a state confirmed Beijing's view that Lee was moving covertly to *de jure* independence. Washington was annoyed that it had received no advance word of such a momentous declaration and worried about its legal and political implications. More seriously, PLA air force fighters undertook flights into the Taiwan Strait and crossed the center line, an informal boundary, and U.S. policymakers worried that when Taiwan jets scrambled to intercept the incoming fighters, an accidental crash might occur.

It turned out that Lee's statement was tied to the upcoming visit of Wang Daohan. Lee understood that political issues would be discussed in more depth than they had before, and, in his view, Taiwan needed to prepare for those discussions by better defining Taiwan's legal status. Beijing had a clear view on that subject: Taiwan was a part of China's sovereign territory and should become a subordinate unit of the PRC, under the one country, two systems model. That position was unacceptable to Taiwan, so the Taiwan side could not afford to have fuzzy views. Indeed, he had said on a couple of public occasions that Taiwan lacked a definite international status. He therefore created a team of experts to research the legal issues and make recommendations. One member of that team was current president Tsai Ing-wen. The team submitted its report to Lee including a draft statement stating key policy principles that he should make in the meetings with Wang and a set of recommendations for follow-up actions, including proposals for constitutional amendments. Lee approved the package, which was to be reviewed by senior officials.

But Lee jumped the gun and used the introductory statement publicly in his *Deutsche Welle* interview. Two substantive points stood out. The first was that Lee was at pains to distinguish the jurisdiction of the ROC government over Taiwan and that of the PRC government over the mainland. But that was not a new assertion, and nor was his later assertion that the ROC was an independent sovereign state.[26] What was new was the link he drew between the territory where elections take place (only in Taiwan and its associated islands) and the enhanced legitimacy of the ROC government. Based on that linkage, he extrapolated, the amendments concerning elections transformed cross-Strait relations into special state-to-state relations.

What is the basis for that last leap of logic? One plausible explanation is that it stemmed from the four requirements for statehood in the Montevideo Convention of 1933: (a) a permanent population, (b) a defined territory, (c) a government, and (d) a capacity to enter into relations with other states.[27] Of those four, the one on which Taiwan's claim of statehood was the weakest was the definition of territorial scope of the ROC. The traditional view of the KMT regime was that both the mainland and Taiwan were ROC's sovereign territories. But the ROC had governed Taiwan only since 1949. Lee's stress on the PRC's and ROC's totally separate jurisdictions, and the assertion that the government derived its legitimacy from elections held only in Taiwan, suggests that he was in effect redefining the sovereign territory of the ROC. To put it differently, if sovereignty derives from the people by their voting in elections, then where the people vote defines the territory of the state.[28]

That Lee was trying to redefine the sovereign territory of the ROC became clear in the early 2000s, when it was revealed that in 1999 Lee's team of experts had also proposed changes in nomenclature, laws, and the constitution to supplement the principles enunciated in his statement. These included (a) the revision and ultimate abolition of the National Unification Guidelines, a one-China document, and (b) ending the use of various formulations that assume or imply a one-China framework (such as "one China, different interpretations" and "one China is the ROC"). The most significant of the suggested changes concerned Article 4 of the constitution, regarding the ROC's territorial scope. That article does not actually specify geographically what the national territory is, but the draft amendment read, "The territory of the Republic of China consists of areas effectively governed by this Constitution," that is, "Taiwan, Penghu, Jinmen, and Mazu."[29] But for two reasons, these changes were never enacted. First, Lee's surprise announcement created a strong negative reaction from Beijing and Washington, leading to a downturn in Taiwan's relations with both. Second, it was not clear by July 1999 whether Lee had both the time and the political support to enact these changes.

There was one more chapter in the saga of Lee Teng-hui's focus on the issue of territory. On April 24, 2000, the NA passed an amendment to the constitution that detailed the process for changing the national territory. The 1946 constitution, which did not provide a detailed geographical definition of the ROC's sovereign territory, had merely stated that any change would have to occur pursuant to a resolution of the NA. The 2000 amendment created a two-step process. First, the LY had to pass the proposal by a three-fourths majority of members present, with a minimum quorum of three-fourths of all members. Second, the measure then had to pass the NA by a three-fourths majority, with two-thirds of the members present. Practically speaking, given the growing parity between the KMT and the DPP, no territorial changes could have passed without the support of both major parties. The net effect of this amendment was that any territorial change would be highly unlikely.[30]

THE 2000 ELECTION SEASON

Taiwan and the United States hold presidential elections in the same year. Up through 2008, Taiwan's election occurred in March. Beginning in 2012, the balloting occurred in January, on the same day as the LY elections. The upshot was that the Clinton administration in 1999 had already started thinking about possible outcomes for the Taiwan elections. In the same year, Republican foreign policy experts began staking out a position on Taiwan that was critical of Clinton's policy.

Based on the KMT's recent election record, it seemed implausible that it would lose. The DPP usually garnered between 40 to 45 percent on an island-wide basis, and its association with the goal of independence was not terribly popular. But the 2000 contest was different. On the one hand, two KMT leaders—Vice President Lien Chan and party heavyweight James Soong—both wished to become Lee Teng-hui's successor. Lee backed Lien, who received the KMT nomination, while Soong ran as an independent. On the other hand, on May 8, 1999, the DPP released a "Resolution on Taiwan's Future" that finessed the issue of independence by asserting that Taiwan was already a "sovereign and independent country," which also happened to be the essence of the KMT position.[31] This modification was engineered by Chen Shui-bian, who served as mayor of Taipei City from 1994 to 1998, and who was emerging as the DPP's presidential candidate.

The Clinton administration early on recognized the possibility that there might be a three-way race and that Chen Shui-bian might win. Chen made two trips to the United States, one in the spring of 1998 and the second in the spring of 1999, both of which allowed him to talk face-to-face with U.S. officials responsible for Taiwan policy and gave them a chance to take his measure. Meanwhile, the Taipei office of AIT intensified its interactions with the DPP in general and Chen's inner circle in particular.

In December 1999, four months before the election, AIT Chairman Richard Bush visited Taipei to convey the U.S. government's view on the election to each of the candidates (Lien, Chen, and Soong) and then to the public. His consistent message was, first, the United States did not have a preference among the three candidates; Taiwan voters should be the ones to pick their president. Second, the United States was prepared to work with whoever was elected. Third, what was important to Washington was not who was elected per se, but whether the new president's policies aligned well with the U.S. interest in the maintenance of peace and stability in the Taiwan Strait. If they did, bilateral relations would be good. If alignment was weak, then there would be discussions to try to close the gap. Another message for the candidates was the importance of good and timely communication. Clearly, the shadow of Lee Teng-hui's July state-to-state declaration hung over this election.

As it happened, Chen Shui-bian's electoral strategy fit well with the guidelines and conduct of U.S. policy. Knowing that the DPP commanded less public support than the KMT, he understood that the best chance for victory was to reach out to middle, undecided voters to gain a sufficient plurality (similar to Tony Blair's "third-way" strategy). His adoption of a relatively moderate position on China policy served that strategy and reduced the DPP's vulnerability due to its past, explicit support of independence.

In the event, Lien and Soong split the KMT vote and Chen Shui-bian squeaked to victory with just under 40 percent of the votes. If the KMT had been united, the

DPP would not have come to power in 2000. The party's initial excitement about gaining power was soon replaced by dread that it lacked any experience in governing on an island-wide basis. Although the Clinton administration had prepared as well as it could for a Chen presidency, the PRC government was unprepared and fearful that Chen might challenge its anti-independence bottom line.

Once Chen Shui-bian was elected, he sought further to reassure the Taiwan public, China, and the United States. In his inaugural address, he stated five steps he would not take while in office as long as Beijing did not intend to use force: declare independence, change the national title (ROC), push to include Lee's two-state formula in the constitution, promote a referendum on independence or unification that would change the status quo, or abolish the National Unification Guidelines or Council. These pledges were known as the "four noes and one not."

As it happened, Chen's victory coincided with the bursting of the global IT bubble, which had a profound effect on Taiwan companies in that sector. The major firms decided that they had to move more of their operations to China to remain internationally competitive. Once the main firms moved, the smaller companies in their respective production networks moved as well. Cross-Strait trade and investment and the number of Taiwan citizens living on the mainland increased accordingly. Some in the DPP opposed this migration, fearing the leverage it might give Beijing, but any steps that the Chen administration took to try to limit investment was circumvented by the ability of Taiwan companies to work through shell companies in third markets.

Meanwhile, in the United States, Republicans worked to make China an issue in the 2000 election. Some labeled the PRC a strategic competitor of the United States, the first time that China had been cast in that light. Some conservatives believed that the United States should be prepared to defend Taiwan simply because it was a democracy, even though its policies might conflict with U.S. interests. Just about all conservatives believed that the Clinton administration had blamed Lee Teng-hui for the tensions of the late 1990s when, in their view, China was the root cause. They advocated strengthening Taiwan's defenses and stating the U.S. defense commitment to Taiwan with greater clarity. They argued that ambiguity in words and deeds, which they associated with the Clinton administration, might lead China to miscalculate U.S. resolve and to underestimate the risk of attacking Taiwan.[32] After George W. Bush became president, he followed up on this recommendation in an interview with ABC News. He said that the United States had an obligation to come to Taiwan's defense. When pressed whether this could involve "the full force of American military," Mr. Bush replied, "Whatever it took to help Taiwan defend theirself [sic]."[33]

CHEN SHUI-BIAN ALIENATES THE BUSH ADMINISTRATION

Chen had hoped that he could elicit cooperation with the KMT in forging a cross-party consensus on mainland policy and work out a conceptual basis for coexistence with Beijing so that the two sides of the Strait could emphasize what they had in common (mainly economic interests) and set aside political disputes. If successful, that strategy would likely broaden the DPP's electoral base and keep Taiwan aligned with U.S. interests.

But both initiatives got nowhere. The KMT was able to maintain a majority or plurality in the LY and so it could block Chen's legislative initiatives. Moreover, the DPP did not handle relations with the KMT well, which deepened mistrust between the two parties and reduced the chances of consensus on China. The PRC focused on the facts that Chen was a minority president, lacked a majority in the LY, and identified with the Deep Green, pro-independence faction within the DPP. So, it stated that unless Chen accepted the "one-China principle" it would not be willing to cooperate with his government, a precondition that it likely knew Chen would reject.[34]

Beginning in the summer of 2002, Chen Shui-bian therefore adjusted both his policy and electoral approach. He correctly assumed that he would face a united opposition in the 2004 election (indeed, Lien Chan and James Soong formed a combined ticket). Chen thus would have to get more than 50 percent of the vote to win reelection in 2004, unlike the 40 percent that was sufficient for victory in 2000. In addition, he switched his electoral strategy from appealing to people whom polls identified as centrist or undecided in their views. Instead, he and the DPP focused on expanding the DPP's hard-core base and then working hard to get it to the polls on election day. In Chen's case, mobilizing the DPP base required playing to the party's fundamentalist, independence-inclined faction (the Deep Greens).

Over the next year, Chen stated a series of policy positions that he knew would be red meat for the fundamentalists:

- He called for legislation to enable holding referendums, a right set forth in the constitution.
- In August 2002, he declared that there was one country on each side of the Strait (i.e., China and Taiwan).
- In May 2003, he called for referendums on domestic policy issues and Taiwan's participation in the WHO, which touched on the issue of Taiwan's sovereignty.
- In September 2003, he called for drafting a new constitution that would, among other things, make Taiwan a "normal country" and approved it through a referendum.
- In October 2003, he asserted that the one-China principle and Taiwan's sovereignty were mutually contradictory.

Chen understood that these statements would anger Beijing, but he likely guessed that they would reinforce his political strategy. He also knew that the United States both expected consultation on sensitive matters such as these policy positions and would probably oppose them, so he chose to leave Washington in the dark. He believed that even if his provocative moves elicited initial U.S. opposition, he would come out in a better position in the long run. Moreover, during the 2002–2003 period, there were people in the Bush administration who were willing to tolerate his edgy pronouncements.

But others were unwilling to be so indulgent. Included in this group was President Bush, whose entire focus after September 11 was on counterterrorism and the war with Iraq. He no longer regarded China as a strategic competitor of the United States but an ally in the war on terror. China saw an opportunity to drive a wedge between Washington and the Chen administration. When PRC President Jiang Zemin met with Bush at the latter's ranch in Crawford, Texas, he complained about Chen's behavior and urged Bush to shift the U.S. position on Taiwan independence from "does not support" to "oppose." Bush agreed, and although the public version of U.S. policy did not change, Bush himself took a decidedly anti-Chen stance for the rest of his presidency.

Up until September 2003, Chen's provocations were just words. But then he turned to actions: he proposed legislation to authorize referendums to be held on election day. Holding referendums could both increase DPP turnout and circumvent the KMT-controlled legislature on politically charged issues. The KMT, afraid of being politically outflanked, sought to outdo the DPP in this effort. Legislation was passed and, at first glance, it seemed that Chen would not be able to hold referendums on sovereignty issues. But he exploited a loophole in the law that allowed him to call for "defensive referendums," which he did. Neither spoke to a seriously debated policy issue.[35]

This whole process panicked the PRC, which appealed to the Bush administration to restrain Chen. Provoked by Chen's actions, Bush made a public statement on December 9, 2003, with PRC Premier Wen Jiabao sitting next to him: "We oppose any unilateral decision by either China or Taiwan to change the status quo [thus toughening the Warren Christopher formulation from May 1996 through the use of the word "oppose"]. . . . [the] comments and actions made by the leader of Taiwan indicate that he may be willing to make decisions unilaterally, to change the status quo, which we oppose."[36]

The referendums were held but failed to pass because less than the required 50 percent of eligible voters participated (the KMT urged its supporters not to do so). The presidential race was close and clouded by a shooting incident right before the election involving Chen and his vice president. But he was declared the winner. A month later, and a month before Chen's inauguration, James A. Kelly, assistant secretary of State for East Asian and Pacific Affairs, issued a tough reiteration of U.S. policy:

> While strongly opposing the use of force by the P.R.C., we must also acknowledge with a sober mind what the P.R.C. leaders have repeatedly conveyed about China's capabilities and intentions. The P.R.C. refuses to renounce the use of force regarding Taiwan despite our consistent representations stating they should do so. P.R.C. leaders state in explicit terms that China considers Taiwan's future a "vital national interest" and that the P.R.C. would take military action in the event Taiwan declares independence. While we strongly disagree with the P.R.C.'s approach, and see military coercion as counter-productive to China's stated intent to seek a peaceful outcome, it would be irresponsible of us and of Taiwan's leaders to treat these statements as empty threats. . . . We encourage the people of Taiwan to regard this threat equally seriously. We look to

President Chen to exercise the kind of responsible, democratic, and restrained leader-ship that will be necessary to ensure a peaceful and prosperous future for Taiwan.

Kelly promised that the United States would "speak bluntly" if Taiwan actions undermined U.S. interests, and specifically expressed concerns about the content and process of any revision of Taiwan's constitution. He signaled that U.S. support on this point was not unlimited.[37]

Beijing issued its own deterrence warning toward the Chen administration in March 2005, in the form of an "Anti-Secession Law." The measure reiterated the key points of PRC Taiwan policy, including what it asserted would be the benefits of unification. But it also set forth the conditions under which the PRC was autho-rized to use "non-peaceful means and other necessary measures to protect China's sovereignty and territorial integrity," if "'Taiwan independence' secessionist forces should act under any name or by any means to cause the fact of Taiwan's separa-tion from China, or that major incidents entailing Taiwan's secession from China should occur, or that possibilities for a peaceful reunification should be completely exhausted."[38] That these "redlines" were stated ambiguously is not terribly surprising, since stating them precisely would be an invitation for a Taiwan leader president to go right up to the line and stop. The problem with their vagueness is that the power to determine whether Beijing's preconditions would be based on the subjective per-ceptions of Beijing leaders, not on the facts of the situation. For example, the pos-sibilities of peaceful unification could be "completely exhausted" not due to anything Taiwan did but because the PRC government refused to offer a proposal that had a realistic chance of being accepted by the Taiwan public and approved through the island's democratic political system.

The KMT sought to gain political capital from the Chen administration's troubled ties with both Beijing and Washington. In April 2005, Lien Chan made the first visit to the mainland by any party chairman since 1949. He met with Hu Jintao, in the latter's capacity as general secretary of the CCP, and they issued a press communiqué on April 29. The two parties agreed to uphold the 1992 consensus, oppose Taiwan independence, pursue peace and stability in the Taiwan Strait, and promote the development of cross-Strait relations. On that basis, and if the KMT regained power, they proposed to resume cross-Strait negotiations on issues of com-mon concern, work toward an end to the state of hostilities, and conclude a peace accord.[39] They also agreed to develop economic exchanges leading to an economic cooperation mechanism, discuss Taiwan's role in the international community, and establish a platform for future party-to-party contact.

There was some risk to this KMT initiative. Those in Taiwan who believed that the KMT had no regard for the interests of the people as a whole could regard the prospect of a KMT administration working with the CCP regime as a form of betrayal. In this case, however, the KMT made a bet that Taiwan companies and the public were tired of the tensions that Chen's political initiatives created and wanted a more normal relationship with the mainland.

Chen's response during his second term was to double down on the political strategy he had formulated to get himself reelected in 2004. Despite corruption scandals involving members of his family and officials in his administration, and broader public dissatisfaction with the negative trend in cross-Strait relations and U.S.-Taiwan relations, he continued to take initiatives that appealed to the DPP base and alienated Beijing and Washington. For example, in January 2006, Chen effectively terminated the National Unification Council, which he had pledged not to do in his 2000 inaugural address. One likely reason Chen took these actions was to ensure the support of the DPP base if impeachment proceedings were initiated in the LY.

From 2004 on, the Bush administration restrained its interactions with the Chen administration and was grudging in the favors it doled out. Ma Ying-jeou, who had emerged as the KMT's presidential candidate for 2008, received a friendly yet private welcome from Bush administration officials when he visited Washington in March 2006. In addition, he was able to make a thorough presentation of his policy proposals in an address at a public event hosted by the Brookings Institution and the Center for Strategic and International Studies.[40] To Taiwan voters, Ma made the case that engagement of the PRC, based on his willingness to accept the 1992 consensus, was a much better way to preserve Taiwan's freedom, prosperity, dignity, and security than Chen Shui-bian's provocative policies.

Ma's DPP opponent in the 2008 election was Frank Hsieh Chang-ting, a party leader who had served as premier and mayor of Kaohsiung. Yet Chen controlled Hsieh's campaign strategy and promoted a referendum calling for Taiwan to seek membership in the UN *under the name Taiwan* (not the ROC), to be held at the time of the March 2008 presidential elections. His likely reason for such an initiative was to appeal to the DPP's fundamentalist faction and to give party supporters an added reason to come out to vote.

The Bush administration strongly opposed Chen's initiative, which prioritized domestic politics over relations with the United States. Even if the referendum passed, there was no chance that a membership application would succeed, since China would vigorously lobby against the proposition that Taiwan was a new state internationally. Thus, the initiative itself unnecessarily increased cross-Strait tensions. In the toughest speech ever delivered on Taiwan policy, Thomas Christensen, deputy assistant secretary of state for East Asian and Pacific Affairs, bluntly stated:

It is the apparent pursuit of name change in the referendum, therefore, that makes the initiative appear to us to be a step intended to change the status quo. Arguments that the referendum, even if passed, would not amount to a pursuit of name change, frankly, strike us as purely legalistic. After all, if the specific nomenclature does not matter, why include it in the referendum in the first place? At a fundamental level, such legalistic arguments from supporters of the referendum make it seem that they do not take seriously Taiwan's commitments to the United States and the international community, are willing to ignore the security interests of Taiwan's most steadfast friend, *and are ready to put at some risk the security interests of the Taiwan people for short-term political gain.* Our bottom line is that the downsides of such an initiative for Taiwan and U.S. interests are potentially large, and, as with any UN referendum, the benefits for Taiwan's international status are non-existent, so we must oppose such an initiative strongly.[41]

The subtext of Christensen's speech was that the United States feared that if the referendum passed, Beijing would regard it as tantamount to a declaration of independence and might undertake a military response. The United States would then face the tough choice of whether to intervene to protect Taiwan despite what it regarded as recklessness on Chen's part. This was not a purely hypothetical scenario. Reportedly, in late 2007 and 2008 PRC officials were expressing higher than average concerns that war really was looming. This raised the question of whether Washington and Beijing were working directly together to constrain Chen. The more precise formulation would be that the two governments were working on parallel tracks in support of a common objective—the avoidance of war.

In the end, the referendum failed because too few people voted for it, and Ma Ying-jeou handily defeated Hsieh Chang-ting by getting 58.4 percent of the vote. Moreover, to the extent that this outcome reflected voters' judgment of Chen's China policy, and it did to some extent, they clearly repudiated him. The KMT won eighty-one seats in the Legislative Yuan to the DPP's twenty-seven.

THE MA YING-JEOU ADMINISTRATION

The combination of the Lien-Hu meeting in 2005 and the KMT's clear-cut electoral victories of 2008 meant that Beijing could set aside its emphasis since 1995 on "opposing independence." In its eyes, "promoting unification" was again the priority. In his inaugural address, Ma affirmed his support for the 1992 consensus and projected a bright future for cross-Strait relations. He vowed that during his presidency, there would be "no unification, no independence, no war" (Ma's so-called three noes). For its part, the PRC had adopted a more gradual approach to unification by including an intermediate phase, what Hu Jintao called "peaceful development."

On December 31, 2008, Hu offered his views on cross-Strait relations in a speech to celebrate the thirtieth anniversary of a statement that the Standing Committee of the National People's Congress had sent to "Taiwan compatriots," urging them to move toward peaceful unification. That was still Beijing's fundamental policy, but Hu demonstrated a realistic understanding that the process would be protracted.

In his speech, Hu stressed in various ways that peaceful development was a long-term process. China needed to "take the long view from an elevated vantage point." The elements of peaceful development—emotional harmony, mutual trust, shared prosperity, and rejuvenation of the Chinese nation—almost by definition required gradualism. Consequently, Hu said, "we should *for a long time to come*, continue to gradually adhere to and comprehensively implement these general policies and guiding principles that have proven to be correct in practice." The two sides should "*gradually* solve the legacy issues in cross-Strait relations and any new issues that arise." To the extent that people in Taiwan misunderstood the mainland or were skeptical of its policies, Beijing should "undo such sentiments and counsel them *with the greatest tolerance and patience.*"[42] By implication, peaceful development would slowly lay the foundation for unification. There was a working consensus between Beijing and Taipei that the two sides should address economic issues first and political ones later, and they should take up easy matters first and difficult ones later.

In this regard, Hu Jintao's December 2008 speech and subsequent cross-Strait interactions clarified the role of the 1992 consensus in Beijing's long-term game plan. Peaceful development and peaceful unification would be two stages of an extended process. Economic and political issues could be addressed during peaceful development, but the 1992 consensus could only be the basis for negotiating economic issues, not political issues. That was because the SEF and ARATS were unable to reach an agreement on the content of the "one-China principle" in developing the 1992 consensus, and from Beijing's point of view, one purpose of political talks was to end that disagreement.

As an indication of the size of the gap, it is worth noting that Ma defined the 1992 consensus as "one China, different interpretations," with his "interpretation" of one China being the ROC. Although most people in Taiwan agreed with Ma's definition, Beijing has never accepted that formulation, in part because it holds that the ROC ceased to exist in 1949. PRC leaders probably let Ma get away with this verbal sleight of hand because they trusted his fundamental intentions. As would become clear, Beijing stuck to its definition of the 1992 consensus that the two sides of the Strait belonged to one China and that they would work together to seek national unification.

In the domain of concrete policy, Taipei and Beijing accomplished a lot during Ma's first term on easier, mostly economic, issues. Working on behalf of the two governments, SEF and ARATS concluded over twenty agreements (Table 1.1). Many of these accords were necessary to establish the basic frameworks for cross-Strait interaction. The opening of mainland tourism to Taiwan was done to give a boost to the Taiwan economy, and soon, groups from the PRC flooded Taiwan hotels, restaurants, luxury stores, and tourist sites. The most important agreement was the Cross-Strait Economic Cooperation Framework Agreement (ECFA), which promised talks to liberalize trade in goods and services and provide for better investment protection.

The United States welcomed the arrival of the Ma administration, in part because he aimed to do what Washington had been advising for years—resume dialogue between the two sides of the Strait. At the time of Ma's inauguration, the Bush administration said that his election provided "a fresh opportunity for Taiwan and China to reach out and engage one another in peacefully resolving their differences," and that it looked forward to working with the new Taiwan leadership. Senator Barack Obama, then campaigning for president, conveyed a letter of congratulations in which he said that Ma's inauguration "holds promise for more peaceful and stable relations between the two sides of the Taiwan Strait."[43]

Table 1.1   Cross-Strait Agreements during the Ma Ying-jeou Presidency

SEF-ARATS Agreements and Other Actions

June 2008
Agreement on Mainland Tourists Traveling to Taiwan
Memo on beginning of passenger charter flights on weekends

July 2008
Decision to ease restrictions on Mainland Chinese tour groups to visit Taiwan

Nov. 2008
Agreement on Food Safety
Agreement on Cross-Strait Air Transport
Agreement on Cross-Strait Sea Transport
Agreement on Cross-Strait Postal Service
Decision to commence charter flights on weekdays starting December 2008

April 2009
Agreement on Joint Crime-Fighting and Judicial Mutual Assistance
Agreement on Financial Cooperation
Agreement on Normalization of Cross-Strait Air Transport

Dec. 2009
Agreement on Cooperation of Agricultural Product Quarantine and Inspection
Agreement on Cooperation in Respect of Standards, Metrology, Inspection, and
    Accreditation
Agreement on Cooperation concerning Fishing Crew Affairs

June 2010
Cross-Strait Economic Cooperation Framework Agreement (ECFA), including the Early
    Harvest Program
Agreement on Intellectual Property Rights Protection and Cooperation

Dec. 2010
Agreement on Medical and Health Cooperation

Oct. 2011
Agreement on Nuclear Power Safety Cooperation, including early-warning mechanism
Joint Opinion on Advancing Negotiations on the Cross-Strait Agreement on Investment
    Protection
Joint Opinion on Strengthening Cross-Strait Industrial Cooperation

Aug. 2012
Agreement on Investment Protection and Promotion
Agreement on Customs Cooperation
Consensus on the personal freedom and safety guarantees

March 2013
Cross-Strait Agreement on Trade in Services (never brought into force)

Feb. 2014
Agreement on Cooperation on Meteorology
Agreement on Cooperation regarding Seismological Monitoring

August 2015
Reciprocal Tax Agreement (signed but never implemented because the legislature did
    not give its approval)

Source: Yasuhiro Matsuda, "Cross-Strait Relations under the Ma Ying-jeou Administration: From Economic to Political Dependence?" *Journal of Contemporary East Asia Studies* 4, no. 2 (January 2015): 3–35.

By and large U.S.-Taiwan relations were positive during the period that Presidents Obama and Ma overlapped. Communications were smooth. Obama approved two large arms packages that altogether totaled over $12 billion. There were also symbolic gestures that reflected the evolution of bilateral ties. Up until 2011, the Taipei Economic and Cultural Representative Office (TECRO) held its annual, public reception to mark the October 10 anniversary of the 1911 revolution and the founding of the ROC in a downtown Washington hotel. For 2011, Taipei requested and Washington approved holding the occasion at Twin Oaks, which had been the ROC ambassador's residence before 1979, and which TECRO used for private events.

There were a couple of points of friction in the bilateral relationship, however. One concerned trade. Taiwan wanted to expand its economic relationship with the United States and other trading partners as a way of balancing its economic ties with the PRC. The office of the USTR was unwilling to consider the idea until Taipei resolved some legacy issues concerning market access for American beef and pork. Ma secured legislation to open the market for the biggest part of the beef trade, but he did not get much in return. On the U.S. side, there was concern about the low level of defense spending within the context of the PRC's continuing military buildup. U.S. officials had begun raising the matter during the Chen administration and stepped up the pressure on Ma's team as the PLA became increasingly capable of going to war. During Ma's time in office, however, the defense share of the total government budget (an indicator of defense's relative priority) hovered around 11 percent. The Pentagon also worried that Taiwan's existing defense strategy was no longer appropriate for a changing threat environment.

Yet Ma did not place defense at the center of his broader strategy for preserving Taiwan's security. Instead, he sought to develop the positive dimensions of cross-Strait relations to the point, he hoped, that Beijing had such a stake in the status quo that it would not dream of going to war. That in turn would create less reason for Taipei to increase defense spending.

But war was not the only thing that Ma had to worry about. More pressing, it turned out, were growing PRC demands for political talks to come to some agreement about the meaning of one China. For example, when Ma administration officials discussed more international space for Taiwan beyond attendance at World Health Assembly (WHA) and International Civil Aviation Organization meetings, Beijing's answer was that this activity was inherently political and that before Taipei could participate in more international organizations, it would have to agree to cross-Strait political talks. Ma Ying-jeou understood that the Taiwan public was not ready for such talks. Moreover, he likely understood that his own interpretation of the ROC as the one China, which Beijing did not accept, meant that a lot of conceptual work would be required to ensure the success of any political talks.

Yet the bigger challenge that President Ma faced was within Taiwan. Several factors combined to bring his mainland policy to a virtual halt. The first was the very nature of Ma's party. The KMT had two major wings that did not always see eye to eye on major issues. One wing was composed more of mainlanders and their offspring, who were based more in the northern part of the island and tied politically to the central government. The other wing was more native Taiwanese by background, based in the south, and dominant in county and local governments. The northern wing was more wedded to Ma's policies than the southern one.

The second challenge was a conflict between Ma and LY Speaker Wang Jin-pyng, a vice chairman of the KMT. Wang was a native Taiwanese from the south and Ma a mainlander from the north. As president, Ma believed that Wang was using his LY position to frustrate his agenda, even though Ma was head of the KMT and though the party had an overwhelming majority in the LY. In the summer of 2013, Ma received information that suggested that Wang was wrongfully disclosing classified information, and he sought to purge Wang. Wang mobilized his supporters and Ma was forced to back down.

Third, and more significant, public opposition was mounting to Ma's mainland policy in general and the service trade agreement in particular. Shelley Rigger summarizes the general trend: "Unlike past critiques that focused on the possibility that overreliance on the mainland market could hollow out Taiwan's economy or give the PRC leverage indirectly through [Taiwanese companies on the mainland], this movement reflected the growing sense that cross-Strait economic cooperation was infiltrating and *directly* reshaping Taiwan politics."[44] The prospect loomed of mainland investment in Taiwan. The loud, brash behavior of the millions of PRC tourists who descended on Taiwan after Ma came to power confirmed for the average Taiwan citizen that each side of the Strait was a different society.

Fourth, Taiwan politics was changing. Civil society groups were proliferating on all manner of issues. Their activists were less willing to work through the institutions of representative democracy and, aided by social media, they created networks of organizations that could be quickly mobilized for direct action against block initiatives they opposed.

These factors combined to create a major conflict over approval of the cross-Strait service trade agreement that had been negotiated under the ECFA framework. There was a dispute both within the LY and between it and Ma over what role the LY members should play regarding the agreement. The KMT gave in and allowed article-by-article review. But continued DPP obstruction caused the relevant KMT committee chair to "lose it" and call for a final vote. That provoked groups of young people opposed to the agreement to break into the LY chamber and occupy it for twenty-three days, which became known as "the Sunflower Movement." At that point, Speaker Wang negotiated an end to the takeover by promising to pass legislation on supervision of cross-Strait economic negotiations. He did not consult with President Ma on this agreement, and to this day no bill has been enacted.

The Sunflower Movement energized Taiwan politics, especially among young people. In the city and county elections held in November 2014, the KMT lost nine jurisdictions and the DPP won seven. Then the KMT struggled to pick a competitive presidential candidate for the 2016 elections. It first picked Hung Hsiu-chu, a northerner with a mainlander background whose China policy was more Beijing-friendly than Ma's had been. Late in the campaign, the KMT replaced Hung with the more mainstream Chu Li-luan. By contrast, the DPP was united and led by Tsai Ing-wen, who reassured voters that she was committed to maintaining the status quo. She won the elections with 56.1 percent of the vote and the DPP captured sixty-eight seats in the LY, the first time it secured an absolute majority.

CONCLUSION

Today's conflict between China and Taiwan had its roots in the struggle between the KMT and CCP that began in the mid-1920s. The first two decades of that struggle had its political dimension, but by and large it was a violent military conflict for control of Mainland China, defined to be the lands over which the last imperial dynasty had held sway at its height. During most of this time, Taiwan, a Japanese colony, was not an object of KMT-CCP contention. During World War II, however, both the ROC government and the KMT in turn called for Taiwan to be returned to China's sovereign territory after the war, and President Franklin Roosevelt agreed. As a result, Japanese officials turned Taiwan over to ROC forces at the war's end.

Mao Zedong's armies defeated Chiang Kai-shek's forces in the war to control the mainland and Chiang moved his government to Taiwan, the only territory left under his control. The newly declared PRC prepared to "liberate" Taiwan, partly because it had been imperial territory but more because it wished to crush the Chiang regime. That plan was abandoned after the United States intervened in the Korean War and then expanded its security assistance to Taiwan. The conflict that ensued had short episodes of military conflict, but it was primarily political: specifically, a contest to see which government would represent the state of China in the international community. With U.S. support, the ROC maintained its primacy for almost two decades, but the PRC took China's seat in the United Nations in October 1971. In late 1978, Washington recognized the PRC as the sole legal government of China, terminated diplomatic relations with Taiwan, pledged that continued ties with Taiwan would be on an unofficial basis, and agreed to terminate its mutual defense treaty with the ROC.

In 1979, therefore, there began a new, political stage in which the PRC sought to convince Taiwan leaders to end the ROC's separate existence and become a part of the PRC under a formula designed in Beijing (one country, two systems). CCP leaders likely felt that Taiwan's position had become so weak and isolated that it would have no choice but to capitulate. But that did not happen. The Reagan administration and all of its successors have worked to improve Taiwan's self-defense capabilities, to counter the modernization of the PLA. Gradually, the whole of the U.S.-Taiwan relationship grew in breadth and depth. Taiwan's democratic transition, which occurred in the late 1980s and early 1990s, constrained the freedom of the island's leaders in negotiations with Beijing. Some of Taiwan's elected leaders took initiatives that Beijing believed were steps toward Taiwan independence, which increased the fears of war temporarily. PRC pessimism turned to optimism with the election of KMT leader Ma Ying-jeou, and the hopes he brought that cross-Strait relations could improve gradually and lead ultimately to unification. But Ma's engagement strategy and Beijing's hope for progress toward a political settlement hit a wall of domestic opposition in Taiwan that led to growing resistance to unification. Events in Hong Kong in 2014–2015 only confirmed doubts in Taiwan about the one country, two systems formula. In early 2016, voters drove the KMT from power and put Beijing's adversaries, Tsai Ing-wen and her DPP in power.

Tsai's election was a serious setback in Beijing's quest for a political resolution to the cross-Strait conflict. Ma's presidency had given PRC leaders hope that a gradual reconciliation, supported by a majority of the Taiwan public was possible. But with the Tsai/DPP victory plus the KMT's inability to produce a credible contender, that strategy was beginning to look like a mirage in the desert. After eight years of "promoting integration," Beijing found itself back to "opposing independence."

NOTES

1. In the West, Taiwan was known as Formosa until into the 1960s.

2. Harry J. Lamley, "Taiwan under Japanese Rule, 1895–1945: The Vicissitudes of Colonialism," in *Taiwan: A New History*, ed. Murray A. Rubenstein (Armonk, NY: M. E. Sharpe, 1999), 201–60.

3. Some PRC strategists today look at Taiwan in a way similar to Chiang Kai-shek.

4. Harry S. Truman, "Statement by the President, Truman on Korea," Wilson Center Digital Archive, June 27, 1950, https://digitalarchive.wilsoncenter.org/document/116192.

5. The members of the Legislative Yuan who represented areas of the mainland were retained in office, on the spurious grounds that it was not possible to hold elections in those districts. As mainlander members died, they were replaced with the runners-up in the original election.

6. The December 15/16 date reflects the fact that the simultaneous announcement of normalization occurred in the evening of December 15 in Washington, by which time it was already the morning of December 16 in Beijing.

7. In addition, the term "Chinese position" was deliberately vague. It could be interpreted to include the government and people on Taiwan but the evolution of opinion on Taiwan rendered that inference tenuous at best.

8. "Taiwan Relations Act," American Institute in Taiwan, April 10, 1979, www.ait.org.tw/our-relationship/policy-history/key-u-s-foreign-policy-documents-region/taiwan-relations-act/.

9. Because the PRC had not yet restored a chief of state position after it had been eliminated during the Cultural Revolution, the Chairman of the National People's Congress, the PRC's legislature, played that role.

10. "Chairman Ye Jianying's Elaboration on Policy Concerning Return of Taiwan to Motherland and Peaceful Unification," September 30, 1981, www.china.org.cn/english/7945.htm.

11. Reagan's memorandum was declassified in 2018. See President Ronald Reagan to Secretary of State George P. Shultz and Secretary of Defense Caspar W. Weinberger, "Arms Sales to Taiwan," American Institute in Taiwan, August 17, 1982, www.ait.org.tw/wp-content/uploads/sites/269/08171982-Reagan-Memo-DECLASSIFIED.pdf.

12. Alan D. Romberg, *Rein in at the Brink of the Precipice: American Policy toward Taiwan and U.S.-PRC Relations* (Washington, D.C.: Henry L. Stimson Center, 2003), 134–37.

13. International Monetary Fund, "Taiwan Province of China: GDP Per Capita, Current Prices (PPP)," *World Economic Outlook*, October 2021, www.imf.org/external/datamapper/PPPPC@WEO/TWN?zoom=TWN&highlight=TWN.

14. Cited in Jay Taylor, *The Generalissimo's Son: Chiang Ching-kuo and the Revolutions in China and Taiwan* (Cambridge, MA: Harvard University Press, 2000), 414.

15. James R. Lilley and Jeffrey Lilley, *China Hands: Nine Decades of Adventure, Espionage, and Diplomacy in Asia* (New York: Public Affairs, 2005), 257.

16. Stephen J. Solarz, "Democracy and the Future of Taiwan," *Freedom at Issue* 77 (March–April 1984): 18–21.

17. Richard C. Bush, *Difficult Choices: Taiwan's Quest for Security and the Good Life* (Wasington, DC: Brookings Institution Press, 2020), 198–99.

18. These occurred in 1942–1943, when the decision was made to return Taiwan to China; in early 1950, when the Truman administration chose not to defend the island against a communist invasion; in 1972, when Nixon made pledges on Taiwan during his China trip; in 1978, when the provisions were made regarding Taiwan in the U.S.-PRC Normalization Communiqué; and in 1982, when the Reagan administration made a formal agreement with Beijing to limit arms sales to Taiwan.

19. One reason for an agreement on the authentication of documents was that Taiwan used a system of dates based on the year the ROC was founded (1912), and China used the Gregorian calendar. Even dates had a political connotation.

20. The bigger difference was that there was absolutely no overlap on the question of *how* Taiwan would fit into a unified China, a difference that exists to this day.

21. The personal goal of at least one senior official in the George H. W. Bush administration was to "break the August 1982 communiqué."

22. According to the guidelines in effect at that time, Taiwan's president and three other senior officials could only make low-profile transits through the United States on their way to another country but they could not make a dedicated trip to the United States itself.

23. Warren Christopher, "American Interests and the U.S.-China Relationship," speech, New York, May 17, 1996), U.S. Department of State, https://1997-2001.state.gov/current/debate/96517qa.html.

24. Richard C. Bush, *One-China Policy Primer*, Brookings Institution, March 2017, www.brookings.edu/research/a-one-china-policy-primer/, pp. 4–5; Bill Clinton, "Full Text of Clinton's Speech on China Trade Bill," speech, Washington, D.C., March 9, 2000, Johns Hopkins University, https://www.iatp.org/sites/default/files/Full_Text_of_Clintons_Speech_on_China_Trade_Bi.htm.

25. Lee Teng-hui, interview by *Deutsche Welle* radio, July 9, 1999, New Taiwan, Ilha Formosa, https://www.taiwandc.org/nws-9926.htm.

26. This is a frequently misunderstood but longstanding element of Taipei's declaratory policy. From the point of view of international law, the gravamen of the formulation is that the ROC was not subordinate to any other state (in this case, the PRC as government of China). Politically, the word "independent" in the formulation was useful in deflecting the demands of some Taiwanese people that there be a declaration of independence. The rebuttal by Lee and other leaders was that we don't need to declare independence because we already are.

27. "Montevideo Convention on the Rights and Duties of States," International Law Students Association, signed December 26, 1933, entered into force December 26, 1934, www.ilsa.org/Jessup/Jessup15/Montevideo%20Convention.pdf.

28. Note that Lee's emphasis on elections implies a popular-sovereignty basis for state formation.

29. Su Chi, *Taiwan's Relations with Mainland China: A Tail Wagging Two Dogs* (New York: Routledge, 2008), 61–62.

30. The process for territorial changes was later altered when the operations of the National Assembly was suspended in 2005. The second stage of the process was now a referendum in which fifty percent of all eligible voters had to approve the measure for it to go into effect. Again, absent a KMT-DPP consensus, any change of territory was politically highly unlikely.

31. See footnote 20.

32. For a 1999 statement by conservatives that concluded, "The Time for Strategic and Moral 'Ambiguity' with Regard to Taiwan Has Passed," see Richard C. Bush, *Untying the Knot: Making Peace in the Taiwan Strait* (Washington, D.C.: Brookings Institution Press, 2005), 129.

33. David E. Sanger, "U.S. Would Defend Taiwan, Bush Says," *New York Times*, April 26, 2001, www.nytimes.com/2001/04/26/world/us-would-defend-taiwan-bush-says.html.

34. Setting such preconditions and requiring an adversary to "declare themselves" (*biaotai*) was a common tactic in the CCP's playbook. Beijing may have understood that politically Chen could not accept the PRC's one-China principle, because one of its elements was that the territory of Taiwan belonged to the state "China." Strategists within the DPP understood that accepting a PRC principle as the price of beginning interactions with Beijing would put them at a permanent negotiating disadvantage.

35. One referendum asked whether Taiwan should acquire more advanced anti-missile weapons if China refused to withdraw its missiles targeting Taiwan. The other asked whether the government should engage in negotiation with Beijing on the establishment of a "peace and stability" framework.

36. Brian Knowlton, "Bush Warns Taiwan to Keep Status Quo: China Welcomes U.S. Stance," *New York Times*, December 10, 2003, www.nytimes.com/2003/12/10/news/bush -warns-taiwan-to-keep-status-quo-china-welcomes-us-stance.html.

37. James A. Kelly, "Overview of U.S. Policy Toward Taiwan," Testimony before the House International Relations Committee, 108th Cong., 1st sess., April 21, 2004, https://2001-2009.state.gov/p/eap/rls/rm/2004/31649.htm.

38. "Anti-Secession Law," Embassy of the People's Republic of China in the United States of America, March 15, 2005, www.mfa.gov.cn/ce/ceus/eng/zt/999999999/t187406.htm.

39. Cross-Strait dialogue had been suspended since 1999, in the wake of Lee Teng-hui's July statement.

40. Ma Ying-jeou, "Taiwan's Role in Peace and Stability in East Asia: A Discussion with Dr. Ma Ying-jeou," remarks, Brookings Institution, March 23, 2006, www.brookings.edu/ events/taiwans-role-in-peace-and-stability-in-east-asia-a-discussion-with-dr-ma-ying-jeou/.

41. Thomas J. Christensen, "A Strong and Moderate Taiwan," speech, U.S.-Taiwan Business Council Defense Industry Conference, Annapolis, Maryland, September 11, 2007, U.S. Department of State, https://2001-2009.state.gov/p/eap/rls/rm/2007/91979.htm. Italics added.

42. Hu Jintao, "Let Us Join Hands to Promote the Peaceful Development of Cross-Straits Relations and Strive with a United Resolve for the Great Rejuvenation of the Chinese Nation," speech, USC US-China Institute, December 31, 2008, USC, https://china.usc.edu /hu-jintao-let-us-join-hands-promote-peaceful-development-cross-straits-relations-and-strive -united. Italics added.

43. Both statements cited in Richard C. Bush, *Uncharted Strait: The Future of China-Taiwan Relations* (Washington, D.C.: Brookings Institution Press, 2013), 2.

44. Shelley Rigger, *The Tiger Leading the Dragon: How Taiwan Propelled China's Economic Rise* (Lanham, MD: Rowman & Littlefield, 2021), 92.

2

U.S.-Taiwan Relations
from 2016 to Present

When Tsai Ing-wen ran for president of Taiwan for the second time after having been defeated in her first attempt, she visited the United States in June 2015. The trip itself was unsurprising; virtually every nonincumbent Taiwan presidential candidate travels to the United States to demonstrate that he or she can maintain good relations with Taiwan's closest partner.[1] For Tsai, however, the visit carried considerable importance because she had failed to win the confidence of the United States during her prior visit in 2011 when she first ran for the presidency. After her meetings in Washington, a senior Obama administration official told the *Financial Times* that Tsai had left U.S. officials doubtful about whether she was willing and able to preserve cross-Strait stability. Scarred by the experience with Chen Shui-bian, the United States wanted greater certainty that it would not get drawn into a future cross-Strait conflict. Such blunt criticism undoubtedly damaged Tsai's bid for the presidency, which she lost to Ma Ying-jeou by five percentage points.

Over the intervening four years, Taiwan's domestic politics shifted considerably as did Washington's views of the PRC. After eight years of KMT rule under Ma, American elites began to see the potential downsides for U.S. interests of closer China-Taiwan relations. Whereas in 2011 Washington thought it was unlikely that Tsai would defeat Ma, in 2015 they forecasted that she would likely win. There also was wariness within the Obama administration about being perceived as attempting to put a finger on the scale to disadvantage Tsai's candidacy in back-to-back elections. This led to a deliberate effort on the part of the Obama administration to avoid allowing any private differences of views to spill into public view. The atmosphere of her later visit was therefore more congenial even before she landed.

Tsai came to Washington better prepared in 2015 and conveyed a more reassuring message. Although the content of her conversations with U.S. officials was kept under wraps, some of the views she conveyed privately were delivered in a public address to an audience at the Center for Strategic and International Studies. In that speech, Tsai stated that there is a broad consensus in Taiwan for maintaining the cross-Strait status quo and said she was committed to a consistent, predictable, and sustainable relationship with China. She pledged to "push for the peaceful and stable development of cross-Strait relations in accordance with the will of the Taiwanese people and the existing ROC constitutional order." Moreover, in a veiled acknowledgment of her earlier missteps, Tsai maintained that "Taiwan should not take the relationship [with the United States] for granted" and promised to have "a proactive diplomatic agenda for peace" and work "with the U.S. to advance our common interests."[2]

Those early signals proved to be reliable indicators of Tsai Ing-wen's policies toward China and the United States during her first six and a half years in office. By eschewing pro-independence policies that could provoke a Chinese attack and by coordinating closely with Washington, Tsai successfully forged a close and trustful relationship with the United States. Satisfying Beijing and preserving stable cross-Strait relations was a different matter altogether.

TUSSLE OVER THE "1992 CONSENSUS"

China didn't trust Tsai because she was leader of the DPP and because she had served as the head of a group of legal experts under former President Lee Teng-hui that formulated the theory that the two sides of the Strait had a "special state-to-state relationship." Moreover, she served as chair of the MAC and vice premier under Chen Shui-bian. Therefore, Beijing set preconditions for continuing the amicable relationship that had existed across the Strait during Ma Ying-jeou's presidency. First, PRC authorities demanded that Tsai would have to reaffirm and adhere to the 1992 Consensus, as Ma had done. Second, they insisted that Tsai accept the "core connotation" of the 1992 Consensus and its "one-China" principle, which the PRC authorities defined as meaning that there is only one China in the world and Taiwan is an inalienable part of China's sovereign territory.

Both demands were politically impossible for Tsai to accept. The DPP, especially the Deep Green faction of the party, had long rejected the 1992 Consensus and she needed DPP support to win power and then govern. Moreover, the DPP strongly disagreed with Beijing's formulation of the "one-China" principle and distrusted the PRC's intentions. Nevertheless, Tsai believed that by providing some reassurances to Beijing, she could prevent cross-Strait relations from deteriorating and work to achieve a new modus vivendi with China. Toward that end, she attempted to address the PRC's concerns in her inaugural address in May 2016.

Regarding the 1992 Consensus, Tsai noted in her speech that various "joint acknowledgments and understandings" had been reached in November 1992 by the respective institutions of two sides of the Strait, not just political parties (i.e., the KMT and the CCP). That was a "historical fact," she maintained, describing the talks as having taken place "in a spirit of mutual understanding and a political attitude of seeking common ground while setting aside differences." Over the subsequent twenty years, she added, "interactions and negotiations across the Strait have enabled and accumulated outcomes which both sides must collectively cherish and sustain."[3]

As for the "core connection" of the 1992 Consensus, Tsai maintained that she was "elected president in accordance with the Constitution of the Republic of China," which assumes the existence of one China. She also pledged that her government would "conduct cross-Strait affairs in accordance with the Republic of China Constitution, the Act Government Relations Between the People of the Taiwan Area and the Mainland Area, and other relevant legislation." The latter statement suggests that the two areas belong to the same country since it defines the "Mainland Area" as the territory of the Republic of China outside the Taiwan Area.

Beijing opted to reject Tsai Ing-wen's carefully crafted reassurances. Perhaps PRC leaders really believed that she was unalterably committed to *de jure* independence, or they calculated that the power balance was in China's favor, so compromise was unnecessary. Another possibility is that Xi Jinping had limited room to maneuver domestically. Just over a year earlier, Xi Jinping had warned that "the earth will move and the mountains will shake" if "the joint political basis across the Straits is destroyed."[4] Yet another possibility, as Richard Bush has averred, "Beijing set the bar of accommodation higher than she could reasonably clear, so that it would not have to develop a modus vivendi with her government through dialogue."[5]

Charging that Tsai was unacceptably ambiguous about the nature of cross-Strait relations, the PRC gave Tsai "an incomplete exam." In June, Beijing suspended all official channels of communication, including those between the "white glove" organizations, Taiwan's SEF and China's ARATS, responsible for official cross-Strait interactions. As the months and years progressed, Beijing imposed a series of punitive economic and diplomatic measures on Taiwan.

Tsai's view of PRC intentions hardened over time, partly as a result of Beijing's heavy-handed approach to Taiwan, but also in response to international developments. One crucial factor was Xi Jinping's 2019–2020 crackdown in Hong Kong, which exacerbated distrust among the Taiwan people toward China and galvanized the radical wing of the DPP to pressure Tsai to adopt pro-independence policies. Another driver was intensified U.S.-China strategic competition and a hardening of Washington's policy toward China, which provided an opportunity for Tsai to strengthen ties with the United States.

The evolution of President Tsai's stance in a decidedly more anti-China direction was reflected in her major speeches. In Tsai's early years as president, she remained committed to sustaining dialogue with the PRC. This was a key message in her first inaugural address, where she called for both sides to "set aside the baggage of history, and reengage in positive dialogue, for the benefit of the people on both sides."[6] Five months later, in her national day speech (celebrated annually on October 10), Tsai laid out "four noes": "Our pledges will not change, and our goodwill will not change. But we will not bow to pressure, and we will not revert to the old path of confrontation."[7] Marking the thirtieth anniversary of cross-Strait exchanges in her

2017 national day speech, Tsai proposed that both sides treasure the "hard-fought results and accumulated goodwill from the past 30 years" and called upon the leaders from both sides to use "political wisdom" to "search for new modes of cross-Strait interactions with determination and patience." She also called for protecting "the Taiwanese people's right to decide their own future."[8]

In her 2018 national day speech, Tsai maintained that China had "seriously challenged the status quo of peace and stability in the Taiwan Strait." Faced with military threats, diplomatic and economic pressure, as well as social infiltration, Tsai called for an overall strategy to bolster Taiwan's national security. At the same time, she provided reassurances to Beijing, Washington, and to the Taiwan public that her government would "neither act rashly to escalate confrontation, nor will we give in." In addition, she said she would "not be provoked into confrontation or conflicts that endanger cross-Strait relations, nor deviate from the will of the people and sacrifice Taiwan's sovereignty."[9]

In a New Year's Day address delivered on January 1, 2019, Tsai demanded that Beijing implement "four musts": (1) "face squarely the reality of the existence of the Republic of China on Taiwan"; (2) respect the commitment of Taiwan's people to freedom and democracy; (3) handle cross-Strait differences peacefully, on the basis of equality; and (4) rely on governments or government-authorized agencies to engage in negotiations. In subsequent speeches, Tsai reasserted these preconditions using the shorthand "peace, parity, democracy, and dialogue."[10]

After winning reelection in a landslide victory in January 2020, Tsai reiterated her willingness to engage in dialogue with China in her second inaugural address and pledged to continue making "the greatest effort to maintain peace and stability in the Taiwan Strait." Asserting that cross-Strait relations had reached "a historical turning point," she maintained that both sides "have a duty to find a way to coexist over the longer term and prevent the intensification of antagonism and differences." Tsai called on Xi Jinping to work jointly with her to stabilize the long-term development of cross-Strait relations, but her appeal fell on deaf ears.[11]

In her national day speech in October 2021, President Tsai again voiced hoped for better cross-Strait relations and promised to "not act rashly," while reminding Beijing that it should have "no illusions that the Taiwanese people will bow to pressure." Tsai maintained that she would continue to fortify national defense "to ensure that nobody can force Taiwan to take the path China has laid out for us," which is neither free nor democratic and would deprive Taiwan's people of their sovereignty.[12]

Tsai reiterated in her New Year's Day address on January 1, 2022, that Taiwan would "neither bow to pressure nor act rashly." She insisted that the use of military means "is absolutely not an option for resolving the differences between our two sides." The path to peacefully and collectively addressing and resolving problems, Tsai said, requires upholding peace and stability in the Taiwan Strait and each side taking care of people's livelihoods.[13]

Later that year, in her national day speech, Tsai delivered a harsher message, condemning China's escalation of pressure on Taiwan in the wake of House Speaker

Nancy Pelosi's visit and its moves "to erase the sovereignty of the Republic of China (Taiwan)." She warned Beijing to not "attempt to divide Taiwanese society by exploiting the fierce competition between our political parties." Only by respecting the commitment of the people of Taiwan to sovereignty, democracy, and freedom can there be a foundation for resuming constructive interaction across the Taiwan Strait, Tsai maintained. Leaving the door to dialogue open, she stated that her government was willing to work with the PRC to find mutually acceptable arrangements for preserving cross-Strait peace and stability as long as there is "rationality, equality, and mutual respect."[14]

In sum, over time as Taiwan's president, Tsai became more suspicious about PRC's intentions and more pessimistic about the prospects for stabilizing and improving cross-Strait relations. Nevertheless, she remained prudent in her approach to China and refrained from making provocations that Beijing could use to justify a violent response. At the same time, Tsai pursued a strategy to bolster Taiwan's national security that included strengthening relations with the United States.

THE PRC'S USE OF COERCION

For Beijing, Taiwan's acceptance of one China has always been the essential first step to addressing any cross-Strait issues. After Tsai Ing-wen's inauguration, the PRC began to take measures aimed at imposing costs on her and the DPP for their refusal to publicly acknowledge that Mainland China and Taiwan belonged to one and the same country. Over time, Beijing relied increasingly on punitive coercive measures, including diplomatic, military, and economic actions. This is in part because its arsenal of tools expanded, but also because its employment of positive inducements has failed to yield results.

In an early sign of Beijing's intention to retaliate against Tsai Ing-wen for her unwillingness to accept its demands, the PRC began to refuse to facilitate the repatriation of Taiwan citizens accused of fraud in third countries. Between April 2016 and August 2017, 270 Taiwan citizens living in Armenia, Cambodia, Indonesia, Kenya, Malaysia, and Vietnam who were accused of committing telecommunications fraud against people in China were deported to China, instead of to Taiwan. This was a departure from the PRC's prior willingness during Ma Ying-jeou's presidency to cooperate with Taiwan on law enforcement matters in countries with which Taiwan does not have diplomatic relations.

Beginning in May 2016, the PRC government quietly urged travel companies to reduce visits to Taiwan by groups of Mainland Chinese tourists. One year later, the total number of PRC tourists visiting Taiwan had dropped by 38.3 percent. Beijing also cut the number of Mainland Chinese students allowed to study at Taiwan universities in 2017 by more than half. Then, on August 1, 2019, the PRC ceased issuing individual travel permits for Taiwan to people from forty-seven major Chinese cities. That year only 2.7 million Mainland Chinese tourists visited Taiwan, down from a peak of over four million in 2015. The number of Mainland Chinese tourists plunged further in 2020 to around 111,000. Fortunately for Taiwan, successful efforts by Taiwan's government to boost travelers from other countries cushioned the blow to the island's tourist industry.

After Tsai's inauguration, Beijing also began to apply trade pressure by denying entry to an unusually high percentage of shipments of food and cosmetic imports from Taiwan for allegedly failing to meet safety standards. Imports of Taiwan's milk-fish, farmed in Tainan's Xuejia district in southern Taiwan—the power base of the DPP—were also suspended in 2016, allegedly due to rising prices after an unusually cold winter in Taiwan. One company in Shanghai had been importing five thousand to six thousand tons of milkfish annually since 2011 to incentivize fish farmers to vote against the DPP.

Chinese trade coercion against Taiwan ebbed for a few years and then resurfaced in February 2020 when Beijing banned imports of Taiwan pineapples, citing the risk of pests that could affect its own crops. Before the ban, virtually all of Taiwan's pineapples were sold to China and 99.79 percent of them had passed inspection. A domestic campaign to increase demand in Taiwan and a surge in exports to Japan more than made up for China's boycott. Despite the failure to impose costs on Taiwan, the PRC halted imports of sugar and wax apples from Taiwan in September, once again due to alleged contamination with harmful bugs. It was no coincidence that pineapples, sugar apples, and wax apples were ranked the top three fruit exports from Taiwan to China in terms of value in 2019.

In June 2022, China suspended imports of Taiwan's grouper, claiming that malachite green, a prohibited chemical used in aquaculture, was detected in samples. Two months later, after Speaker Pelosi's visit to Taiwan, Beijing expanded its trade bans to cover more than two thousand individual Taiwan food products, including vegetables, cookies, cakes, drinks, and fresh seafood. Since food comprises only a tiny fraction of Taiwan's exports to the PRC, the impact on its economy was not consequential, though individual companies suffered losses. Beijing turned the screws further in December 2022, suspending imports of alcoholic beverages from select Taiwan companies.

Even as the PRC imposed economic pressure on Tsai and her DPP supporters, it continued to offer positive inducements to the private sector and tried to court young people to promote cross-Strait economic integration and influence Taiwan's politics. In February 2018, the PRC rolled out "31 Measures" aimed at (1) bypassing Tsai Ing-wen's DPP leadership and instead directly providing opportunities for Taiwan's businesses and individuals in China; and (2) attracting Taiwan investment and luring top Taiwan talent to move to the PRC. As it turned out, according to Taiwan's MAC, the effect of the thirty-one measures a year after they were launched was minimal. For example, in 2018, Taiwan businesspeople invested US$8.5 billion in China, representing an 8.1 percent fall from the previous year, and the third consecutive year of negative growth.

In 2019, just two months before Taiwan's presidential elections, Beijing announced twenty-six additional incentives to entice Taiwan talent and companies. The new measures were ostensibly to provide enterprises and individuals from

Taiwan with the same treatment as those from Mainland China. For example, Taiwan firms were supposed to be granted equal treatment in financing, trade remedies, export credit insurance, import and export facilitation, and standards formulation. Taiwan individuals were similarly offered equal treatment in areas such as consular protection, agricultural cooperation, transportation, communication charges, culture and sports, and admissions and examinations. Taiwan's outbound investment in China rebounded in 2020, rising 42 percent, after plunging 51 percent in 2019 over the previous year. The increase was likely a result of China's success in controlling the COVID-19 pandemic that year and its relatively rapid economic recovery, rather than a result of the twenty-six measures.

The deterioration of cross-Strait relations and the questionable effectiveness of such preferential measures did not stop Beijing from providing economic incentives to Taiwan and encouraging cross-Strait integration. On an inspection tour of the southeastern province of Fujian located opposite Taiwan in March 2021, Xi Jinping exhorted provincial officials to "be bold in exploring new paths for integrated cross-Strait development," including by implementing policies that would enhance Taiwan people's livelihoods to advance economic and social integration across the Taiwan Strait.[15]

In a possible sign of escalating PRC economic coercion, the Taipei-based Far Eastern Group, a conglomerate with business operations in China, was fined almost US$14 million in November 2021, ostensibly for environmental, health and safety, land use, and other violation of PRC laws. The real reason for the fines, as made clear by Chinese officials and state media, was Far Eastern's donations to Taiwan's ruling DPP. The action against Far Eastern came a few weeks after Beijing announced it would sanction Taiwanese politicians who push for independence as well as companies that provide them with financial support. Asked about the punishment of Far Eastern, a spokesperson for Beijing's Taiwan Affairs Office said that China "will absolutely not allow people who support Taiwan independence or destroy cross-Taiwan Strait relations to make money in the mainland, who dare bite the hand that feeds them."[16] Ironically, the Far Eastern Group's CEO, Douglas Hsu, comes from a Mainland Chinese family. The episode marked the first time that the PRC undertook punitive economic measures against Taiwan that could have significant negative impact on Chinese economic interests. Beijing's willingness to incur costs may signal a new and more dangerous phase in cross-Strait relations.

Another tactic being employed by the PRC to pressure Taipei is the arbitrary detention of Taiwan residents visiting China. According to the SEF, in the three years and four months after Tsai Ing-wen's inauguration in May 2016, there were 149 reports of Taiwan citizens who had gone missing after traveling to the PRC. The most well-known case was that of human rights activist Lee Ming-che who disappeared in March 2017 and was later sentenced to five years in prison for "state subversion." Lee was released after completing his prison term and returned to Taiwan in April 2022. Of the remaining missing individuals, as of October 2020, 101 had either returned home or informed Taiwan officials about their detention. The whereabouts of forty-eight individuals remain unknown.

Another consequence of Beijing's coercive response to the Tsai administration was a rollback in the gains that had been made in Taiwan's participation in international organizations during the Ma Ying-jeou era. In late May 2016, just over a week following Tsai's inauguration, her new minister of health attended the WHA meeting in Geneva, marking the eighth time that Taiwan joined the annual meeting as an observer. However, a Chinese official maintained that this was a "special arrangement under the one-China principle" and warned that future participation in international organizations would only take place if Tsai acknowledged the "1992 Consensus." Beijing has blocked Taiwan's participation since then, including after the onset of the COVID-19 pandemic when the Group of Seven (G7) for the first time backed Taiwan's inclusion in the WHA.

Taiwan was also not invited to participate in the UN's International Civil Aviation Organization's (ICAO) Council Assembly in 2016, which it had attended three years earlier as a guest of then-ICAO Council President Roberto Kobeh-Gonzalez. Similarly, despite being allowed to participate in previous years, individuals from Taiwan were excluded from the annual conference of the UN's International Labor Organization and meetings of the Food and Agriculture Organization of the UN's Committee on Fisheries. In May 2017, Taiwan's delegation was forced to leave a meeting of the Kimberly Process held in Perth, Australia, after PRC officials at the meeting raucously protested their participation.

Taiwan's nongovernmental organizations (NGOs) have also felt the pinch. In 2016, the chairman of the Taiwan Foundation for Rare Disorders, a Taiwan NGO dedicated to the treatment of rare diseases, was barred from a UN-affiliated meeting because of an objection from Beijing. Although Taiwan has not succeeded in its bid to join the UN Framework Convention on Climate Change (UNFCCC) as an observer, ten of its NGOs are accredited as civil society observers and have been allowed to participate in major conferences. In recent years, however, even Taiwan's NGOs have occasionally been barred from UNFCCC meetings. For example, the Taiwan Youth Climate Coalition was prevented from attending the opening ceremony of the UN climate talks in Glasgow, Scotland, known as COP26.

In addition to intensifying its efforts to curtail the ability of Taiwan NGOs to take part in international organizations that require sovereignty for membership, the PRC has stepped up pressure on NGOs from around the world to use what it calls the "correct terminology for Taiwan Province" on their websites.[17] At the May 2021 session of the UN Economic and Social Council's (ECOSOC) Committee on NGOs, the applications of seven NGOs for UN consultative status, which permits NGOs to participate in UN proceedings, were deferred due to objections from Beijing concerning the terminology used for Taiwan on their websites. Even a small, private high school in Colorado was ordered to refer to Taiwan as a province of China before it could get approval to take part in a UN commission. Yet no UN provision requires NGOs or other groups to take a particular stance on the status of Taiwan.

Another way in which Beijing attempted to both punish Tsai and pressure her to accede to Chinese demands was by poaching Taiwan's diplomatic partners.

Beginning in the 1970s, the PRC and Taiwan competed for diplomatic recognition from nations around the world using checkbook diplomacy. The main trend, however, was countries switching diplomatic allegiance to Beijing, which the PRC encouraged through the use of financial incentives. During the eight years of Chen Shui-bian's presidency, Beijing persuaded nine countries to break diplomatic ties with Taiwan and recognize the PRC but had a net loss of six. Under the eight years of Ma Ying-jeou's rule, Taipei and Beijing reached a tacit understanding to halt their competition for recognition from each other's diplomatic partners.

That "diplomatic truce" ended even before Tsai's inauguration. In March 2016, Beijing reestablished diplomatic ties with Gambia, a country in West Africa, which had broken ties with Taiwan in 2013 but wasn't recognized by the PRC at the time due to the truce with Ma. Over the next five years, China wooed away eight of Taipei's diplomatic partners: Sao Tome and Principe in December 2016, Panama in June 2017, Burkina Faso, the Dominican Republic, and El Salvador in 2018, the Solomon Islands and Kiribati in 2019, and Nicaragua in 2021. This left only thirteen countries and the Holy See (Vatican City) with full diplomatic relations ties with Taiwan.

Since the late 1990s, the PLA has been preparing for contingencies in the Taiwan Strait to deter, and if necessary, compel Taiwan to abandon moves toward *de jure* independence. At the same time, the PLA is amassing capabilities to unify Taiwan with the PRC by force, while deterring or denying intervention by a third party, most likely the United States. One of the goals of China's 2015 military reforms was to build a military capable of carrying out complex joint operations such as invading and occupying Taiwan. The PLA's focus on preparing for using violence against Taiwan is evidenced by its development of a force structure that is aimed at sea control, amphibious warfare, and power projection. As part of its wide-ranging campaign to pressure Taiwan and the Tsai administration, and to warn the United States not to challenge PRC sovereignty or embolden Taipei to pursue independence, the Chinese military has continually conducted military operations and training near Taiwan. For example, according to the U.S. Department of Defense's 2021 China Military Power Report, the PLA conducted joint amphibious assault exercises near Taiwan in 2020. China's aircraft carrier, the *Liaoning*, along with its escort ships, sailed through the Taiwan Strait.[18] China's Zhurihe Training Base in Inner Mongolia contains a huge mockup of a portion of downtown Taipei, including full-size recreations of the Presidential Office Building and Ministry of Foreign Affairs.

On March 31, 2019, two PLA Air Force (PLAAF) J-11 fighters deliberately crossed the median line of the Taiwan Strait for the first time in two decades. The median line was drawn by the United States in 1955, and although it is not an official boundary, it had been tacitly observed by both China and Taiwan with a few exceptions since 1958. After that violation, sorties by Chinese military aircraft into Taiwan's Air Defense Identification Zone (ADIZ) have occurred at ever higher rates and with increasing frequency, with occasional median line crossings. Between September 17, 2020, when Taiwan's Ministry of National Defense began publishing daily, detailed reports on the PLA's flights into Taiwan's ADIZ, and September

30, 2021, Chinese military aircraft entered Taiwan's ADIZ on nearly 250 days. In August 2022, 444 Chinese aircraft crossed into Taiwan's ADIZ – more than twice the number of aircraft of the previous record month (196 aircraft in October 2020). Sorties are conducted by various types of military aircraft from the PLAAF and PLA Navy, and occasionally include nuclear-capable bombers.

There is no single reason for the PRC's brazen military activity around Taiwan. On some occasions, Chinese aggressive operations appear to be intended to signal Beijing's displeasure over U.S. arms sales to Taiwan and high-level visits by American officials to Taiwan, such as the visits by U.S. Secretary of Health and Human Services Alex Azar and Under Secretary of State Keith Krach in 2020. At other times, however, a specific trigger has been absent. Training Chinese pilots, collecting intelligence on Taiwan's response mechanisms, wearing down Taiwan's pilots and maintenance crews, intimidating the Tsai administration, and inducing psychological despair among Taiwan's populace are all likely PRC objectives.

In addition to its expanding toolkit for economic, diplomatic, and military coercion, Beijing has continued to develop and implement its "Three Warfares" concept, composed of psychological warfare, public opinion warfare, and legal warfare, which is designed to demoralize adversaries in peacetime and during conflicts. The "Three Warfares" has been an element of PRC operation planning against Taiwan since at least 2003. As part of this strategy, China has stepped up its influence operations, including disinformation campaigns, which are aimed at undermining the resolve of the Taiwan military and people to defend themselves. Disinformation is also being used to influence Taiwan's politics. One analysis of the rapid rise in popularity of Han Kuo-yu, who won the 2018 Kaohsiung mayoral race, later became the KMT's losing presidential candidate in 2020, and subsequently was recalled from his mayorship, attributed his mayoral victory to "a campaign of social media manipulation orchestrated by a mysterious professional cybergroup in China."[19]

Beijing has also blatantly used more traditional forms of media in Taiwan to influence public opinion. Investigative reporting has uncovered that the PRC's Taiwan Affairs Office directed managers at the pro-Beijing *China Times* and CTi-TV regarding what issues to cover in their stories.[20] In May 2019, a delegation of anti-Tsai Ing-wen Taiwan media executives visited Beijing and was received by CCP Politburo Standing Committee member Wang Yang, who has responsibility for policy toward Taiwan. Wang told the group: "Now as we want to realize peaceful unification, one country, two systems, we need to rely on the joint efforts of our friends in the media. I believe you understand the situation. History will remember you."[21]

United Front tactics remain a mainstay of the PRC's strategy to influence Taiwan's politics and society. CCP efforts to identify potential sympathizers within the KMT and force a "united front" with them to weaken its adversary date to the CCP-KMT civil war. According to Vincent Chen, deputy director-general of Taiwan's National Security Bureau, there are at least twenty-two pro-unification organizations and political parties in Taiwan, some of which have connections to organized crime and networks that extend to local temples, Taiwan businessmen in the mainland, or Taiwan youth.[22]

All these forms of coercion are examples of "gray zone" tactics, which are measures used to exert pressure while remaining below the threshold of use of force to avoid a legitimate conventional military response. Within the gray zone, which a study by the Center for Strategic and International Studies defines as "the contested arena somewhere between routine statecraft and open warfare," the PRC is employing a broad range of levers to gain a strategic advantage over Taiwan and any country that might try to intervene in a conflict in the Taiwan Strait.[23]

One consequence of PRC coercion against Taiwan was an increase in the perceived unfriendliness of China toward Taiwan's government and the Taiwan people as measured in public opinion polls conducted or commissioned by Taiwan's MAC. In August 2019, China's perceived unfriendliness toward Taiwan's people exceeded 51 percent for the first time since the poll was first conducted in December 2010. In August 2022, China's perceived unfriendliness toward the Taiwan people was 66.6 percent and its perceived unfriendliness toward the Taiwan government was 80.1 percent.[24] In addition to the PRC's increased reliance on coercion in its strategy toward Taiwan, Beijing's crackdown on democracy advocates in Hong Kong likely contributed to the increased negativity in Taiwan's perceptions of PRC unfriendliness toward the government and people.

XI JINPING'S TAIWAN STRATEGY

In October 2013 Xi Jinping met with Ma Ying-jeou's envoy, former Taiwan Vice President Vincent Siew, on the margins of the APEC leaders meeting in Bali. It was his third meeting with a representative from Taiwan since assuming the post of CCP general secretary a year earlier. Reports from Chinese state media on their discussion cited Xi as calling for Beijing and Taipei to maintain the momentum of "peaceful development of relations across the Taiwan Strait," a reference to the policy guideline set by his predecessor Hu Jintao. "Both sides of the Strait belong to one family," the Chinese leader said, and urged the strengthening of political mutual trust. Xi then made an unprecedented statement: "the issue of political disagreements that exist between the two sides must reach a final resolution, step by step, and these issues cannot be passed on from generation to generation." He also reiterated the PRC's willingness to "make reasonable and fair arrangements" for "equal consultations" with Taiwan on cross-Strait issues within the framework of "one China."[25] This may have been a signal that Xi Jinping aspired to make progress toward reunification during his tenure in power, perhaps by opening cross-Strait political talks, or even unifying the two sides of the Strait. It may also have reflected Xi's unhappiness that Ma Ying-jeou had been unwilling to start political talks, as Beijing had requested.

Despite this possible indication of impatience or even ambition—which Xi only repeated once in the succeeding nine years—the PRC has continued to pursue a policy that prioritizes preventing Taiwan's *de jure* independence over the goal of achieving reunification. Beijing professes to remain confident in its capacity to achieve this priority objective, even as it lays the groundwork for its long-term aim of unifying Taiwan with the motherland. Xi frequently reaffirms that he is committed to the pursuit of peaceful reunification, while occasionally noting that use of force is an option if all peaceful means are exhausted. Statements on Taiwan by Xi Jinping, such as in his speeches in 2021 on the CCP's 100th anniversary and the 110th anniversary of the 1991 Xinhai Revolution, underscore China's determination to reunify the country; to defend national sovereignty and territorial integrity; and to adhere to one country, two systems, the one-China principle, and the 1992 Consensus. These declarations echo statements by earlier PRC leaders.

Xi Jinping's messages to President Biden in their first virtual meeting in November 2021 included a sharp warning that "whoever plays with fire will get burnt" and an admonition not to use Taiwan to contain China, but did not signal an urgency to achieve unification. Regarding that longer-term goal, Xi said, "We have patience and will strive for the prospect of peaceful reunification with utmost sincerity and efforts," adding the caveat that if China's hand is forced by "separatist forces for Taiwan independence," it "will be compelled to take resolute measures."[26] When the two leaders met on the margins of the G20 Leaders' Summit in Bali, Indonesia in November 2022, Xi Jinping emphasized that the "Taiwan question" is "the core of China's core interests" and the "first red line that must not be crossed in China-U.S. relations."[27]

In his first ten years in power, Xi Jinping gave only one comprehensive speech laying out his thinking about, and policy toward, Taiwan. That speech was delivered on January 2, 2019, on the occasion of the fortieth anniversary of a message that the standing committee of the National People's Congress (the PRC's legislature) sent to its "Taiwan compatriots" announcing the shift from the policy of liberation to one of peaceful unification. The main thrust of Xi's speech was that reunification was a historical inevitability and Beijing would continue to rely primarily on persuasion and economic integration. For example, Xi proposed that "integrated cross-Strait development" be deepened to consolidate the foundation for unification. "Integrated cross-Strait development" is a modification of "peaceful development of cross-Strait relations," and was introduced in 2017 as a response to the DPP's return to power. The revised policy focuses on bringing the people of Taiwan and the mainland closer together through social and economic interaction. In that vein, Xi called for creating a common market and greater cooperation in infrastructure, industrial standards, education, healthcare, and other areas. In addition, Xi stressed the importance of shared language, origin, and race, because "between loved ones, there is no knot of perception that cannot be untied."[28]

On the tougher side, Xi warned against any effort to separate Taiwan from Mainland China. "Taiwan independence is an adverse current of history and is the road to ruin . . . and will only bring immense catastrophe to Taiwan," he maintained, citing the need to "adhere to the one-China principle and safeguard the prospect of peaceful unification." As for how unification should be achieved, Xi reaffirmed that "peaceful reunification and one country, two systems" was the "best approach," but he called for exploring a "Taiwan version" of "one country, two systems." PRC experts later pointed to this as a gesture of good will toward

Taiwan that they hoped would open the door to thinking creatively about future cross-Strait integration. They failed to realize the disastrous impact Beijing's policies toward Hong Kong would later have on Taiwan's assessment of its ties with China.

Another central message of Xi's January 2 speech that can be traced to prior Chinese leaders is that the goal of restoring China to great power status is hampered by Taiwan's separate existence. "The Taiwan issue," he said, "is an outcome of a weak China and a country in turmoil." Asserting that "our country must be reunified, and will surely be reunified," Xi maintained that achieving reunification was "an inevitable requirement for realizing the rejuvenation of the Chinese nation in the new era." This linkage between unification and the country's rejuvenation, which Xi Jinping dubbed early on as the "Chinese Dream," was first made by Xi in his political report to the 19th Party Congress in October 2017 and was repeated in Xi's political report to the 20th Party Congress in October 2022. A White Paper entitled "The Taiwan Question and China's Reunification in the New Era," released by Beijing in August 2022 – the first White Paper on PRC policy toward Taiwan in two decades – also stated that reunification is "indispensable" for the realization of China's rejuvenation.[29]

Whether tying Taiwan unification with national rejuvenation means that Xi's 2049 target for the latter is now a hard deadline for the former is a subject of heated debate both inside and outside China. Xi would be ninety-five years old in 2049, and even if he is still alive, he is unlikely to be China's top leader. His successor could introduce a new narrative, for example, by persisting in calling for reunification, but claiming that national rejuvenation is attainable as long as Taiwan is not permanently separated from Mainland China.

The more important determinant of whether Beijing remains patient in its pursuit of reunification with Taiwan is whether the PRC views time as on its side. A judgment that the window for reuniting with Taiwan is closing—for example, due to the absence of a viable political party in Taiwan that supports one China—could require a shift in strategy aimed at using all possible means to compel reunification. Alternatively, if the PRC remains confident that time is on its side, it is more likely to conclude that using force against Taiwan presents unnecessary and unacceptable risks. In that regard, it is notable that the Resolution of the CCP on the Major Achievements and Historical Experience of the Party Over the Past Century that was adopted at the Sixth Plenum on November 11, 2021, stated that, "We have maintained the initiative and the ability to steer in cross-Strait relations. For realizing China's complete reunification, time and momentum are always on our side."[30]

As Xi Jinping's first decade in power nears its end, the risk of a PRC military invasion of Taiwan exists but is far from certainty or even a high probability in the coming years. China's redline for the use of military force to seize and control the island remains an effort by Taiwan to change its legal identity. In the near term, intensified coercion against Taiwan is more likely than a full-scale invasion. Yet the danger is growing that the PRC will use limited military actions to bolster China's redline and warn Taiwan and the United States against crossing it.

An important signal of PRC intentions may come when the CCP issues the "Comprehensive Plan for Resolving the Taiwan Problem in the New Era," which was mentioned for the first time in the third resolution on party history issued in November 2021 at the CCP Central Committee Sixth Plenum. Early indications in Chinese state media suggest that the Comprehensive Plan may be largely a repackaging of current policy, but it cannot be ruled out that a more coercive and even more aggressive approach could be afoot.

Future PRC policy toward Taiwan, whether formulated by Xi Jinping or his successors, will be influenced by numerous factors, including: (1) the CCP's confidence in the PLA's ability to seize and control Taiwan at an acceptable cost; (2) the CCP's assessment of the risk of Taiwan independence; (3) the relative weight of PRC domestic challenges, including the economy and social stability; and (4) the CCP's assessment of U.S. intentions toward China and Taiwan, and the durability of the U.S. one-China policy.

U.S. POLICY TOWARD TAIWAN UNDER TRUMP

President-elect Donald Trump's December 2, 2016, phone call with Taiwan's President Tsai Ing-wen only lasted a few minutes and was primarily an exchange of congratulatory pleasantries. According to some accounts, it was added to Trump's call sheet at the last minute without any prior discussion of potential fallout. Other versions claim Trump placed the call after huddling with his advisors based on the belief that talking to Taiwan's president would increase his leverage over Beijing. Whatever the truth, there is no doubt that Trump didn't expect the call to backfire. The episode ended up poisoning Trump on Taiwan and weakening the hawks on his team who favored using Taiwan as a weapon against China, according to Josh Rogin, author of *Chaos under Heaven.*

Regardless of whether the initial plan was to use Taiwan to gain an advantage over China, Trump clearly decided to give it a shot. In an interview with Fox Sunday News on December 11, 2016, he explained that abiding by the one-China policy only made sense if he could "make a deal with China having to do with other things, including trade." Beijing responded with a curt message: the "one-China principle" is "non-negotiable."[31] Even after Trump's inauguration, there would be no substantial communication whatsoever between China and the United States until the newly elected American president repaired the damage that he had caused with his Taiwan call. Trump, who hoped to persuade Xi to meet him at his Mar-a-Lago estate, had no choice but to do a volte-face. The PRC stonewalled proposals from the White House to arrange an introductory call between the two leaders until Trump agreed to reaffirm the U.S. one-China policy. After an arranged phone call with Xi Jinping, the White House issued a statement that said, "President Trump agreed, at the request of President Xi, to honor our one-China policy."[32]

Henceforth, Trump would be cautious on any issue related to Taiwan. Two months after the call with Xi, Trump told Reuters that he would "certainly want to speak to [Xi] first before taking another call from Tsai."[33] Throughout his presidency, Trump's reaction to policy decisions involving Taiwan ranged from contempt to fury and occasionally indifference. Former Trump National Security Advisor John Bolton related in *The Room Where It Happened* that Trump often used the analogies of the tip of one of his Sharpies and his Resolute Desk to compare Taiwan and China. When Trump learned that a deputy assistant secretary of state's visit to Taipei had prompted a PRC government protest, he was incensed and demanded to know why he hadn't been informed in advance. On several occasions, Trump delayed notifying Congress of arms sales approvals to Taiwan to avoid angering Beijing.

President Trump had a long-standing antipathy to U.S. alliances and their associated defense commitments. He privately questioned whether the U.S. should plan to come to Taiwan's defense under any circumstances. In Bob Woodward's book on the first year of the Trump administration, *Fear: Trump in the White House*, he relates a meeting at which Trump and his national security team discussed the nature and rationale for U.S. treaty alliances. After initially inquiring what the United States gets by maintaining a large military presence on the Korean Peninsula, Trump said, "Even more than that, what do we get from protecting Taiwan, say?" In another episode, when a senator warned the president about the possibility of a Chinese invasion of Taiwan, Trump reportedly said that "Taiwan is like two feet from China. . . . We are eight thousand miles away. If they invade, there isn't a fucking thing we can do about it."

President Trump's reluctance to take measures in support of Taiwan that could set back ties with Beijing persisted until early 2020. The signing of the phase one U.S.-China trade deal in January and the spread of COVID-19 to the United States and the rest of the world in the ensuing weeks and months soured Trump on China. After praising China in a tweet in January for "working very hard" to control the virus, Trump explicitly blamed the Chinese government in March for the pandemic, claiming it could have been contained within Chinese borders if Beijing had fully shared information about the outbreak.

There was no consensus in the Trump administration about Taiwan policy or any other foreign policy issue, for that matter. His advisors were divided, and they often pursued their own agendas while deliberately keeping President Trump out of the loop. Most of the time, however, senior administration officials worked earnestly to strengthen Taiwan's security and U.S.-Taiwan ties because they believed that Taiwan and the bilateral relationship have value on their own merits. Occasionally, however, Taiwan was seen as a card to be played in the intensifying U.S. strategic competition with China.

During the four years of Trump's presidency, many policy steps were taken to enhance U.S.-Taiwan relations and signal strong U.S. backing for Taiwan. In March 2018, Deputy Assistant Secretary of State Alex Wong—the U.S. official that roused Trump's ire—visited Taipei and delivered a speech alongside President Tsai. In his remarks, Wong asserted that the United States wished "to strengthen our ties with the Taiwan people and to bolster Taiwan's ability to defend its democracy," adding that, "Our commitment to these goals has never been stronger."[34]

When the United States dedicated its sprawling new building in Taipei a few months later, Marie Royce, an Assistant Secretary of State for Educational and Cultural Affairs, was sent by the State Department to attend the ceremony. She said that "The new office complex is a symbol of the strength and vibrancy of the U.S.-Taiwan partnership in the 21st century."[35] Several senior U.S. officials had tried to persuade President Trump to include a cabinet member in the U.S. delegation, but he reportedly vetoed the idea due to concerns about setting back trade talks with China.

The dispatch of a cabinet secretary came more than two years later, after Trump abandoned hope of extracting more trade concessions from Beijing and denounced China for spreading what he called the "China virus" or the "kung flu." U.S. Secretary of Health and Human Services Alex M. Azar II visited Taipei in August 2020, marking the first time visit by a U.S. cabinet member to Taiwan since 2014 and the highest-level visit by an American official to the island since 1979. U.S. officials said the visit was intended to highlight Taiwan's success in containing the spread of the coronavirus. One month after Azar's visit, the Trump administration sent a special envoy to Taiwan to attend a memorial service for former President Lee Teng-hui. The envoy, Keith Krach, undersecretary for economic growth, energy, and the environment, was the highest-level official from the State Department to visit Taiwan since the United States broke diplomatic ties with Taipei.

In the first publicly announced meeting between U.S. and Taiwan national security advisors since 1979, U.S. National Security Advisor John Bolton met with his Taiwan counterpart NSC Secretary General David Lee in May 2019. The visit by Lee to Washington, D.C., was kept under wraps until after he had departed the United States. Taipei was surprised when Trump administration officials encouraged them to publicize the visit and Lee's schedule in Washington. In another likely first, Rear Admiral Michael Studeman, director of J2, which is responsible for intelligence at the U.S. Indo-Pacific Command, visited Taiwan in November 2020.

In addition to continuing to hold long-established bilateral dialogues with Taiwan, such as the political-military talks, consultations on Taiwan's participation in international organizations, and the special channel talks, the Trump administration created new mechanisms to expand communication and cooperation between Washington and Taipei. One of those forums was the U.S.-Taiwan Consultations on Democratic Governance in the Indo-Pacific region, which was launched in September 2019 and co-led by Taiwan's Foreign Minister Joseph Wu and Deputy Assistant Secretary of State Scott Busby, the senior-most official in the Bureau of Democracy, Human Rights, and Labor. The impetus behind the new mechanism was the U.S. desire to deepen cooperation with Taiwan on governance matters in the Indo-Pacific. During the rollout, AIT Director Brent Christensen described the new dialogue mechanism as linked to the U.S. vision for a free and open Indo-Pacific (FOIP). He specifically noted that Taiwan had an important role to play in the FOIP strategy's three pillars: economics, security, and governance.[36] Complementing the Democratic Governance dialogue, a year later the Trump administration established a financing framework to strengthen cooperation on infrastructure development in the Indo-Pacific.

Another new bilateral mechanism, the U.S.-Taiwan Economic Prosperity Partnership Dialogue (EPPD), was launched in November 2020. A five-year agreement was inked to promote cooperation on health, technology, and security. The forum was the Trump administration's response to President Tsai Ing-wen's decision the previous summer to lift remaining restrictions on the import of American beef and pork. Taipei had hoped that Tsai's politically courageous act would be followed by a U.S. decision to initiate talks on a Free Trade Agreement (FTA), or at least resume the Trade and Investment Framework Agreement (TIFA) talks, but the USTR refused to sign on. Since the State Department's portfolio included economics, but not trade, the new forum was intended to focus on issues like 5G security, semiconductors, as well as investment screening and science and technology. As crucial issues in the bilateral relationship that also have global implications, the EPPD was a welcome addition but wasn't a substitute for trade agreements. Nor did it solve the negative impact on Taiwan of Trump-imposed tariff surcharges on steel and aluminum imports from around the world. The tariffs, which were aimed at curbing the alleged dumping of Chinese steel and aluminum products in the United States, were imposed in March 2018 under Section 232 of the Trade Expansion Act of 1962. Taipei fought hard to secure a tariff exemption but was unsuccessful.

Bilateral cooperation was also advanced in other areas. The Trump administration, through AIT, signed bilateral agreements with Taiwan to further cooperation on intellectual property rights enforcement, international parental child abduction, health, international education focused on Mandarin and English training, and science and technology. In addition, Taiwan's Ministry of Foreign Affairs and AIT issued a joint statement in March 2020 outlining efforts to cooperate in the research and development of tests, medicines, and vaccines for COVID-19, as well as in the exchange of medical supplies.

Trump's Department of Defense (DoD) was especially forward-leaning in its support for Taiwan. In his speech at the Singapore Shangri-La Dialogue in June 2017, Defense Secretary James Mattis maintained that his department was "steadfastly committed to working with Taiwan and with its democratic government" to fulfill U.S. obligations under the TRA. Although the message was unexceptional, it was the first time that a U.S. Secretary of Defense had mentioned Taiwan at the annual forum since its inception in 2002.

DoD broke new ground in U.S. support for Taiwan, however, when it released the Indo-Pacific Strategy Report on June 1, 2019. The report was described as an "implementation document" for the Department's role in the Trump administration's FOIP vision. The section of the report that focused on Taiwan opened with "The United States has a vital interest in upholding the rules-based order, which includes a strong, prosperous, and democratic Taiwan." Taiwan was referred to as a country with which the United States has a security partnership, in a section that also included Singapore, New Zealand, and Mongolia, all of which were described as "reliable, capable, and natural partners of the United States" that are "actively taking steps to uphold a free and open international order."[37] The designation of Taiwan as a country was a break from the way Taiwan has historically been described in U.S.

official documents. Some U.S. officials privately claimed that it was an oversight, but it is more likely that the language used was purposeful. Also notable was that the approach elevated the centrality of Taiwan's role in the rebalance to Asia relative to the Obama administration.

In another change in the way that Taiwan was handled compared to prior administrations, Trump's DoD made public many military operations and defense-related engagements with Taiwan that had previously been kept secret. In an unprecedented move, the U.S. Army posted a video on its official Facebook page on June 16, 2020, showing Green Berets from the elite 1st Special Forces Group training on the island of Taiwan with counterparts from Taiwan's army.[38] A Chinese newspaper in Singapore reported that the U.S. military had confirmed that the video depicted Green Berets taking part in an exercise known as "Balance Tamper" in Taiwan.[39] The following year, after Trump had already left office, it was reported that about two dozen members of U.S. special operation and support troops together with a contingent of Marines had been "secretly operating in Taiwan to train military forces there" for at least a year.[40]

In another example, the *South China Morning Post* revealed that it had tried, but failed, to obtain data on U.S. Navy transits through the Taiwan Strait until the U.S. Pacific Fleet provided it to the newspaper in May 2019. The U.S. Navy began announcing transits of the Taiwan Strait by U.S. warships in July 2018 and has continued the practice ever since. Taiwan Strait transits by U.S. navy ships totaled twenty-nine and thirty-nine in President Obama's first and second terms, respectively.[41] During Trump's four years in office, there were thirty such transits.

The Trump administration notified Congress of twenty proposed major Foreign Military Sales cases for Taiwan, with a combined value of $18.3 billion. Among the most significant notifications was the approval in August 2019 of 66 new F-16V fighter aircraft. The Obama administration had considered selling new fighter jets to Taiwan but decided instead to help Taiwan refurbish its existing fleet of 145 F-16s.

Another noteworthy weapons sale was the October 2020 decision to sell Taiwan 135 Standoff Land Attack Missile Expanded Response (SLAM-ER) Missiles and eleven High Mobility Artillery Rocket System (HIMARS). Observers widely viewed both weapons systems as providing Taiwan with offensive capabilities to strike Chinese air and amphibious assets deployed along China's eastern coast. Prior arms sales had been clearly defensive or within a gray area that enabled the United States to support the sale as consistent with the provision of the 1979 TRA that stated, "It is the policy of the United States . . . to provide Taiwan with arms of a defense character." The approval of offensive arms was the result of the dramatic shift in the cross-Strait military balance and a rethinking of what Taiwan would need to defend itself under the new circumstances.

Beijing's aggressive attempts to poach Taiwan's diplomatic partners prompted the Trump administration to take more proactive steps to help Taipei staunch the flow. After the Dominican Republic, El Salvador, and Panama shifted diplomatic allegiance to the PRC, the State Department recalled the chiefs of mission from all three nations "to discuss ways in which the United States can support strong, independent, democratic institutions throughout Central America and the Caribbean."[42] Following talks in Washington, D.C., an official U.S. statement warned countries throughout the region against pursuing "economic agreements and relationships with unfamiliar partners whose methods lack a proven, positive track record."[43]

U.S. officials considered, but then rejected, taking measures to penalize some of the countries that had severed diplomatic ties with Taiwan. For example, the administration deliberated the possibility of reducing foreign aid and imposing visa restrictions on officials in El Salvador, but the proposal was nixed due to concerns that San Salvador would retaliate by withdrawing its help to stop the flow of illegal immigrants to the United States.

The Trump administration also criticized Beijing's push to compel foreign companies to use language on their websites and other promotional materials indicating Taiwan is part of China. When the China Civil Aviation administration demanded that thirty-six foreign airlines, including some American carriers, respect Chinese sovereignty and not refer to Taiwan as a country, the White House pushed back, publicly calling the move "Orwellian nonsense" and demanded that the PRC "stop threatening and coercing American carriers and citizens."[44]

Trump officials also stepped up efforts to help Taiwan expand its participation in international organizations. That push, however, was consistent with U.S. policy since 1994 to back Taiwan's membership in international organizations that do not require statehood as a condition of membership and to encourage Taiwan's meaningful participation in international organizations where its membership is not possible.

In the spring of 2020, the United States launched a campaign to rally its allies to restore Taiwan's status as an observer at the WHA at the annual meeting, which was scheduled for mid-May. At the time, Taipei had outperformed almost all other governments in controlling the number of COVID-19 cases—on April 1, Taiwan had only 329 total cases and five deaths. The U.S. campaign was led by Secretary of State Mike Pompeo, who publicly called on all nations to support Taiwan's inclusion "as an observer at the WHA and in other relevant United Nations venues" and appealed to WHO Director-General Tedros Adhanom Ghebreyesus to invite Taiwan. Japan, Australia, and New Zealand joined the United States in pushing for Taiwan's observer status.[45] The State Department also initiated a "#TweetforTaiwan" crusade on Twitter that retweeted a tweet by President Tsai Ing-wen about Taiwan's success in combatting the virus and criticized the PRC's lack of transparency about COVID-19. According to *Foreign Policy*, the United States and Japan pressed Australia, the United Kingdom, France, and Germany to join in signing a letter to WHO Director Tedros, but in the end, no letter was sent.[46] Trump's animus toward America's European allies and his castigation of the WHO were likely factors in the U.S. inability to get support from any European countries. In the face of strong opposition from the PRC, the U.S. campaign was unsuccessful.

Nevertheless, the Trump administration made some headway in drumming up international support for expanding Taiwan's interactions with countries that aren't among its diplomatic allies through a program called the Global Cooperation Training Framework (GCTF). Created in 2015, the GCTF began as a U.S.-Taiwan endeavor to provide a platform that enables Taiwan to contribute to transnational problem-solving and share its expertise with partners across the region in a wide variety of fields, including public health, law enforcement, disaster relief, energy, women's empowerment, digital economy and cyber security, media literacy, and good governance. During Trump's term in office, Japan became an official GCTF partner in March 2019 and henceforth co-hosted all GCTF workshops. In 2019 and 2020, Sweden, Australia, Guatemala, and the Netherlands co-hosted events. In addition, the GCTF platform was upgraded from a regionally focused program to a global one, with the first workshop outside Taiwan held in Palau in 2019 and a virtual workshop held with Guatemala in 2020.

The Trump administration continued the practice of permitting Taiwan's president to transit the United States on visits to countries with which it retained official diplomatic relations. In the summer of 2018, Tsai transited the United States en route to Paraguay and Belize, two of Taiwan's remaining diplomatic allies. During her brief stopover, Tsai was permitted to give a short speech standing in front of a piece of the Berlin Wall at the Ronald Reagan Presidential Library. For the first time, journalists accompanying the Taiwan president's entourage were allowed to report onsite and conduct live broadcasts. In another unprecedented step, Tsai also inspected the Taipei Economic and Cultural Office in Los Angeles. On her return transit, Tsai toured NASA's Johnson Space Center in Houston, Texas, marking the first time that a leader of Taiwan was allowed to visit an American government facility. Providing Tsai with a bit more latitude than previous U.S. administrations was yet another example of the Trump administration's increased support for Taiwan.

President Tsai's second inauguration in May 2020 presented another opportunity for senior Trump administration officials to demonstrate their support. Due to the coronavirus pandemic, the United States did not send an official delegation; instead, numerous dignitaries sent virtual messages of congratulations alongside messages from representatives from forty-six other countries. Among those American officials who sent messages was U.S. Secretary of State Mike Pompeo, which marked the first time a senior American official had publicly congratulated a Taiwan president on an election victory. Pompeo said that Tsai's "courage and vision in leading Taiwan's vibrant democracy is an inspiration to the region and the world."[47] He was joined by U.S. House Speaker Nancy Pelosi, Acting Senate President Chuck Grassley, and Joe Biden in offering well-wishes.

Under the Obama administration and its predecessors, the U.S. one-China policy was usually described as based on the three U.S.–China Joint Communiqués and the TRA, in that order. On a few occasions, Obama administration officials included the Reagan administration's "Six Assurances" as part of the catechism, and even put the TRA first. For example, in 2011, then-Assistant Secretary of State for East Asia Kurt Campbell told Congress that "the Taiwan Relations Act, plus the so-called 'Six Assurances' and the three Communiqués, form the foundation of our overall approach." At other times, officials shied away from including the Six Assurances as among the pillars of U.S. policy toward Taiwan. When asked in a congressional hearing about whether the Obama administration is committed to the Six Assurances, Campbell's successor, Danny Russel, avoided reaffirming that the Six Assurances remain an essential pillar of the U.S. one-China policy, characterizing them as merely "an important part" of Washington's U.S. approach.

First conveyed by the Reagan administration in 1982, the Six Assurances emphasized that Washington had not set a date certain for ending arms sales to Taiwan and that the United States had not agreed to consult with the PRC on such sales. They also included a pledge that the United States would not play a mediation role between Beijing and Taipei and maintained that the United States had not agreed to take any position regarding sovereignty over Taiwan.

The Trump administration made the "Six Assurances" a mainstay of the U.S. one-China policy, which officials invariably included as the third element after the TRA and the three U.S.-China Communiqués. In August 2020, the Trump administration declassified documents relating to the Six Assurances from 1982, various versions of which had been in the public domain for years. The purpose, according to Assistant Secretary of State for East Asian and Pacific Affairs David R. Stilwell, was to "prevent and reverse [the] PRC's squeezing of Taiwan's international space." Declassification also served to underscore that the United States is a reliable partner, while reaffirming a long-standing U.S. policy of taking no position on Taiwan's sovereignty. One of the documents—an internal presidential memorandum issued by President Ronald Reagan, clarified that the president's intent in the August 1982 U.S.–China Joint Communiqué was to tie the reduction of U.S. arms sales to Taiwan on the continued commitment of China to the peaceful solution of cross-Strait differences. "It is essential," Reagan wrote, "that the quantity and quality of the arms provided Taiwan be conditioned entirely on the threat posed by the PRC."[48]

In response to growing PRC pressure on Taiwan, the U.S. Congress introduced a significant number of bills aimed at strengthening Taiwan's security during the Trump administration. Although several pieces of legislation became law, none of them required major changes to U.S.–Taiwan policy. The enacted laws did not give the president any authority that he would not already claim under U.S. law. However, they had an outsized impact on views of U.S. policy in China and Taiwan. The PRC attached great significance to congressional legislation, believing that the executive and legislative branches of the U.S. government were working hand-in-glove to use Taiwan as a weapon against China. In Taiwan, the public likely overestimated the importance of U.S. legislation, concluding that U.S. support for Taiwan was so strong that it could prevent any harm from coming to Taiwan.

The 2018 National Defense Authorization Act (NDAA) asked the president to consider reciprocal port calls by the U.S. and Taiwan navies, but did not mandate them. The Taiwan Travel Act, adopted in 2018, stated only that it "should be the policy of the United States to permit higher level officials to meet with their Taiwan counterparts and allow high-level officials from Taiwan to come to the United States and meet with their counterparts." That same year, the Asia Reassurance Initiative Act asked the president to "conduct regular transfers of defense articles to Taiwan that are tailored to meet the existing and likely future threats from the People's Republic of China" and "encourage the travel of high-level United States officials to Taiwan." The NDAAs for 2019, 2020, and 2021 reaffirmed the policies and directives covered in other Taiwan-related legislation and called for briefings and reports on specific matters of concern to Congress. For example, the NDAA of 2021 called for executive branch officials to brief relevant congressional committees annually on arms sales to Taiwan as well as provide reports on the feasibility of establishing a medical security partnership with the Ministry of Defense of Taiwan.[49]

In 2020, the Taiwan Allies International Protection and Enhancement Initiative (TAIPEI) Act included language suggesting that the executive branch back Taiwan's participation in UN-affiliated agencies such as the WHO and membership in organizations that do not require sovereignty as a condition for joining. It also requested that other states be rewarded or punished for breaking, preserving, or upgrading ties with Taiwan. The Taiwan Assurance Act of 2021 maintained that Taiwan plays a vital role in the U.S. "Free and Open Indo-Pacific Strategy" and appropriated $3 million to support activities under the GCTF.

One of the Trump administration's final policy decisions regarding Taiwan was rescinding long-standing guidance on executive branch contacts with Taiwan. The guidelines regulating interactions between American diplomats, servicemembers, and other officials with their Taiwan counterparts had been in place for decades, though they had been periodically updated. In a press statement, Secretary of State Pompeo termed the guidance "self-imposed restrictions of our permanent bureaucracy."[50] The sudden elimination of the guidelines left U.S. diplomats uncertain about how to interact with counterparts from Taiwan. Political appointees started publicly tweeting about their meetings with Taiwan officials. Some diplomats likely erred on the side of caution and continued following the guidelines, while others may have postponed meetings until the policy was clarified. The Biden administration reimposed the guidelines, albeit in a revised form.

For the most part, Trump administration policies toward Taiwan were intended primarily to strengthen bilateral ties and bolster the island's security, not to use Taipei as a weapon against China. But there were instances in which senior Trump officials deliberately attempted to use Taiwan to bludgeon Beijing, putting Taiwan in the crosshairs of U.S.-China strategic competition. The most blatant example was a January 6, 2020, press statement by Secretary of State Pompeo on the mass arrests in Hong Kong. After condemning the arrests and demanding the release of the pro-democracy activists, Pompeo announced that U.S. Ambassador to the United Nations Kelly Craft would soon visit Taiwan, which he described as "a reliable partner and a vibrant democracy that has flourished despite CCP efforts to undermine its great success," adding that "Taiwan shows what a free China could achieve."[51] In the end, the Craft visit was canceled, along with all other travel by senior State Department officials that was planned for the final week of the Trump administration. Since Taiwan virtually always bore the brunt of Beijing's punishment, the cancellation spared it another round of retaliatory actions by China, which had reacted to the announcement by warning the United States against "playing with fire."

In instances where administration officials took actions aimed at strengthening Taiwan on its own merits, the impact on Taiwan's security of policy decisions was not always carefully weighed. For example, before March 2019, Beijing tacitly recognized the center line of the Taiwan Strait and PLA aircraft rarely crossed it and infrequently flew in Taiwan's ADIZ. Since then, aircraft intrusions across the median line of the Taiwan Strait increased and PLA warplanes began flying almost daily in Taiwan's ADIZ. Furthermore, for the first time, a PRC Foreign Ministry spokesperson asserted in September 2020 that no median line in the Taiwan Strait exists. In addition to eroding Taiwan's security, responding militarily to the increased air activity has been costly. According to former Taiwan Defense Minister Yen Te-fa, the cost to Taiwan of scrambling jets to respond to PLA warplanes approaching the ADIZ was NT$25.5 billion (approximately US$921 million) in 2020.[52]

It is also uncertain whether Taipei was consulted by Washington prior to undertaking unprecedented steps that could provoke strong PRC retaliatory responses, which were usually carried out against Taiwan, not the United States. For example, Taipei appeared to be taken by surprise when the U.S. DoD issued its Indo-Pacific Strategy report that referred to Taiwan as a country.

Throughout the Trump administration there was tension between the members of his administration, who strongly supported strengthening Taiwan's security and bilateral ties, and the president, whose antipathy to Taiwan was an open secret. This tension created uncertainty about how the United States would respond if strains in cross-Strait relations intensified and reached a level that required presidential involvement.

HOW TSAI ING-WEN MANAGED RELATIONS WITH THE UNITED STATES IN THE TRUMP ERA

President Tsai Ing-wen recognized that the Trump administration posed both risks and opportunities for Taiwan. She sought to carefully manage the relationship with the United States to avoid Taiwan becoming a pawn in the intensifying U.S.-China competition or being harmed by Washington's confrontational approach to Beijing. At the same time, Tsai tried to take advantage of the potential to strengthen relations with the United States, which became increasingly important as cross-Strait relations deteriorated.

Only days after her phone call with President-elect Trump, Tsai downplayed the significance of the call, saying that it was "a way for us to express our respect for the U.S. election as well as congratulate President-elect Trump on his win." Meeting with a small group of American reporters in Taipei, she insisted that "one phone call does not mean a policy shift."[53] It was a smart move that was aimed at heading off increased tensions with Beijing. It was early in Tsai's tenure, and she still hoped to persuade the PRC to maintain amicable cross-Strait ties. In her national day speech just two months earlier, she had called upon the leaders from both sides to use "political wisdom" to "search for new modes of cross-Strait interactions with determination and patience."

When President Trump opted to reaffirm the U.S. one-China policy after dangling the possibility that he might not do so, Tsai was likely relieved. A crisis in U.S.-China relations over Taiwan would not have served Tsai's interests. However, fundamentalists in her party who had long pushed for policies that would enable Taiwan to achieve formal independence saw the Trump administration as a rare chance to make strides toward that goal. One disgruntled politician, Parris Chang, told *The Economist*, "She hasn't shown she can seize the opportunity."[54] If Trump had jettisoned the one-China policy, Tsai would have come under even greater pressure from the DPP's "Deep Greens" to declare independence.

As plans solidified for the Trump-Xi summit at the Mar-a-Lago estate on April 6–7, 2017, concerns arose in the Tsai administration that Taiwan could get thrown under the bus and its interests irrevocably harmed. Trump's urgency to reduce the bilateral trade deficit with China and obtain Xi's cooperation to pressure North Korea to end its nuclear weapons program sparked apprehension that Taiwan could be used as a bargaining chip in the context of a broader deal. Then-Foreign Minister David Lee publicly warned the United States to refrain from signing a fourth joint communiqué with China.[55] Such fears were not unprecedented—virtually every U.S.-China summit prompts worries in Taipei about a deal that could be detrimental to Taiwan's interests. Taipei's public airing of its concerns was unusual, however, and suggested that Tsai wasn't yet fully confident in her relations with the new administration. That changed over the months and years to come.

During Trump's four-year term in office, Tsai successfully navigated the risks and secured gains for Taiwan. As relations with Beijing deteriorated, Tsai concluded that the optimal way to protect Taiwan's security was to forge closer ties with the United States. She sought help from Washington to strengthen Taiwan's security, economy, and international participation, and, in most cases, received a positive response. The one area where the Trump administration fell short was in trade; Tsai's push for launching negotiations on a bilateral free trade agreement failed to make progress.

Tsai convinced her American interlocutors that she was a reliable partner and could help the Trump administration advance its agenda. Moreover, when the United States was hit hard by the COVID-19 pandemic, Taiwan proved to be a good friend, donating millions of masks and other supplies to the United States. As Beijing ramped up pressure on Taipei, Tsai persisted in her policy of preserving the cross-Strait status quo and refrained from pursuing provocative policies that could have drawn the United States into a conflict. Compared to the unpredictability of the Trump administration, Tsai chartered a steady path.

Whereas Donald Trump's defeat in the November 2020 presidential election was greeted with relief by many of America's treaty allies, his loss created some anxiety in Taipei, especially in the ruling DPP. Trump's tough policies toward China were generally quite popular in Taiwan and the U.S.-Taiwan relationship had gone from strength to strength. Taipei's concerns were not based on any specific evidence that suggested Joe Biden would be softer on China or less supportive of Taiwan.

Instead, they emanated from Taipei's prior experience with Democratic administrations, which had sometimes prioritized ties with Beijing in decision-making on arms sales to Taiwan and other issues, as well as a widespread assessment that the Obama administration didn't do enough to push back against increasingly assertive PRC policies, such as the militarization of the South China Sea. Just days prior to the election, Lai I-chung, president of the Taiwan National Security Bureau's think tank, the Prospect Foundation, and former DPP foreign policy director, told the *Washington Post* that, "The lack of the deeper understanding on the issue of Taiwan by Biden advisors is something that causes a lot of concern here."[56]

Biden sought to allay these concerns during the campaign in an op-ed published in the *World Journal*, the largest circulation Chinese language newspaper in the United States, where he pledged that if elected, U.S. policy in the region would include "deepening our ties with Taiwan." Biden described Taiwan as "a leading democracy, major economy, technology powerhouse—and a shining example of how an open society can effectively contain COVID-19."[57] As the U.S. election neared, Taipei remained worried, but as it turned out, Taiwan's fears were not borne out.

BIDEN INHERITS TENSE U.S.-CHINA AND CROSS-STRAIT RELATIONSHIPS

The Biden administration inherited an acrimonious relationship with Beijing. President Trump placed tariffs on approximately $360 billion worth of products from China, which set in motion a tit-for-tat trade war. Other actions taken against China included restricting Chinese businesses from purchasing American technology, imposing sanctions on Chinese companies, and barring U.S. investment in Chinese firms with ties to the PRC military. Already rocky bilateral ties deteriorated sharply after the onset of the COVID-19 pandemic, which Trump insisted Beijing could have been contained within China's borders.

In one example of worsening relations, the United States ordered China to close its consulate in Houston, Texas, in July 2020, charging its diplomats with enabling economic espionage and the attempted theft of scientific research. China retaliated by shuttering the U.S. consulate in Chengdu. The same month, Secretary of State Pompeo declared that Beijing's claims in the South China Sea were "completely unlawful" and condemned Chinese bullying to control offshore resources in waters that it had no legal claim to.

The Trump administration also belatedly took action against China's human rights violations. For most of his presidency, Trump was reluctant to punish China for its human rights breaches, despite mounting evidence that at least one million Uyghurs and other Muslim minorities were being held in mass detention camps against their will. Although some officials in his administration favored using the 2016 Global Magnitsky Human Rights Accountability Act to impose penalties on Chinese officials, Trump refrained from doing so for several years because he didn't want to disrupt the potential for a major trade deal with Beijing.[58] But after the phase one trade agreement was signed and the coronavirus spread to the United States, Trump took the gloves off on human rights. In the summer of 2020, the United States blacklisted several Chinese companies and sanctioned multiple officials from China citing human rights abuses in Xinjiang. Beijing retaliated by imposing unspecified "reciprocal counter-sanctions" on current and former representatives from a range of U.S. organizations that work on human rights, Hong Kong, and other contentious issues in the U.S.-China relationship.

Before his election victory, Biden's campaign declared that the Chinese government's oppression of Uyghurs and other ethnic minorities in Xinjiang was a genocide and that presidential candidate Joe Biden "stands against it in the strongest terms."[59] On its last full day in power, the Trump administration formally adopted that position. Moreover, Trump's imposition of sanctions on China for its egregious human rights violations, although slow in getting started, provided a base that the incoming Biden team could build on.

Another arena of bitter U.S.-China contention was Hong Kong. Beijing's imposition of the National Security Law in Hong Kong on June 30, 2020, which effectively ended the former British colony's separate legal system, prompted the Trump administration to take a raft of measures aimed at making China pay a price. In July, Trump signed into law the Hong Kong Autonomy Act, a bill to sanction Chinese officials, businesses, and banks responsible for undermining Hong Kong's freedoms. He also signed an executive order that declared a national emergency with respect to the situation in Hong Kong. Trump subsequently imposed sanctions on numerous Chinese officials for their alleged role in crushing dissent in Hong Kong.

During the presidential transition, Chinese State Councilor and Foreign Minister Wang Yi delivered a speech to the Asia Society in New York titled "Reorient and Steer Clear of Disruptions for a Smooth Sailing of China-U.S. Relations." The problems in the bilateral relationship, Wang explained, were due to the wrong policies pursued by the United States, and the strategic miscalculations that some U.S. politicians have about China. Wang called for U.S. policy toward China to "return to objectivity and sensibility as early as possible." As for China's policy, Wang found no fault, and described Beijing as pursuing a policy toward the United States that is "always stable and consistent."[60] This theme of blaming the United States for all the ills in the bilateral relationship would be heard again and again after Biden took office.

The Biden team also inherited a strained cross-Strait relationship. The trajectory of cross-Strait relations, and the concomitant trend of Tsai Ing-wen securing greater support from the Trump administration, led the PRC to increasingly resort to coercive tactics. Beijing's more aggressive policies prompted many observers to argue that Xi Jinping's approach to Taiwan was not just guided by fear of the island's separation from China, but instead by ambition to unite the country as part of Xi's "China Dream" of national rejuvenation. Flights by PLA aircraft near Taiwan and military exercises aimed at honing PLA capabilities as well as intimidating Taiwan were conducted more frequently. After large-scale air and naval exercises in September 2020, the spokesman for China's Taiwan Affairs Office defended the drills, calling Taiwan a "sacred" and "inseparable" part of China.[61] Following the thirteenth passage of a U.S. warship through the Taiwan Strait, the PRC dispatched its newest aircraft carrier, the *Shandong*, to transit the same waters.

Beijing's decision to crush dissent in Hong Kong through the implementation of the National Security Law reaffirmed what was already the majority view in Taiwan that "one country, two systems" was an unacceptable formula for cross-Strait unification. A 2019 survey conducted by the Election Study Center of National Chengchi University in Taiwan found that 90 percent of respondents had very low confidence in Chinese leaders' assurances that under the "one country, two systems" plan, life in Taiwan would remain unchanged, and the government and the military would be governed by Taiwan. Unsurprisingly, the survey found a high correlation between Taiwan people's views of life in Hong Kong and their confidence in Beijing's pledges.[62]

The PRC's insistence on presenting "one country, two systems" as the only model for unification with Taiwan and President Tsai Ing-wen's unwillingness to accept the "1992 Consensus" made an easing of cross-Strait tensions unlikely, at least until Taiwan's next presidential election in 2024, and perhaps beyond. While Beijing blamed Taipei for changing the cross-Strait status quo, the PRC had done much to undermine it. When Joe Biden assumed office on January 20, 2021, cross-Strait relations were at their lowest point since the 1995–1996 third Taiwan Strait crisis, while the U.S.-Taiwan relationship was closer and stronger than at any time since 1979.

Trump's propensity for acting unilaterally and disregarding the interests of U.S. allies had placed the United States in a more isolated position internationally and weakened Washington's hand in dealing with China. The U.S. announcement of its withdrawal from several international organizations, including the UN Human Rights Council and the WHO, also imperiled Washington's ability to influence Chinese behavior. Biden asserted during the campaign and after his election victory that one of his top foreign policy priorities would be rehabilitating U.S. alliances. "The best China strategy, I think, is one which gets every one of our—or at least what used to be our—allies on the same page," he told *New York Times* columnist Thomas Friedman, adding, "It's going to be a major priority for me in the opening weeks of my presidency to try to get us back on the same page with our allies."[63]

Not all U.S. relationships with other countries suffered under Trump, however, in part because Beijing's more assertive behavior turned some countries that might have preferred a hedging strategy more firmly against China. Nations like Japan, which was facing growing pressure from the Chinese military and coast guard in the East China Sea, and Australia, which was being targeted by Beijing with economic coercion, were two notable examples. India also welcomed a tougher U.S. approach to China after deadly clashes took place between Indian and Chinese troops along their disputed border in June 2020. The growing willingness of some countries to push back against China's assertiveness suggested that forging coalitions to impose costs on Beijing for its behavior might be possible. Along with the trade tariffs, these coalitions presented the incoming Biden administration with potential sources of leverage in future negotiations with China.

BIDEN ADMINISTRATION POLICY TOWARD TAIWAN

President Biden's national security team judged that the Trump administration bequeathed a robust U.S.-Taiwan relationship, and they were eager to build on it. Recognizing that Taipei was uneasy about the Democrats' return to power, key individuals who would later assume senior positions in the Biden administration proactively took steps to reassure Taiwan that the United States would remain a reliable partner. Less than two weeks after Biden's victory, Antony Blinken—former deputy secretary of state in the Obama administration and soon to be Biden's secretary of state—accepted a congratulatory phone call from Bi-khim Hsiao, Taiwan's representative in the United States. Hsiao tweeted about the phone conversation on social media, presumably with the permission of the Biden transition team.

In a firm signal of support for Taiwan, the incoming Biden administration arranged for an invitation for Representative Hsiao to attend President Biden's inauguration. It marked the first time since Washington severed diplomatic ties with Taiwan in 1979 that Taipei's representative in the United States was formally invited to a presidential inauguration by the Joint Congressional Committee on Inaugural Ceremonies. The circumstances under which the TECRO representative participated in prior U.S. presidential inaugurations were different and less official.

Both Secretary of State-Designate Blinken and Secretary of Defense-Designate Lloyd Austin highlighted their support for Taiwan during their respective confirmation hearings on January 19. Blinken maintained that "the commitment to Taiwan is something that we hold to very strongly" and noted that "he would also like to see Taiwan playing a greater role around the world, including in international organizations."[64] Austin said that U.S. "support to Taiwan has been rock solid over the years" and pledged that he would "make sure that we're living up to our commitments to support Taiwan's ability to defend itself."[65] The term "rock solid" was henceforth used frequently by Biden administration officials.

In what may have been an early effort by the PRC to test the Biden administration, just days after Biden was sworn into office the PRC flew eight nuclear-capable bombers, four fighter jets, and an anti-submarine aircraft into Taiwan's ADIZ. Echoing Austin, a spokesman for the White House declared that the U.S. commitment was "rock solid." The State Department issued a lengthy statement:

> The United States notes with concern the pattern of ongoing PRC attempts to intimidate its neighbors, including Taiwan. We urge Beijing to cease its military, diplomatic, and economic pressure against Taiwan and instead engage in meaningful dialogue with Taiwan's democratically elected representatives.
>
> We will stand with friends and allies to advance our shared prosperity, security, and values in the Indo-Pacific region—and that includes deepening our ties with democratic Taiwan. The United States will continue to support a peaceful resolution of cross-strait issues, consistent with the wishes and best interests of the people on Taiwan. The United States maintains its longstanding commitments as outlined in the Three Communiqués, the Taiwan Relations Act, and the Six Assurances. We will continue to assist Taiwan in maintaining a sufficient self-defense capability. Our commitment to Taiwan is

rock-solid and contributes to the maintenance of peace and stability across the Taiwan Strait and within the region.[66]

Although not played up at the time, the statement marked a shift in U.S. rhetorical policy.[67] Washington had long supported peaceful resolution of cross-Strait issues, but it had been years since a U.S. official had stated that the resolution had to be "consistent with the wishes and best interests of the people on Taiwan." A version of that formulation had originally been used by President Bill Clinton,[68] but during the George W. Bush administration, the policy was revised so it called for peaceful resolution of cross-Strait issues consistent with the wishes of people on both sides of the Taiwan Strait. By quietly reviving the original language, the Biden administration signaled its support for Taiwan's democratic system, which enables the people's wishes and interests to register their views, and discarded the fiction that the PRC government represents the wishes and interests of the people living in Mainland China.

The episode showed that there was an emerging consensus in the United States that Taiwan's security was under threat and that Washington needed to clearly signal to Beijing its determination to preserve peace and stability in the Taiwan Strait. Halfway into the first week of the Biden administration, Taipei's worries that it might not receive strong support from the new team in the White House were already significantly allayed.

In the ensuing months, the United States continued to signal strong backing for Taiwan. President Biden expressed concern about the PRC's increasingly assertive actions toward Taiwan in his first phone call with Xi Jinping in February.[69] Increasing Chinese military pressure on Taiwan led U.S. officials to issue a sharp public warning in April. As China flew multiple military aircraft near Taiwan and a Chinese aircraft carrier group conducted exercises close to the island, the White House described China's activity as "potentially destabilizing."[70] Referring to Chinese actions directed at Taiwan as aggressive, Secretary of State Blinken cautioned Beijing that any attempt to try to change the status quo in the Western Pacific by force would be a "serious mistake."[71]

The "Interim National Security Strategic Guidance," issued by the White House on March 3, provided further evidence of continuity with Trump's policies toward Taiwan. The "Interim National Security Strategic Guidance" called Taiwan "a critical economic and security partner" and pledged that the United States would support the island in line with long-standing American commitments.[72] In April, in what a White House official called a "personal signal" of the president's commitment to Taiwan and its democracy, Biden dispatched former U.S. Senator Chris Dodd and former Deputy Secretaries of State Richard Armitage and James Steinberg to Taiwan to mark the forty-second anniversary of the TRA.[73]

The Trump administration's elimination of the guidelines for contacts between U.S. officials and their Taiwan counterparts in the final weeks of Trump's presidency was quietly welcomed by Biden officials. The rules had been cumbersome; Taiwan officials weren't permitted to enter the State Department, for example, so American officials had to meet them in restaurants and hotels. Moreover, the net effect of the contact guidelines was that interaction between U.S. and Taiwan diplomats in third countries was relatively uncommon, which many believed did not serve U.S. interests. At the same time, however, Biden officials recognized that it was necessary to have some guidelines in place to ensure that the U.S. one-China policy remained credible.

On April 9, the State Department issued new "contact guidelines" to define what interactions would be permissible between U.S. government officials and their Taiwan counterparts. A one-paragraph statement emphasized that the new guidelines were intended "to encourage U.S. government engagement with Taiwan that reflects our deepening unofficial relationship." Calling Taiwan a "vibrant democracy and an important security and economic partner that is also a force for good in the international community," the statement noted that the liberalized guidance was consistent with the U.S. unofficial relationship with Taiwan. In addition, it noted that the new guidance would enable effective implementation of the U.S. one-China policy, which, the statement, maintained, "is guided by the Taiwan Relations Act, the three Joint Communiqués, and the Six Assurances." The decision to list the TRA ahead of the Joint U.S.-China Communiqués was a change from the statement issued by the State Department only six weeks prior and was undoubtedly a deliberate signal of firm support for Taiwan.[74]

The liberalized guidelines for contacts between U.S. and Taiwan officials were consistent with a general trend of more loosely interpreting what constituted permissible interactions, while still maintaining Washington's pledge to Beijing as part of normalization in 1979 to conduct unofficial ties with Taiwan. They were also deemed necessary to manage an increasingly substantive relationship. In an episode less than two weeks before the issuance of the new guidelines that stretched the credibility of that pledge, however, the United States sent its ambassador to Palau, John Hennesey-Niland, to accompany a delegation led by the Palauan president to Taipei. It was the first time that a sitting American envoy to a third country traveled to Taiwan in an official capacity since the United States broke ties with Taiwan. It wasn't clear whether the visit had been approved by the interagency process that coordinates policy-making and implementation or indeed whether it was following the new guidelines. In any case, the practice seemed to be an aberration rather than a harbinger of a new policy.

Over Biden's first year, the new bilateral mechanisms that were launched under the Trump administration were sustained, and new structures of cooperation were formed. In March, an agreement was signed to boost cooperation between U.S. and Taiwan coast guards, which included a working group to improve communications and share information on coast-guard-related efforts. The move followed the PRC's passing of a law that allows its coast guard to use lethal force on foreign vessels operating in Chinese waters, which, in the South China Sea presumably includes waters disputed by other claimants.

On the trade front, after a five-year hiatus, the United States and Taiwan held a virtual round of the TIFA Council at the end of June. The meeting marked a resumption of high-level trade engagement and covered a broad range of issues. To strengthen work aimed at countering forced labor in global supply chains, a new Labor Working Group was established. The readout issued by USTR made no mention of discussions aimed at signing a bilateral FTA.[75] In December 2021, Taiwan dodged a bullet when a referendum failed to pass that proposed reimposing the ban on imports of pork and beef containing ractopamine due in part to the Tsai administration's staunch opposition. Yet although USTR stated in official reports released in May 2022 that it planned to intensify its engagement with Taiwan, the office remained mum on the question of whether the two sides might begin talks on a bilateral FTA. USTR did uphold its pledge to deepen the U.S. trade and economic relationship with Taiwan the following month when it launched the U.S.-Taiwan Initiative on 21st Century Trade, which aims to develop "an ambitious roadmap for negotiations for reaching agreements with high-standard commitments and economically meaningful outcomes."[76] The talks kicked off November 8-9, 2022 and made progress on four of the eleven areas on the trade agenda: trade facilitation, anti-corruption standards, trade between U.S. and Taiwan small and medium enterprises, and good regulatory practices.

The ongoing global shortage of semiconductors due in large part to the coronavirus epidemic led to closer cooperation between the United States and Taiwan on semiconductor supply chains. In December 2021, Taipei and Washington established a new Technology Trade and Investment Collaboration framework to develop commercial programs and strengthen critical supply chains by promoting two-way investment. The creation of such bilateral mechanisms was relatively easy; bringing Taiwan into multilateral coalitions was far more difficult, however, even when initiated by the United States and focused on economic cooperation. In May 2022 the Biden administration did not include Taiwan when it launched the Indo-Pacific Economic Framework (IPEF) because some regional partners were uncomfortable with extending an invitation to Taiwan while excluding the PRC.

As COVID-19 cases surged in Taiwan in 2021, the United States sent 2.5 million vaccine doses to Taiwan in June and an additional 1.5 million doses in November. U.S. officials accused the PRC of attempting to block vaccine purchases by Taiwan for political reasons, which Beijing denied. Three U.S. senators announced the pending delivery of the first batch when they visited Taiwan in June, noting that the United States was happy to repay gratitude to Taiwan for its donations of personal protective equipment and other supplies to the United States in the early days of the pandemic.

The year 2021 marked the fiftieth anniversary of the PRC's becoming permanent on the UN Security Council and occupying a seat in the UN General Assembly. On October 25, 1971, with the passage of UN Resolution 2758, the PRC replaced the ROC at the United Nations and became "the only lawful representatives of China to the United Nations." Since the mid-2000s, Beijing has distorted the meaning of that Resolution as part of an effort to insert its one-China principle into the UN system. The Biden administration publicly pushed back against the PRC's effort to use Resolution 2758 to circumscribe Taiwan's meaningful participation in the United Nations. In a press statement, Secretary of State Antony Blinken argued that the exclusion of Taiwan in the work of the United Nations and its related bodies undermines its effectiveness. He called for all UN Member States to join the United States in "supporting Taiwan's robust, meaningful participation throughout the UN system and in the international community consistent with our 'One-China;' policy, which is guided by the Taiwan Relations Act, the three Joint Communiqués, and the Six Assurances."[77] Deputy Assistant Secretary of State for East Asian and Pacific Affairs Rick Waters went even further in a public event hosted by the German Marshall Fund of the United States. "The People's Republic of China has misused Resolution 2758 to prevent Taiwan's meaningful participation," he asserted, citing Taiwan being blocked not only from participating in the WHO, but also from participating in ICAO and the International Criminal Police Organization.[78]

Like the Trump and Obama administrations, Biden's government made a concerted push to expand Taiwan's participation in international organizations, especially UN-affiliated agencies. The main target of the effort was aimed at persuading U.S. allies to publicly support reviving Taiwan's observer status in the WHA, the top decision-making body of the WHO. A significant achievement in this regard was achieved in May 2021, when the countries of the G7—Britain, Canada, France, Germany, Italy, Japan, and the United States—for the first time voiced their joint support for Taiwan's participation in the WHO. The communiqué issued after the G7 Foreign and Development Ministers meeting declared support for "Taiwan's meaningful participation in the World Health Organization forums and the World Health Assembly," noting that the international community should be able to benefit from the experience of all partners, including Taiwan's successful contribution to the tackling of the COVID-19 pandemic."[79] Although the PRC again blocked Taiwan from participating in the WHA, the PRC was put on notice that its practice of excluding Taiwan from the world's global health organization was coming under growing international criticism.

In the runup to the seventy-fifth WHA in May 2022, President Biden signed into law a bill directing the Secretary of State to develop a strategy to regain observer status for Taiwan in the WHO. In addition, Secretary of State Blinken issued a statement strongly advocating for the WHO to invite Taiwan to participate as an observer. Over seventy countries around the world joined the United States in calling for Taiwan's participation in the WHA. Nevertheless, Beijing rejected the appeal and insisted that the matter be handled per Beijing's narrow interpretation of the one-China principle.

Greater progress was made in expanding and elevating the GCTF. Australia joined the United States, Taiwan, and Japan as a full partner in October 2021. In addition, more like-minded countries co-hosted GCTF workshops, including the United Kingdom, Canada, Israel, and Slovakia. The first GCTF-affiliated franchise workshop was held in the Czech Republic in September 2021. At the end of 2022, 6,302 individuals from one hundred and twenty-five countries across five continents had participated in GCTF workshops since the program's inception in 2015.

The Biden administration continued the Trump administration's policy of trying to help Taiwan retain its remaining diplomatic partners, although it did so primarily through quiet diplomacy rather than public threats. When Xiomara Castro was running for president in Honduras, she pledged to shift diplomatic ties from Taipei to Beijing, which she claimed would give Honduras access to economic opportunities, PRC-made COVID-19 vaccines, and low-cost medicine. To forestall the move, which would have further increased Chinese influence in the region as well as diminished Taiwan's role, the United States dispatched Assistant Secretary for Western Hemisphere Affairs Brian Nichols to Honduras just prior to the elections. After Castro won, her government signaled that it would prioritize relations with the United States and therefore would not establish diplomatic relations with China. It remained uncertain whether that decision would stick.

The United States was unable to prevent Nicaragua from abandoning Taiwan, however. In December Managua announced that it was breaking ties with Taipei and reestablishing diplomatic ties with the PRC. The populist, anti-U.S. Sandinista regime was the target of a multitude of U.S. sanctions and viewed aligning with China as an attractive option. In addition to Honduras, Taiwan's remaining diplomatic allies in Latin America include Belize, Guatemala, Haiti, Paraguay, Saint Lucia, Saint Kitts and Nevis, and Saint Vincent and the Grenadines. Its diplomatic allies in other regions are Eswatini, the Holy See, the Marshall Islands, Tuvalu, Nauru, and Palau.

As Washington's concerns increased about Chinese military pressure on Taiwan and the potential for PRC use of force against the island, the Biden administration sought to enlist the support of its allies to signal Beijing that its actions were not cost-free and that it would pay a high price if it attacked Taiwan. The campaign began with the inclusion of statements supporting the preservation of cross-Strait peace and stability in joint statements with other countries. The first such joint statement was signed by President Biden and Japanese Prime Minister Yoshihide Suga in March. It was the first time since 1969 that the Taiwan Strait had been mentioned in a U.S.-Japan leaders' statement. Two months later, similar language was included in a joint statement signed by Biden and Korean President Moon Jae-in. When President Biden traveled to Europe in June 2021, two of the three statements he signed included mention of Taiwan, both of which were unprecedented. The Carbis Bay G7 Summit Communiqué underscored "the importance of peace and stability across the Taiwan Strait, and encourage[d] the peaceful resolution of cross-Strait issues."[80] The U.S.-EU Summit Statement contained identical language.[81] There was no reference to Taiwan in the Brussels Summit Communiqué that was issued after the meeting of the NATO's North Atlantic Council, however.

The joint statement issued at the Australia-U.S. (AUSMIN) ministerial consultations in September included a lengthy paragraph on Taiwan that referenced Taiwan as "a critical partner for both countries." The statement noted U.S. and Australian support for Taiwan's "meaningful participation in international organizations" as well as "peaceful resolution of cross-Strait issues without resorting to threats or coercion." Both countries also expressed their commitment to strengthen donor coordination with Taiwan in the Pacific.[82]

In addition to these policy statements, the Biden administration successfully coordinated military engagements and activities with its allies and partners to bolster deterrence in the Taiwan Strait and in the broader Indo-Pacific region. For example, seventeen naval ships from six different countries—the United States, United Kingdom, Japan, New Zealand, the Netherlands, and Canada—conducted a joint military exercise off the Japanese island of Okinawa in October 2021. That same month, American and Canadian warships sailed together through the Taiwan Strait.

As strengthening Taiwan's security assumed greater urgency, the Biden administration took various steps to signal its commitment to preserving peace in the Taiwan Strait. U.S. warships made eleven transits through the Taiwan Strait, sailing monthly between January and November during Biden's first year in office. In 2022, U.S. warships conducted nine Taiwan Strait transits. On two separate days in July 2021, U.S. military aircraft landed in Taiwan to deliver supplies to the American Institute in Taiwan. Proposed U.S. arms sales to Taiwan that were notified to the U.S. Congress in 2021–2022 totaled $3.8 billion. The potential weapons deals included anti-ship Harpoon missiles, air-to-air Sidewinder missiles, and more advanced Patriot air-defense missiles along with radar and support equipment.

Under growing pressure to demonstrate to the Taiwan people that they have U.S. backing, President Tsai Ing-wen confirmed in an interview with CNN in October that American troops have been deployed to Taiwan in small numbers for training purposes. It was the first time that a Taiwan president had acknowledged such cooperation between the two militaries.

In policy statements regarding Taiwan, U.S. officials attempted to warn the PRC against attacking Taiwan, but also reassure Beijing that Washington did not support Taiwan independence. Since there was little concern that Tsai Ing-wen would take provocative measures toward China, the United States didn't see the need to warn Taipei, but it did try to reassure Taiwan that the United States would not sacrifice the island's interests for the sake of good relations with Beijing. Getting the balance right and delivering consistent messages was challenging. At times, policy statements and actions appeared to be unclear and even contradictory.

When asked in a public event hosted by the Asia Society in early July 2021 whether the United States is giving Taiwan too much love, Biden's Indo-Pacific Coordinator Kurt Campbell said that the United States supports "a strong unofficial relationship with Taiwan," but asserted that, "We do not support Taiwan independence." Campbell insisted that he and his colleagues "fully recognize and understand the sensitivities involved here."[83]

Statements by President Biden suggested otherwise, however. During an August 2021 interview with ABC News, Biden suggested, incorrectly, that the United States has a treaty commitment to defend Taiwan. He said that the United States made a "sacred commitment" to respond to an invasion or action against our NATO allies, adding, "Same with Japan, same with South Korea, same with Taiwan." The comment was quickly walked back by a senior administration official who said that U.S. policy with regard to Taiwan had not changed. In October, Biden muddied the policy waters further by telling reporters that he and Xi Jinping had agreed to "abide by the Taiwan agreement." Since there is no such thing as a joint U.S.-China agreement on Taiwan, Biden left everyone guessing as to what he meant, and the White House press secretary reiterated that U.S. policy is guided by the TRA. Later that month, President Biden mistakenly told a town hall that the United States has a commitment to come to Taiwan's defense if it is attacked by China. He repeated that position in a May 2022 press conference in Tokyo standing alongside Japanese Prime Minister Kishida Fumio. In a CBS "60 Minutes" interview the following September, Biden pledged that he would send U.S. troops to defend Taiwan "if in fact there was an unprecedented attack."

In the most egregious misstatement of U.S. policy on Taiwan to date, President Biden told reporters in November 2021 that Taiwan "makes its own decisions," and that the island is "independent." After he was advised to correct the record, Biden explained that he did not intend to encourage Taiwan independence, but instead was urging Taipei to do what the "Taiwan Act requires." "Let them make up their mind," the president stated. Only a few hours earlier, Biden and Xi Jinping had held their first meeting, albeit virtually. The White House's readout said that Biden had reaffirmed the U.S. one-China policy and reassured Xi that the United States does not support Taiwan independence. In the *60 Minutes* interview the following year, Biden reiterated that "Taiwan makes their own judgments about their independence," adding that the U.S. was not encouraging Taiwan to go independent, but "That's their decision." In all these instances, the White House stated that the president's remarks did not signal a change in U.S. policy.

Since assuming office, Secretary of State Blinken has twice inadvertently referred to Taiwan as a country in testimony to Congress. At a March 10, 2021, House Foreign Affairs Committee hearing on the Biden administration's foreign policy agenda, he described Taiwan as "a country that can contribute to the world, not just its own people."[84] Six months later, on September 13, Blinken again referred to Taiwan as a country. Asked whether the United States will "have the backs of our friends" in Ukraine and Taiwan, the secretary replied, "Absolutely, we stand by our commitment to both countries."[85] Such gaffes are not inconsequential since they undermine the credibility of the U.S. one-China policy, which could result in a hardening of Beijing's policies.

Another episode of policy confusion took place when Assistant Secretary of Defense for the Indo-Pacific Ely Ratner suggested in testimony to Congress that while the United States might not back Taiwan independence, it has a strategic interest in keeping Taiwan separate from the PRC. Ratner described Taiwan as "a critical node within the first island chain (in the Western Pacific), anchoring a network of U.S. allies and partners . . . that is critical to the region's security and critical to the defense of vital U.S. interests in the Indo-Pacific."[86] The statement prompted critics to charge that Ratner had departed from long-standing U.S. policy of not opposing Taiwan's unification with China and remaining agnostic about how the two sides of the Strait settle their differences as long as they do so peacefully and without coercion. If the United States blatantly opposed the integration of Taiwan with the PRC, that could induce Beijing to recalibrate its policy and opt to resolve the Taiwan issue through use of force.[87]

By contrast, the Biden administration's handling of Taiwan's participation in the Summit for Democracy in December 2021 provided an example of adept management of the sensitive nature of policy toward Taipei and Beijing. Taiwan's inclusion recognized the progress that the island has made in creating a vibrant democracy that delivers good governance to its people. Washington afforded Taiwan's government and its people dignity, but also differentiated it from countries with which the United States has diplomatic relations. Although most of the 110 invitees were leaders from democracies around the world, the two participants invited from Taiwan were Digital Minister Audrey Tang and Taiwan's Representative to the United States Bi-khim Hsiao. In accordance with the U.S. unofficial relationship with Taiwan and its one-China policy, both Tang and Hsiao joined the virtual summit with background images that did not include the ROC flag or other symbols of sovereignty.

The Biden administration also adroitly threaded the needle of providing reassurance to Taipei without provoking Beijing when Russian President Vladimir Putin invaded Ukraine on February 24, 2022, raising fears among Taiwan's people that they could be abandoned if the PRC attacked. Those fears were partly stoked by Chinese disinformation narratives that included the slogan "Ukraine today, Taiwan tomorrow." President Biden dispatched a delegation of former senior defense and security officials to the island led by former chairman of the Joint Chiefs of Staff Adm. Mike Mullen (Ret.), to reaffirm America's support for Taiwan.

In President Biden's first two years in office, policy toward Taiwan was formulated based on the broader policy priorities of emphasizing the Indo-Pacific region, strengthening relations with allies and partners, and bolstering democratic resilience. Taiwan was the beneficiary of these organizing principles of the Biden administration's foreign policy, and the U.S.-Taiwan relationship deepened as a result. At the same time, however, the Biden administration fell short in some areas. The absence of a clear trade policy redounded negatively for Taipei, which had hoped to launch negotiations with the United States on trade agreements that would not only further solidify bilateral ties, but also might encourage other countries to follow in the United States' footsteps. Taiwan's exclusion from IPEF was also a major disappointment for Taiwan. In addition, despite efforts to present a contrast with the Trump administration in terms of professionalism, coordination, and discipline, the Biden administration's rhetorical imprecision regarding Taiwan was notable. The inconsistent and occasionally contradictory statements on Taiwan by the president and senior officials more closely resembled the Trump administration than any previous administration since 1979 and at best created confusion in both Beijing and Taipei.

IS STRATEGIC AMBIGUITY OUTDATED?

Ever since the U.S.-ROC Mutual Defense Treaty ended on January 1, 1980, the United States has been vague about whether and under what circumstances the United States would defend Taiwan. Breaking the treaty, which included a commitment by both Washington and Taipei to "act to meet the common danger" in response to an armed attack against territories of either of the parties in the West Pacific, was required under the terms of normalization of diplomatic relations between the United States and the PRC.[88] Henceforth, the U.S. policy of "strategic ambiguity" was deemed sufficient to deter the PRC from attacking Taiwan based on the premise that China's leaders must make worst-case assumptions about U.S. resolve. After Taiwan's democratization and the emergence of the DPP as a political force, ambiguity was also viewed as necessary to dissuade Taipei from pursuing pro-independence policies that could provoke a PRC attack and draw the United States into a conflict. This policy of "dual deterrence" has served American interests for over four decades. In recent years, however, the PLA's development and deployment of military capabilities aimed at deterring or, if necessary, defeating U.S. intervention in a Taiwan contingency, along with further advancement in its capabilities to invade Taiwan, has prompted an intense debate among national security experts about whether the U.S. policy of "strategic ambiguity" is sufficient to preserve peace in the Taiwan Strait.

The push to change U.S. policy to "strategic clarity"—making explicit that the United States would respond to any Chinese use of force against Taiwan—began with the publication of an article by Congressman Mike Gallagher. Writing for the *National Review* on May 11, 2020, he argued for ending the forty-year-old policy of strategic ambiguity. Calling for "a declaratory statement of policy committing the United States to the defense of Taiwan," Gallagher acknowledged that such an approach had inherent risks, but he maintained that complacency posed an even greater hazard.[89]

The "strategic clarity" argument gained momentum when Richard Haass and David Sacks advocated a change in policy in the pages of *Foreign Affairs* in September 2020. The authors argued that purposeful ambiguity would no longer deter an increasingly assertive China with growing military capabilities. They proposed that the White House issue a presidential statement and accompanying executive order that reiterates Washington's support for its "one-China" policy, but also unequivocally states that the United States would defend Taiwan if it came under Chinese armed attack. At the same time, the authors maintained that the United States needed to modify its force posture and make preparing for a Taiwan contingency a top priority for DoD planners.[90]

Proponents of adopting strategic clarity were given a boost in March 2021, when Admiral Philip Davidson, then-commander of the U.S. Indo-Pacific Command, warned that the danger of a cross-Strait war was real and growing. Testifying at a hearing convened by the Senate Armed Services Committee, Davidson asserted that the threat of a PRC attack on Taiwan "is manifest during this decade, in fact, in the next six years." His testimony set off a firestorm of debate about the risk of war in the Taiwan Strait. Two weeks later, Admiral John Aquilino, the nominee to succeed Davidson who was subsequently confirmed as commander of U.S. Indo-Pacific Command, stopped short of endorsing the six-year time frame, but maintained that "this problem is much closer to us than most think."

Chairman of the Joint Chiefs of Staff General Mark Milley weighed into the discussion at another congressional hearing in June. He argued that Xi Jinping and his military are aware that an invasion of Taiwan "would be extraordinarily complicated and costly." Milley also distinguished between capabilities and intent, asserting that Xi had moved up the target for developing capabilities to seize Taiwan from 2035 to 2027 but that the PRC did not currently have the intent to seize Taiwan in the next year or two. Milley acknowledged that intent could change quickly but expressed doubt that an invasion would happen "out of the blue."[91]

Some advocates of strategic clarity echoed a concern that emerged in the U.S. defense community that the shift in the U.S.-China and cross-Strait military balances in the PRC's favor has opened a window of opportunity over the next decade for the PLA to seize and control Taiwan. According to this line of reasoning, if the PLA waits too long, it may lose the chance to reunify the country. Xi Jinping himself has signaled impatience by asserting that differences between Taiwan and Mainland China must not be passed on to the next generation. Beijing's assessment that the United States is in decline and war-weary was frequently cited as one of the reasons that Beijing could attack in the near term. The U.S. withdrawal from Afghanistan and its decision to not send troops to defend Ukraine even before Russia invaded provided additional justifications for a Chinese calculation that the United States would not come to Taiwan's defense. A spate of articles cited war games by the Pentagon and the RAND Corporation that concluded a U.S.-China military clash over Taiwan would result in a U.S. defeat and a Chinese takeover of Taiwan in just days or weeks. Since there was no quick military fix available to shore up deterrence, adopting "strategic clarity" was an attractive solution.

Experts on the other side of the argument maintained that providing Taiwan with an ironclad security guarantee was not in America's interests. Beijing would likely view the rhetorical shift as a violation of the terms of normalization of diplomatic relations and a threat to Chinese sovereignty. Xi Jinping would come under pressure to attack now while the PLA has the upper hand. Revising U.S. rhetorical policy would therefore provoke, not deter a Chinese attack. Proponents of preserving "strategic ambiguity" contended that China's priority was preventing Taiwan independence and that unification was a long-term goal. Moreover, Taiwan is first and foremost a political problem left over from the CCP-KMT civil war, these experts argued, and it is in Beijing's interest to achieve unification without bloodshed, if possible. PRC strategy is aimed at inducing a sense of despair among the Taiwan people so that they eventually conclude that their only viable future is to unify with the mainland. To achieve this goal, Xi Jinping is relying increasingly on coercive tools. In his book titled *Difficult Choices*, Richard Bush dubbed that strategy "coercion without violence."

Moreover, experts opposing a policy change suggested that Xi recognizes that attempting to take Taiwan by force presents unacceptable risks. Military conflict with the United States could escalate to attacks on each other's homelands and involve a nuclear exchange. The PLA could get bogged down in a long war, both with the United States and Taiwan. A large portion of its navy could be destroyed, and many thousands of lives could be lost. A cross-Strait war could set back the fulfillment of Xi's other goals, such as making China a global leader in innovation by 2035 and achieving national rejuvenation by 2049. A decision by Beijing to use force against Taiwan could instill fear in countries that have territorial disputes with China and encourage them to join anti-China coalitions. U.S. allies could jointly impose punishing economic sanctions on China that draw from the playbook used against Russia after its February 24, 2021, invasion of Ukraine, including banning Chinese banks from making or receiving international payments using the SWIFT messaging service, travel bans and asset freezes on individuals, restrictions on high-tech exports to China, and bans on imports of select products from China.

Some experts also asserted that a policy of "strategic clarity" could embolden a future leader of Taiwan to push for independence, which would likely provoke a PRC attack and pull in the United States. It might also result in Taiwan doing less to prepare to defend the island since its military could be confident that the United States would ride to the rescue.

The debate over "strategic ambiguity" versus "strategic clarity" appears to be taking place in Congress, academia, and think tanks, but not in the executive branch of the Biden administration. U.S. officials signaled that they believed there were no compelling reasons to change American policy. U.S. policy coordinator for the Indo-Pacific Kurt Campbell stated publicly that there were "significant downsides" to a declaration that the United States would defend Taiwan under all circumstances. Instead, Campbell said, "The best way to maintain peace and stability is to send a really consolidated message that involves diplomacy, defense innovation and our own capabilities to the Chinese leadership, so they don't contemplate some sort of ambitious, dangerous provocative set of steps in the future."[92]

As experts debated the advisability of revising U.S. declaratory policy regarding the defense of Taiwan, attention within the legislative and executive branches increasingly focused on the Taiwan military's lack of sufficient capability to defend the island. In her second inaugural address in May 2020, President Tsai Ing-wen reaffirmed Taipei's commitment to developing asymmetric capabilities and pledged to implement defense reforms that would enable the military to achieve its strategic objective of multidomain deterrence. She also reversed the trend of declining defense budgets. But given the severe threat that Taiwan faces from the PRC, many believe that Taipei's spending on defense, which in 2023 is a proposed US$18.31 billion (if the special budget for procurement of new fighter jets is included) or roughly 2.4 percent of GDP, falls far short of Taiwan's needs.

Many observers in the United States doubt that Taiwan is continuing to implement the Overall Defense Concept, an innovative asymmetric warfighting framework introduced in 2017 by former chief of the Taiwan General Staff, Admiral Lee Hsi-min. Whereas the term was included in key Taiwan military documents for several years, it does not appear in either the 2021 Quadrennial Defense Review (QDR) or the National Defense Report. In at least one sign of a departure from an emphasis on developing asymmetric capabilities, the QDR says the ministry is planning to deter an invasion by threatening to retaliate with long-range missile strikes against the Chinese mainland.

Taiwan's military continues to face enormous challenges, including inadequate resources, low readiness, ineffective reserves, and a troubled transition to an all-volunteer force. While some recent procurements such as coastal defense cruise missiles and mobile artillery are consistent with an asymmetric approach and the U.S. push for Taiwan to buy a small number of large, expensive weapons systems and larger quantities of small mobile, survivable lethal weapons, not all acquisitions fit this pattern. For example, under a US$1.42 billion deal that was approved in 2019, Taiwan will receive a delivery of 108 Abrams tanks between 2023 and 2026. Many experts argue that Taiwan should instead acquire more access denial weapons, including anti-aircraft missiles, ballistic missile defenses, naval mines, and drones, that can stop, or even deter, a Chinese invasion.

Support for Taiwan in the U.S. Congress is at an all-time high, but debates persist among members over how to best ensure Taiwan's security. Numerous bills focused on Taiwan were introduced in the 117th Congress (2021–2022), including the Taiwan Invasion Prevention Act, the Taiwan Partnership Act, the Taiwan PLUS Act, the Taiwan Relations Reinforcement Act, the Taiwan Defense Act of 2021, the Arm Taiwan Act, and the Taiwan Policy Act. However, only four enacted laws contained Taiwan provisions: (1) a law that directed the Secretary of State to develop a strategy to regain observer status for Taiwan in the WHA; (2) the Consolidated Appropriations Act, 2022, which barred using funds made available by the Act to create, procure, or display any map that inaccurately depicts the territory and social and economic system of Taiwan and its island groups; (3) the National Defense Authorization Act (NDAA) for FY2022, which required the executive branch to submit reports and briefings to Congress but did not mandate major policy changes; and (4) the NDAA for FY2023, which included the Taiwan Enhanced Resilience Act (TERA) that authorized up to $10 billion in Foreign Military Financing grants through 2027 for key capabilities and training for Taiwan and authorized another $1 billion in equipment from U.S. military stockpiles, among other provisions.

The Ukraine war created an unprecedented sense of urgency about the potential for a PRC attack on Taiwan and led to a reinvigorated effort by the U.S. DoD to push Taiwan to implement military reforms that would deny the PLA the ability to seize and control the island. The war underscored the need for Taiwan to bolster its self-defense capability by investing in asymmetric capabilities that are resilient, mobile, distributed, and cost-effective. Particularly salient lessons of the war for Taiwan are the necessity to prioritize civil defense preparations and accelerate reform of the military reserve system. Heightened concern about a possible Chinese invasion of the island before the end of the decade also prompted the United States to pressure Taiwan to revise its acquisition strategy to focus almost exclusively on the counter-invasion scenario. Acceding to U.S. preferences, Taipei abandoned a plan to purchase 12 MH-60R anti-submarine helicopters.

SPEAKER PELOSI TRAVELS TO TAIWAN

Speaker of the House of Representatives Nancy Pelosi landed in Taiwan on August 2, 2022, marking the first time that a House speaker visited Taiwan in twenty-five years. Biden administration officials tried, but failed, to persuade Pelosi to postpone or cancel her trip. Xi Jinping reportedly asked the U.S. president to prevent the Speaker from traveling to Taiwan.[93] However, Biden demurred, largely because of his respect for the independence of Congress that he developed during his thirty-six years in the Senate. President Biden instructed the U.S. military to warn Pelosi of the risks of making of the trip and told reporters that "The military thinks it's not a good idea right now." Nevertheless, Pelosi decided to proceed with her visit as planned.

After Pelosi's twenty-four-hour stay in Taiwan, the PLA held four days of live-fire military drills and rehearsed capabilities to impose a blockade around Taiwan. At least five ballistic missiles were launched over Taiwan that splashed into six closure zones east of Taiwan that bracketed the island and its key ports. Another five ballistic missiles fired by the PLA splashed down in Japan's EEZ, the first time that Chinese missiles landed within 200 nautical miles of Japanese territory. Dozens of Chinese warplanes and naval ships crossed the median line of the Taiwan Strait. China also flew drones over Taiwan's outlying Kinmen Island and military helicopters flew past Pingtan Island, one of Mainland China's closest points to Taiwan.

The Biden administration accused Beijing of overreacting and using the Pelosi visit to Taiwan as a pretext to conduct aggressive military activity and change the status quo in the Taiwan Strait, a position that was echoed in a statement by the G7 countries. Over the ensuing weeks and months it became clear that China had in fact created a "new normal" in its military posture around Taiwan. The tempo of PLA activity around Taiwan increased and cyberattacks on the island surged. Chinese navy ships joined military aircraft in routinely operating across the Taiwan Strait center line and closer to the edge of Taiwan's territorial waters and airspace. Whatever short term benefits had accrued to Taipei from Pelosi's brief stopover quickly dissipated, leaving Taiwan's security in greater danger than before her visit.

CONCLUSION

There has been more continuity than change in the Biden administration's approach to Taiwan. Concern about rising PRC coercion against Taiwan, the perceived need to strengthen deterrence, and a desire to support Taiwan's democracy have been the primary drivers of Biden's policy toward Taiwan. Growing U.S.-China strategic competition, in tandem with rising cross-Strait tensions, has provided an impetus for closer ties between Washington and Taipei. With the end of Trump's presidency, Taipei no longer has to fear being used as a bargaining chip in a U.S.-China deal. The Biden administration has provided regular signals of reassurance of U.S. support for Taiwan and allayed concerns that the Democrats' return to power would be accompanied by greater emphasis on U.S.-China cooperation that could damage Taiwan's interests.

Tsai Ing-wen has carefully navigated the choppy waters of growing U.S.-China rivalry and increasing cross-Strait friction. Her persistent commitment to preserving the cross-Strait status quo and to strengthening Taiwan's democracy, prosperity, and security has made her a reliable partner for the United States. For Taiwan, forging closer ties with the United States has brought many tangible benefits, including more frequent and higher-level official interactions, increased U.S. support for Taiwan's international participation, greater U.S. efforts to rally the support of its allies for Taiwan, enhanced U.S. efforts to help Taiwan keep its diplomatic allies, and more robust U.S. support for Taiwan's defense and security.

Over the Trump administration and the first two years of the Biden administration, the scope of cooperation between the United States and Taiwan expanded significantly. The creation of bilateral mechanisms to coordinate on such issues as health, supply chains, coast guards, and democratic governance provides a stronger base for the future growth of U.S.-Taiwan relations. Closer coordination on cyber, disinformation, and other growing security threats also contribute to deeper ties.

The strengthening of U.S.-Taiwan ties, while necessary and backed by both Taipei and Washington, has nevertheless come at a price. Chinese pressure on Taiwan, which began in earnest when Tsai became president, has increased substantially in response to more visible and significant U.S.-Taiwan cooperation. Beijing's diplomatic, military, and economic coercion against Taiwan have mounted as the PRC seeks to punish Taipei and warn against further provocations that harm Chinese interests. Defending and protecting Taiwan from PRC coercion has now become one of the most challenging tasks for Washington and Taipei.

NOTES

1. Every candidate who is not currently serving as president, vice president, premier, or vice premier is permitted to visit the United States. Individuals in those positions may be permitted to transit the United States en route to another destination.

2. Tsai Ing-wen, "Tsai Ing-wen 2016: Taiwan Faces the Future," speech, Washington, D.C., June 3, 2015, CSIS, www.csis.org/events/tsai-ing-wen-2016-taiwan-faces-future.

3. Tsai Ing-wen, "Inaugural Address of ROC 14th-Term President Tsai Ing-wen," speech, Taipei, Taiwan, May 20, 2016, Office of the President, Republic of China (Taiwan), https://english.president.gov.tw/News/4893.

4. Xinhua [新华社], "Setting the Tone for Cross-Strait Relations and Showing Sincerity and Goodwill—Taiwan Public Opinion Hotly Discusses General Secretary Xi Jinping's Latest Speech to Taiwan [定调两岸关系　展现真情善意—台湾舆论热议习近平总书记最新对台讲话]," Embassy of the People's Republic of China in the United States of America, March 6, 2015, www.mfa.gov.cn/ce/ceus//chn/zt/twwt/t1243153.htm.

5. Richard C. Bush, *Difficult Choices: Taiwan's Quest for Security and the Good Life* (Washington, D.C.: Brookings Institution Press, 2021), 329.

6. Tsai Ing-wen, "Inaugural Address of ROC," 14th-term President Tsai Ing-wen, speech, Taipei, Taiwan, May 20, 2016, Office of the President, Republic of China (Taiwan), https://english.president.gov.tw/News/4893.

7. Tsai Ing-wen, "President Tsai's 2016 National Day Address," speech, Taipei, Taiwan, October 10, 2016, Office of the President, Republic of China (Taiwan), https://english.president.gov.tw/News/4997.

8. Tsai Ing-wen, "President Tsai Delivers 2017 National Day Address," speech, Taipei, Taiwan, October 10, 2017, Office of the President, Republic of China (Taiwan), https://english.president.gov.tw/News/5231.

9. Tsai Ing-wen, "President Tsai Delivers 2018 National Day Address," speech, Taipei, Taiwan, October 10, 2018, Office of the President, Republic of China (Taiwan), https://english.president.gov.tw/News/5548.

10. Tsai Ing-wen, "President Tsai's New Year's Talk for 2019," speech, Taipei, Taiwan, January 1, 2019, Office of the President, Republic of China (Taiwan), https://english.president.gov.tw/News/5618.

11. Tsai Ing-wen, "Inaugural Address of ROC 15th-Term President Tsai Ing-wen," speech, Taipei, Taiwan, June 20, 2020, Office of the President, Republic of China (Taiwan), https://english.president.gov.tw/News/6004.

12. Tsai Ing-wen, "President Tsai Delivers 2021 National Day Address," speech, Taipei, Taiwan, October 10, 2021, Office of the President, Republic of China (Taiwan), https://english.president.gov.tw/News/6175.

13. Tsai Ing-wen, "President Tsai Delivers 2022 New Year's Address," speech, Taipei, Taiwan, January 1, 2022, Office of the President, Republic of China (Taiwan), https://english.president.gov.tw/News/6209.

14. Tsai Ing-wen, "President Tsai Delivers 2022 National Day Address," speech, Taipei, Taiwan, October 10, 2022, Office of the President, Republic of China (Taiwan), https://english.president.gov.tw/News/6348.

15. "Xi Urges Chinese Province to Deepen Ties with Democratic Taiwan," *Bloomberg*, March 25, 2021, www.bloomberg.com/news/articles/2021-03-25/xi-urges-chinese-province-to-deepen-ties-with-democratic-taiwan?sref=e0X6oOeR.

16. Lawrence Chung, "Fines on Taiwan's Far Eastern Group Fan Fears of More Retaliation by Beijing over Political Donations," *SCMP*, November 24, 2021, www.scmp.com/news/china/politics/article/3157108/fines-taiwans-far-eastern-group-fan-fears-more-retaliation.

17. Jessica Drun and Bonnie S. Glaser, "The Distortion of UN Resolution 2758 to Limit Taiwan's Access to the United Nations," German Marshall Fund, March 2022, https://www.gmfus.org/sites/default/files/2022-03/Drun%26Glaser-distortion-un-resolution-2758-limit-taiwans-access.pdf.

18. Office of the Secretary of Defense, *Military and Security Developments Involving the People's Republic of China*, U.S. Department of Defense, 2021, https://media.defense.gov/2021/Nov/03/2002885874/-1/-1/0/2021-CMPR-FINAL.PDF.

19. Paul Huang, "Chinese Cyber-Operatives Boosted Taiwan's Insurgent Candidate," *Foreign Policy*, June 26, 2019, https://foreignpolicy.com/2019/06/26/chinese-cyber-operatives-boosted-taiwans-insurgent-candidate/.

20. Katherin Hille, "Taiwan Primaries Highlight Fears over China's Political Influence," *Financial Times*, July 16, 2019, https://www.ft.com/content/036b609a-a768-11e9-984c-fac8325aaa04.

21. Hille, "Taiwan Primaries Highlight Fears."

22. Vincent W. F. Chen, "Republic of China, Taiwan's Unique Status Shall Not Perish: CCP's Influence Operations against Taiwan," presentation, Jamestown Foundation's Ninth Annual China Defense and Security Conference, Carnegie Endowment for International Peace, Washington, D.C., October 15, 2019, https://www.youtube.com/watch?v=yVvOhJ2P6n0.

23. "Gray Zone Project," CSIS, www.csis.org/programs/gray-zone-project.

24. Chen Yufu and Jonathan Chin, "Public Perception of Chinese Hostility Soars," *Taipei Times*, August 19, 2022, https://www.taipeitimes.com/News/taiwan/archives/2022/08/19/2003783794.

25. "China's Xi Says Political Solution for Taiwan Can't Wait Forever," Reuters, October 6, 2013, www.reuters.com/article/us-asia-apec-china-taiwan/chinas-xi-says-political-solution-for-taiwan-cant-wait-forever-idUSBRE99503Q20131006.

26. "President Xi Jinping Had a Virtual Meeting with US President Joe Biden," Ministry of Foreign Affairs of the People's Republic of China, November 16, 2021, www.fmprc.gov.cn/mfa_eng/zxxx_662805/202111/t20211116_10448843.html.

27. "President Xi Jinping Meets with U.S. President Joe Biden in Bali," Ministry of Foreign Affairs of the People's Republic of China, November 14, 2022, https://www.fmprc.gov.cn/mfa_eng/zxxx_662805/202211/t20221114_10974686.html.

28. Xi Jinping, "Working Together to Realize Rejuvenation of the Chinese Nation and Advance China's Peaceful Reunification," speech, Beijing, China, January 2, 2019, Taiwan Affairs Office, www.gwytb.gov.cn/wyly/201904/t20190412_12155687.htm.

29. "The Taiwan Question and China's Reunification in the New Era," The Taiwan Affairs Office of the State Council and The State Council Information Office, The People's Republic of China, August 2022, https://english.news.cn/20220810/df9d3b8702154b34bbf1d451b99bf64a/c.html.

30. "Full Text of the Chinese Communist Party's New Resolution on History," *Nikkei Asia*, November 19, 2021, https://asia.nikkei.com/Politics/Full-text-of-the-Chinese-Communist-Party-s-new-resolution-on-history.

31. "'One China' Principle Is Non-Negotiable: Beijing," Reuters, January 14, 2017, www.reuters.com/article/us-usa-trump-china/one-china-principle-is-non-negotiable-beijing-idUSKBN14Y0N4.

32. Mark Lander and Michael Forsythe, "Trump Tells Xi Jinping U.S. Will Honor 'One China' Policy," *New York Times*, February 9, 2017, www.nytimes.com/2017/02/09/world/asia/donald-trump-china-xi-jinping-letter.html.

33. Jeff Mason, Stephen J. Adler, and Steve Holland, "Exclusive: Trump Spurns Taiwan President's Suggestion of Another Phone Call," Reuters, April 28, 2017, www.reuters.com/article/us-usa-trump-taiwan-exclusive/exclusive-trump-spurns-taiwan-presidents-suggestion-of-another-phone-call-idUSKBN17U05I.

34. Alex Wong, "Remarks by Deputy Assistant Secretary of State Alex Wong at the American Chamber of Commerce in Taipei Hsieh Nien Fan," speech, Taipei, Taiwan, March 21, 2018, American Institute in Taiwan, www.ait.org.tw/remarks-deputy-assistant-secretary-state-alex-wong-american-chamber-commerce-taipei-hsieh-nien-fan/.

35. "American Institute in Taiwan Inaugurates New Office Complex in Taipei," Ministry of Foreign Affairs, Republic of China, Taiwan, June 13, 2018, https://nspp.mofa.gov.tw/nsppe/news.php?post=136061&unit=376.

36. W. Brent Christensen, "Opening Remarks by AIT Director W. Brent Christensen at the U.S.-Taiwan Consultations on Democratic Governance in the Indo-Pacific Region," speech, Taipei, Taiwan, September 12, 2019, American Institute in Taiwan, www.ait.org.tw/opening-remarks-by-ait-director-w-brent-christensen-at-the-u-s-taiwan-consultations-on-democratic-governance-in-the-indo-pacific-region/.

37. "The Department of Defense Indo-Pacific Strategy Report: Preparedness, Partnerships, and Promoting a Networked Region," U.S. Department of Defense, June 1, 2019, https://media.defense.gov/2019/Jul/01/2002152311/-1/-1/1/DEPARTMENT-OF-DEFENSE-INDO-PACIFIC-STRATEGY-REPORT-2019.PDF.

38. Joseph Trevithick, "Army Releases Ultra Rare Video Showing Green Berets Training in Taiwan," *The Drive*, June 29, 2020, www.thedrive.com/the-war-zone/34474/army-releases -ultra-rare-video-showing-green-berets-training-in-taiwan.

39. "Taiwan's Ministry of Defense Confirms U.S. Military in Taiwan to Assist in Train-ing [台国防部证实美军在台协助训练]" *Lianhe Zaobao [联合早报]*, June 29, 2020, www .zaobao.com.sg/realtime/china/story20200629-1064895.

40. Gordon Lubold, "U.S. Troops Have Been Deployed in Taiwan for at Least a Year," *Wall Street Journal*, October 7, 2021, www.wsj.com/articles/u-s-troops-have-been-deployed -in-taiwan-for-at-least-a-year-11633614043.

41. John Power, "US Warships Made 92 Trips through the Taiwan Strait since 2007," *SCMP*, May 3, 2019, www.scmp.com/week-asia/geopolitics/article/3008621/us-warships -made-92-trips-through-taiwan-strait-2007.

42. Edward Wong, "U.S. Recalls Top Diplomats from Latin America as Worries Rise over China's Influence," *New York Times*, September 8, 2018, www.nytimes.com/2018/09/08/us /politics/us-latin-america-china.html.

43. Gardiner Harris, "U.S. Weighed Penalizing El Salvador over Support for China, Then Backed Off," *New York Times*, September 29, 2018, https://www.nytimes.com/2018/09/29/ world/americas/trump-china-taiwan-el-salvador.html.

44. "Statement from the Press Secretary on China's Political Correctness," Trump White House archive, May 5, 2018, https://trumpwhitehouse.archives.gov/briefings-statements/ statement-press-secretary-chinas-political-correctness/.

45. Michael R. Pompeo, "Secretary Michael R. Pompeo at a Press Availability," U.S. Department of State (archived, 2017–2021), May 6, 2020, https://2017-2021.state.gov/ secretary-michael-r-pompeo-at-a-press-availability-5/index.html.

46. Colum Lynch, "WHO Becomes Battleground as Trump Chooses Pandemic Confron-tation Over Cooperation," *Foreign Policy*, April 29, 2020, https://foreignpolicy.com/2020/04 /29/world-health-organization-who-battleground-trump-taiwan-china/.

47. Michael R. Pompeo, "Taiwan's Inauguration of President Tsai Ing-wen," U.S. Department of State (archived 2017–2021), May 19, 2020, https://2017-2021.state.gov/ taiwans-inauguration-of-president-tsai-ing-wen/index.html.

48. President Ronald Reagan to Secretary of State George P. Shultz and Secretary of Defense Caspar W. Weinberger, "Arms Sales to Taiwan," American Institute in Taiwan, August 17, 1982, www.ait.org.tw/wp-content/uploads/sites/269/08171982-Reagan-Memo -DECLASSIFIED.pdf.

49. "National Defense Authorization Act for Fiscal Year 2021," H.R. 6395, 116th Cong., (December 2020), www.govtrack.us/congress/bills/116/hr6395/text.

50. Michael R. Pompeo, "Lifting Self-Imposed Restrictions on the U.S.-Taiwan Relation-ship," U.S. Department of State (archived, 2017–2021), January 9, 2021, https://2017-2021 .state.gov/lifting-self-imposed-restrictions-on-the-u-s-taiwan-relationship/index.html.

51. Michael R. Pompeo, "On the Mass Arrests of Democracy Advocates in Hong Kong," U.S. Department of State (archived, 2017–2021), January 6, 2021, https://2017-2021.state .gov/on-the-mass-arrests-of-democracy-advocates-in-hong-kong/index.html.

52. David Spencer, "Taiwan Needs a Strategy to Counter China's Grey-Zone Tactics," *Taiwan News*, December 26, 2020, www.taiwannews.com.tw/en/news/4084689.

53. Lavanya Ramanathan and Simon Denyer, "Taiwan's Leader Says Call with Trump Didn't Reflect U.S. Policy Change," *Washington Post*, December 6, 2016, www.washington-post.com/world/taiwans-leader-says-trumps-phone-call-is-not-a-policy-change/2016/12/06/ c7ffd012-bb7f-11e6-817f-e3b588251d1e_story.html.

54. "America's Affirmation of the One-China Policy Pleased Taiwan, Too," *The Economist*, February 18, 2017, www.economist.com/asia/2017/02/16/americas-affirmation-of-the-one-china-policy-pleased-taiwan-too.

55. Judy Lin, "Taiwan Govt Voices Concerns over Rumors of U.S.-China Signing 4th Communiqué," *Taiwan News*, March 23, 2017, www.taiwannews.com.tw/en/news/3123758.

56. Gerry Shih, "Taiwan Frets Over How a Biden Administration Would Deal with China," *The Washington Post*, October 30, 2020, www.washingtonpost.com/world/asia_pacific/biden-china-election-taiwan-obama/2020/10/30/44e55488-0868-11eb-8719-0df159d14794_story.html.

57. "Biden's Letter to the United Daily News Will Deepen Relations with Taiwan [拜登投書聯合報系 當選將深化與台灣關係]," *United Daily News [聯合報]*, October 22, 2020, https://udn.com/news/story/121687/4955258?from=udn_ch2_menu_v2_main_index. The *World Journal* is owned by *United Daily News*, a newspaper published in Taiwan.

58. Jonathan Swan, "Exclusive: Trump Held Off on Xinjiang Sanctions for China Trade Deal," *Axios*, June 21, 2020, www.axios.com/trump-uighur-muslims-sanctions-d4dc86fc-17f4-42bd-bdbd-c30f4d2ffa21.html.

59. Zachary Basu, "Biden Campaign Says China's Treatment of Uighur Muslims Is 'Genocide,'" *Axios*, August 25, 2020, www.axios.com/biden-campaign-china-uighur-genocide-3ad857a7-abfe-4b16-813d-7f074a8a04ba.html.

60. Wang Yi, "Reorient and Steer Clear of Disruptions: For a Smooth Sailing of China-U.S. Relations," speech, Asia Society, New York, December 19, 2020, Ministry of Foreign Affairs of the People's Republic of China, www.fmprc.gov.cn/mfa_eng/wjb_663304/wjbz_663308/2461_663310/202012/t20201219_468835.html.

61. "China Says Military Drills Near Taiwan Were a 'Necessary Action,'" Reuters, September 15, 2020 www.reuters.com/article/us-china-politics-taiwan/china-says-military-drills-near-taiwan-were-a-necessary-action-idUSKBN2670DG.

62. T. Y. Wang, "Hong Kong National Security Law: The View From Taiwan," *The Diplomat*, July 2, 2020, https://thediplomat.com/2020/07/hong-kong-national-security-law-the-view-from-taiwan/.

63. Thomas L. Friedman, "Biden Made Sure 'Trump Is Not Going to Be President for Four More Years,'" *New York Times*, December 2, 2020, www.nytimes.com/2020/12/02/opinion/biden-interview-mcconnell-china-iran.html.

64. Antony Blinken, "Nomination of Hon. Antony J. Blinken to Be U.S. Secretary of State—Part I," Testimony before the Senate Committee on Foreign Relations, 117th Cong., 1st sess., January 19, 2021, www.govinfo.gov/content/pkg/CHRG-117shrg43890/html/CHRG-117shrg43890.htm.

65. Austin Lloyd, "To Conduct a Confirmation Hearing on the Expected Nomination of: Lloyd J. Austin III to Be Secretary of Defense," Testimony before the Senate Committee on Armed Services, 117th Cong., 1st sess., January 19, 2021, www.armed-services.senate.gov/download/transcript-1192021.

66. Ned Price, "PRC Military Pressure against Taiwan Threatens Regional Peace and Stability," U.S. Department of State, January 23, 2021, www.state.gov/prc-military-pressure-against-taiwan-threatens-regional-peace-and-stability/.

67. The shift in policy had been previewed during the presidential transition. A Biden transition official told the *Financial Times* that "Once in office [Biden] will continue to support a peaceful resolution of cross-Strait issues consistent with the wishes and best interests of

the people of Taiwan." See Katrina Manson, "US Risks Enraging China by Easing Limits on Taiwan Relations," *Financial Times*, January 9, 2021, www.ft.com/content/debd932f-48f7 -4933-a596-a4663b442002.

68. Clinton said that the United States should be "absolutely clear that the issues between Beijing and Taiwan must be resolved peacefully and with the assent of the people of Taiwan." See "Full Text of Clinton's Speech on China Trade Bill," *New York Times*, March 9, 2000 (archived), https://archive.nytimes.com/www.nytimes.com/library/world/asia/030900clinton -china-text.html.

69. "Readout of President Joseph R. Biden, Jr. Call with President Xi Jinping of China," The White House, February 10, 2021, www.whitehouse.gov/briefing-room/statements-releases /2021/02/10/readout-of-president-joseph-r-biden-jr-call-with-president-xi-jinping-of-china/.

70. "White House Says China's Moves around Taiwan 'Potentially Destabilizing,'" Reuters, April 9, 2021, www.reuters.com/world/china/white-house-says-chinas-moves -around-taiwan-potentially-destabilizing-2021-04-09/.

71. "Blinken Warns of China's 'Increasingly Aggressive Actions' against Taiwan," Reuters, April 11, 2021, www.reuters.com/world/china/blinken-warns-chinas-increasingly-aggressive -actions-against-taiwan-2021-04-11/.

72. "Interim National Security Strategic Guidance," The White House, March 3, 2021, www.whitehouse.gov/briefing-room/statements-releases/2021/03/03/interim-national -security-strategic-guidance/.

73. David Brunnstrom and Michael Martina, "Biden Sends Unofficial Delegation to Taiwan in 'Personal Signal,'" Reuters, April 13, 2021, www.reuters.com/world/china/biden -sends-unofficial-delegation-taiwan-underscore-commitment-white-house-2021-04-13/.

74. Ned Price, "New Guidelines for U.S. Government Interactions with Taiwan Counterparts," U.S. Department of State, April 9, 2021, www.state.gov/new-guidelines-for-u-s -government-interactions-with-taiwan-counterparts/.

75. "United States and Taiwan Hold Dialogue on Trade and Investment Priorities," Office of the United States Trade Representative, June 30, 2021, https://ustr.gov/about-us /policy-offices/press-office/press-releases/2021/june/united-states-and-taiwan-hold-dialogue -trade-and-investment-priorities.

76. "United States and Taiwan Announce the Launch of the U.S.-Taiwan Initiative on 21st-Century Trade," Office of the United States Trade Representative, June 1, 2022, https://ustr.gov/about-us/policy-offices/press-office/press-releases/2022/june/united-states -and-taiwan-announce-launch-us-taiwan-initiative-21st-century-trade.

77. Antony Blinken, "Supporting Taiwan's Participation in the UN System," U.S. Department of State, October 26, 2021, www.state.gov/supporting-taiwans-participation-in -the-un-system/.

78. The German Marshall Fund of the United States, "UN Resolution 2758 Turns 50: Implications for Taiwan," YouTube Video, 8:18, October 21, 2021, www.youtube.com/ watch?v=G0rqjDd8npA&t=498s.

79. "G7 Foreign and Development Ministers' Meeting: Communiqué, London, 5 May 2021," UK Foreign, Commonwealth and Development Office, May 5, 2021, www.gov.uk/government /publications/g7-foreign-and-development-ministers-meeting-may-2021-communique/g7-for eign-and-development-ministers-meeting-communique-london-5-may-2021.

80. "Carbis Bay G7 Summit Communiqué," The White House, June 13, 2021, www.white house.gov/briefing-room/statements-releases/2021/06/13/carbis-bay-g7-summit-communique/.

81. "U.S.-EU Summit Statement," The White House, June 15, 2021, www.whitehouse .gov/briefing-room/statements-releases/2021/06/15/u-s-eu-summit-statement/.

82. "Joint Statement on Australia-U.S. Ministerial Consultations (AUSMIN) 2021," U.S. Department of State, September 16, 2021, www.state.gov/joint-statement-on-australia-u-s-ministerial-consultations-ausmin-2021/.

83. "Kurt Campbell: U.S. and China Can Co-Exist Peacefully," Asia Society Policy Institute, July 6, 2021, https://asiasociety.org/policy-institute/kurt-campbell-us-and-china-can-co-exist-peacefully.

84. Antony Blinken, "The Biden Administration's Priorities for U.S. Foreign Policy," C-SPAN, Testimony before the House Foreign Affairs Committee, 117th Cong., 1st sess., March 10, 2021, www.c-span.org/video/?509633-1/house-foreign-affairs-committee-hearing-biden-administration-foreign-policy-priorities.

85. Antony Blinken, "The U.S. Withdrawal from Afghanistan," C-SPAN, Testimony before the House Foreign Affairs Committee, 117th Cong., 1st sess., September 13, 2021, www.c-span.org/video/?514505-1/secretary-blinken-afghanistan-withdrawal-inherited-deadline-not-inherit-plan.

86. Ely Ratner, "Statement by Dr. Ely Ratner Assistant Secretary of Defense for Indo-Pacific Security Affairs," Testimony before the Senate Committee on Foreign Relations, 117th Cong., 1st sess., December 8, 2021, www.foreign.senate.gov/imo/media/doc/120821_Ratner_Testimony1.pdf.

87. See, for example, Paul Heer, "Has Washington's Policy toward Taiwan Crossed the Rubicon?" *The National Interest*, December 10, 2021, https://nationalinterest.org/feature/has-washington%E2%80%99s-policy-toward-taiwan-crossed-rubicon-197877, and Michael Swaine, "US Official Signals Stunning Shift in the Way We Interpret 'One China' Policy," Responsible Statecraft, May 21, 2022, https://responsiblestatecraft.org/2021/12/10/us-official-signals-stunning-shift-in-the-way-we-interpret-one-china-policy/.

88. "Mutual Defense Treaty between the United States and the Republic of China," opened for signature December 2, 1954, The Avalon Project at the Yale Law School, https://avalon.law.yale.edu/20th_century/chin001.asp.

89. Mike Gallagher, "It's Time to Stand with Taiwan," *The National Review*, May 11, 2020, www.nationalreview.com/2020/05/taiwan-deserves-united-states-support/.

90. Richard Haass and David Sacks, "American Support for Taiwan Must Be Unambiguous," *Foreign Affairs*, September 2, 2020, www.foreignaffairs.com/articles/united-states/american-support-taiwan-must-be-unambiguous.

91. Mark Milley, "General Milley, Secretary Austin Full Testimony Transcript on 2022 Budget Request," Testimony before the House Armed Services Committee, 117th Cong., 1st sess., June 23, 2021, www.rev.com/blog/transcripts/general-milley-secretary-austin-full-testimony-transcript-on-2022-budget-request.

92. Demetri Sevastopulo and Kathrin Hille, "Washington Shies Away from Open Declaration to Defend Taiwan," *Financial Times*, May 4, 2021, www.ft.com/content/26b03f60-ac06-4829-b2ed-da78ac47116a.

93. Yasmeen Abutaleb and Tyler Pager, "Chinese Leader Asked Biden to Prevent Pelosi from Visiting Taiwan," *Washington Post*, August 20, 2022, https://www.washingtonpost.com/politics/2022/08/20/nancy-pelosi-biden-taiwan/.

3

Charting the Future of U.S.-Taiwan Relations

AMERICA'S TOP INTERESTS AND OBJECTIVES IN TAIWAN

After waves of conflict across Asia from the late nineteenth century through the 1970s, the past four decades have been characterized by a long peace—a period when interstate tensions have simmered below the level of armed conflict and countries have been able to concentrate national energies on improving the livelihoods of their peoples. This period produced historic rates of economic growth across Asia, leading to dramatic improvements in human welfare in every country except North Korea.[1] Asia has emerged as the engine of the world economy, now accounting for nearly 60 percent of global growth. U.S. exports to Asia create more jobs than any other region. It is home to five U.S. treaty allies and critical security partners such as Taiwan. It is widely accepted in the United States that Asia will be the most consequential region for America's security and prosperity in the twenty-first century.

One of the greatest threats to the long peace in Asia is a conflict in the Taiwan Strait. For decades, Washington has organized its diplomacy and its military capabilities to uphold its abiding interest in preserving peace and stability in the Taiwan Strait. This has required the United States to deter China from using force against Taiwan and also Taiwan from seeking *de jure* independence—the two paths that could lead to conflict.

America's focus on upholding peace and stability has provided enabling conditions for a dramatic increase in prosperity on both sides of the Taiwan Strait, as well as for Taiwan's democratic transformation. It also has eased Japanese anxieties about becoming strategically flanked by China through annexation of Taiwan. This, in turn, has allowed Japan to concentrate its national focus on its own economic

101

progress and the development of the region, where Japan remains a leading source of foreign direct investment.

Taiwan has emerged as a key partner for the United States in its own right. In 2020, the United States traded more with Taiwan than it did with India or France. American companies depend upon Taiwan-produced semiconductors to sustain their supply chains and continue to innovate and grow. There are deep levels of cooperation on science and technology, public health, and educational issues. The United States and Taiwan partner to share best practices with countries around the world regarding democratic governance and defending against external political interference. U.S. and Taiwan experts also stand shoulder-to-shoulder whenever crises emerge, whether in Iraq, Syria, or Afghanistan, or in response to disease outbreaks in Africa or elsewhere. Washington views Taiwan's resilience in the face of Beijing's intensifying pressure as an important symbol for the region and the world of the strength of democratic values for protecting freedoms and advancing well-being. U.S. support for Taiwan also is enshrined in U.S. law in the TRA. As a point of comparison, none of these aforementioned conditions applied to America's relationship with Ukraine prior to Russia's February 2022 invasion.

The United States views its interests as being best served by a strong and moderate Taiwan. As former U.S. official Tom Christensen previously explained, "Anything that makes Taiwan stronger and safer is good for the United States, and, for obvious reasons, is also good for the people of Taiwan. Anything that places such peace and stability at risk runs directly against the interests of the United States."[2]

Taiwan's security is of profound significance for America's future. Because the Taiwan Strait is a potential flashpoint, it commands Washington's unblinking attention. And as American and Chinese forces have reached greater parity in their capacity to destroy each other's forces, neither side can have absolute confidence in their ability to prevail over the other in a conflict.[3]

In addition to the sobering risk of major loss of life, a 2021 study by the Council on Foreign Relations concluded that a cross-Strait conflict "would likely produce a global recession, if not a depression. It would disrupt Asian and international trade, sever major supply chains, and could collapse international financial systems. This would produce deeply painful economic consequences for U.S. allies, who trade more with China than they do with the United States. One study estimates that a single year of U.S.-China conflict could cause American GDP to decline by 5–10 percent."[4]

Given the scale of the stakes involved, it is understandable why U.S. officials have sought to underscore that Taiwan's security is not just an "internal matter" for China, or an annex of U.S.-China competition, but rather an issue of major consequence for the international system and global economy. Taiwan now accounts for "92 percent of the world's most advanced semiconductor manufacturing capacity."[5] Chips produced in Taiwan power everything from consumer goods to cars, computers, and satellites. Taiwan thus occupies a central position in global value chains. There is no substitute for Taiwan in the world for production of these critical inputs to the global economy. Reflecting this reality, world leaders increasingly have been underscoring publicly that Taiwan's security is a matter of global concern.

There is growing international recognition of the global benefit of Taiwan remaining integrated into the international community as a leading innovative power, a democratic success story, and a key contributor of global public goods. There also is broad bipartisan consensus within the United States that American interests are served by deepening and strengthening relations with Taiwan within the bounds of America's long-standing framework of unofficial relations.

America's policies are designed to mitigate risks resulting from unilateral changes to the status quo in the Taiwan Strait, such as a Chinese attack on Taiwan. They also are intended to ensure Taiwan's capability to preserve its political and economic autonomy and its dynamism as a free society until leaders on both sides of the Taiwan Strait can resolve differences peacefully and in a manner that is acceptable to the Taiwan public. Given Taiwan's democratic system, the support of the Taiwan people will be necessary to ratify any adjustment to the nature of relations between Taipei and Beijing.

FUTURE CROSS-STRAIT SCENARIOS AND IMPLICATIONS FOR AMERICAN INTERESTS

America's capacity to preserve peace and stability in the Taiwan Strait increasingly is being stressed by China's growing capabilities to act on its ambitions. Beijing has made no secret of its long-standing goal of unifying Taiwan with the mainland, including by force if necessary.

Chinese President Xi Jinping rhetorically has included unification as an element of achieving "national rejuvenation," a goal that China's leaders have set to reach by the centenary of the founding of the PRC in 2049. Actuarial tables suggest a low likelihood that Xi Jinping will remain in power in 2049. Nevertheless, there is little doubt that unification is a consolidated objective among the top leadership that will persist following Xi's departure. Every Chinese leader since Mao Zedong has signaled determination to unify Taiwan with the mainland. There is still debate within the expert community, though, about whether the CCP leadership has set a deadline for unification that could compel the use of force if it is not yet achieved.

Much of the forecasting of China working toward a deadline for unification rests on an assumption that China will act militarily once it has confidence in its capacity to prevail. Such an assumption that capabilities will drive decisions on use of force is itself a debatable proposition given the indivisible risks China would face if it were to initiate a military assault on Taiwan. China does not have any shield for its economy from potential financial fallout from initiating aggression. Beijing also does not have any near-term solutions to its dependency on imports of fuel and food to support its economy and its people. As the case of Russia has shown, the U.S. and its partners possess significant nonmilitary capacity to target other powers' vulnerabilities when compelled to do so.

Other experts base their assumptions about use of force on President Xi Jinping needing to achieve unification before he concludes his time in power to cement his position in the pantheon of Chinese leaders. This also is a debatable proposition, particularly given the range of other goals Xi has identified as desired legacy achievements apart from unification of Taiwan. Additionally, as chapter 2 explains, recent authoritative documents such as the Chinese Communist Party's Sixth Plenum Resolution in 2021 and Xi's work report to the 20th Party Congress in 2022 have signaled the opposite of urgency, instead emphasizing that "time and momentum are always on our [China's] side" to achieve unification with Taiwan.

Nevertheless, the situation in the Taiwan Strait is dynamic, not static. Many of the elements of the status quo since U.S.-China diplomatic recognition in 1979 have been eroding and likely will continue to do so in the foreseeable future. As former U.S. National Intelligence Officer for Asia John Culver observed, these elements include:

- Taiwan's domestic political and identity development, where public support for the "1992 consensus" has diminished in recent years.
- The emergence of full-blown U.S.-China strategic rivalry, which increases Taiwan's attraction to both major U.S. political parties as a litmus test of "standing up to China."
- China's own emergence as a great power with clear military dominance over Taiwan and seeming military parity [along China's periphery] with the United States.[6]

This erosion of the post-1979 cross-Strait status quo coincides with China's determined efforts in recent years to field military capabilities to project force out to the first-island chain, and eventually beyond it. Rising powers often seek to gain strategic depth in their immediate periphery, so, unsurprisingly, China would seek to gain greater control over adjacent waters and airspace. At the same time, China's investment in military force projection capabilities is prompting efforts by the United States and Taiwan to strengthen deterrence.

China's efforts to exert greater control over its periphery have been accompanied by a revived focus at home on ideology and nationalism as cohesive agents of society. These trends have manifested in a sweeping series of countrywide actions, including crackdowns on lawyers, celebrities, and entrepreneurs; scrutiny of the loyalties of non-Han minorities, particularly in Xinjiang and Tibet; the elimination of Hong Kong's special status; and intensification of multi-spectrum pressure on Taiwan. Beijing's growing emphasis on ideology and nationalism also bled into China's diplomacy, giving rise to greater pugnacity on the part of senior Chinese officials in pushing back against any country perceived to be undermining China's interests or national dignity through its words or actions.

The central point is that the broader context of the cross-Strait situation is evolving. As such, any meaningful evaluation of the future needs to grapple with various scenarios that may emerge. Although there are a limitless number of potential scenarios, we will examine seven hypothetical trajectories for the next decade. These scenarios are divided into two categories—economic and political-military futures—and are organized within each category along a spectrum from less to more conflictual.

ECONOMIC SCENARIOS

Taiwan Deepens Economic Dependence on China

In this scenario, Beijing solidifies its role as the economic anchor-weight of Asia. Through its membership in the Regional Comprehensive Economic Partnership (RCEP), entry into the Comprehensive and Progressive Trans-Pacific Partnership (CPTPP), and deepened trade and investment links with countries across Asia through Belt and Road Initiative (BRI) activities, Beijing generates gravitational pull for supply chains to run through China. Beijing also pushes for Chinese regulations and specifications to be used in products and services across the region.

The costs for Taiwan's economy of remaining apart from Asia's economic integration grow, as all of Taiwan's direct competitors are under the umbrella of Asian economic integration and able to benefit from trade and regulatory liberalization of membership. To remain competitive, many leading Taiwan companies move some operations within the walls of new regional trade regimes to benefit from lower regional trade barriers.

This pivot toward seeking to maximize benefits from regional trade integration leads to a hollowing out of some industries in Taiwan. China's growing demand for Taiwan products and services reverses efforts under the Tsai administration to seek to diversify Taiwan's supply chains and trade relationship away from the mainland. Such a shift likely also produces a tailwind for KMT politicians, who favor lowering tension with the mainland to allow Taiwan to benefit economically from China's rise.

Taiwan's economic integration with the mainland causes Beijing to gain confidence that its strategy of "integrated development" with Taiwan is making progress in pulling Taiwan closer. This deepening cross-Strait economic integration leads Chinese policymakers to judge that Taiwan's leading economic players will become more invested in exerting political influence inside Taiwan to oppose *de jure* independence or permanent separation, given the existential risk that such actions would pose to the continued viability of their businesses in the mainland. It also reinforces Beijing's confidence that Taiwan's leaders will move directionally toward acknowledging that Taiwan's only viable long-term path to security and prosperity runs through Beijing. Such acceptance by Taiwan's leaders of the criticality of cross-Strait economic integration for Taiwan's long-term security and prosperity gives China's leaders confidence that their approach is working and that further escalation of pressure on Taiwan can be postponed.

There is a real risk in this scenario that Beijing could overestimate the leverage that deepening economic integration offers, failing to recognize that such integration on its own is a necessary but not sufficient condition for Beijing to advance its cross-Strait political goals. This could cause Chinese leaders later on to revert to ratcheting up military and other forms of pressure to try to push Taiwan into political talks leading to a new shared understanding of the nature of cross-Strait relations.

In a scenario of substantially deepening cross-Strait economic links, Washington likely would sharpen pressure on Taiwan to reduce sales of semiconductors and related parts, equipment, and know-how to the mainland as part of its efforts to limit China's capacity to develop military technologies that could harm the United States and its security partners. Beijing would be tempted to respond by increasing coercive pressure on Taiwan to make available key inputs for China's continued technological development.

Taiwan's greater emphasis on fostering commercial links with the mainland likely would bring to a head a long-simmering debate in Washington about America's response to cross-Strait economic integration. One view is that deepening cross-Strait integration should compel the United States to liberalize trade with Taiwan, including potentially through a bilateral trade agreement, to incentivize Taiwan to diversify its trade flows away from the mainland. Such a step would set a predicate that other partners, such as Japan and Australia, potentially could follow. A more national security-centered view is that the United States should respond to deepening cross-Strait integration by intensifying the urgency of its efforts to "re-shore" production of key capabilities, including cutting-edge semiconductor chips, to the United States or allied countries. Such efforts would be designed to preempt any future situation whereby China wields influence over America's access to Taiwan-produced chips. Sharper U.S. incentives or disincentives for transferring production of cutting-edge chips outside of Taiwan would put stress on U.S.-Taiwan relations.

Deglobalization and U.S.-China Economic Decoupling Lead to Taiwan's Growing Isolation

In this scenario, the United States and China descend into deep rivalry and both seek to reduce reliance on the other, including by seeking to dramatically reduce exposure to the other's economy. Leaders in both capitals frame decoupling decisions as necessary costs to shore up vulnerability from actions by the other. Isolationist and autarkic trends accelerate and spread to the European Union (EU). EU policy on China frays, as Hungary, Greece, and others rebuff attempts to form an EU consensus to address Chinese behavior and instead signal their prioritization on profiting from China's economic expansion. This leads each European country to pursue its own economic benefit-maximizing policies toward China.

With the United States, China, and the EU going their own ways, the open global trading system begins to atrophy. Major economies begin to deprioritize adherence to WTO rules and conventions, leading to the emergence of a race to the bottom dynamic. The reliability of the International Monetary Fund as lender of last resort comes up for question as countries begin to express doubts about whether the United

States or China would approve assistance to countries it views as being supportive of the other major power.

As the world increasingly cleaves into regional spheres of influence, Beijing grows more aggressive in its efforts to limit American influence in Asia. China uses economic incentives and disincentives to pressure Asian countries to reduce their engagement with the United States. Beijing begins to insist that foreign companies choose between doing business in China or Taiwan. Chinese officials also intensify regulatory and procedural scrutiny of Taiwan companies operating in the mainland that previously made campaign contributions to politicians that Beijing deems as being pro-independence.

China also becomes more risk tolerant of challenging U.S. naval and air presence operations inside the first island chain, leading to a rise in incidents involving U.S. and Chinese surface naval and air platforms. U.S. officials privately signal to Taiwan leaders that they expect to have access to Taiwan ports and airfields in event of emergency. If such private requests become public, they could prompt Beijing to warn publicly that it would take punitive military measures against Taiwan if it offers aid and access to U.S. forces. This could lock all three sides into an escalatory dynamic that none of them seek, but all find difficult to escape.

The fragmentation of the global economy reduces productivity worldwide and places downward pressure on Taiwan's global supply chain-dependent economy. Debates grow sharper inside Taiwan about whether Taiwan should respond to slowing global growth by pursuing economic opportunities on the mainland. Intensifying security competition between the United States and China in areas adjacent to Taiwan puts Taiwan in a bind—they either support U.S. presence operations in the region and attract China's ire or become more muted about U.S. military activities and draw concerns from Washington about falling into Beijing's orbit. This dynamic polarizes views inside Taiwan about the proper balance between maintaining relations with the United States and with China, leading to increasingly fractious domestic debates about how Taiwan should situate itself in Asia and in the world.

POLITICAL-MILITARY SCENARIOS

Negotiated Political Settlement between Taiwan and the PRC

Reaching an uncoerced political settlement likely would require Beijing to make wholesale adjustments to its negotiating posture, beginning with an abandonment of its "one country, two systems" formula for governing cross-Strait relations. Following Beijing's trampling of Hong Kong's separate system in 2020, this concept likely has become permanently poisoned in Taiwan as an organizing principle for a cross-Strait political settlement. Reaching a peaceful settlement likely also would require Beijing to make explicit that it does not view Taiwan the same as Hong Kong; Beijing will not seek to impose a hierarchical relationship on Taiwan as it did in its insistence that Hong Kong is subordinate to Beijing. Taiwan's voters almost certainly would never ratify an arrangement that places Taiwan in an inferior position to the mainland or that cedes decisions about how Taiwan governs itself to Beijing. Without broad public support from the Taiwan people, no peaceful settlement will be possible.

Put differently, a political settlement likely will remain out of reach until China's leaders choose to redefine "unification" as something resembling a confederation or commonwealth or friendly but separate relationship such as that exists between the United States and Canada. Any type of peaceful political settlement thus would require China's leaders to abandon long-standing positions, which the current generation of leaders has shown little openness to do. As such, any process leading to a peaceful settlement might have to wait until a new generation of leaders in Beijing emerges, or longer.

Taiwan's leaders similarly would need to show flexibility—or tolerance of ambiguity—on several key principles. They would need to accept limits on Taiwan's security relationship with the United States, such as by committing that Taiwan will not be used as a base of operations for U.S. military forces. They also would need to find a formulation on sovereignty questions that allowed for there to be a broad enough interpretation of China's sovereign territory to accommodate the PRC's and the ROC's definition of national boundaries.

Efforts to move down this track likely will not materialize in the near-term. Neither side appears motivated to make such drastic compromises now. The politics on both sides of the Strait argues against being a first-mover in the direction of mutual accommodation. Given the extremely low likelihood of this scenario materializing in the coming decade, there is no need for the United States to declare opposition to a peaceful resolution now and aggravate relations with Beijing, and with some in Taiwan, in the process.

Adaptation of Status Quo

The post-1979 cross-Strait status quo has been mutually unsatisfying to all three sides, but it has met the baseline requirement for all three parties and has allowed conflict to be averted. Beijing has not been able to reach its objective of unification, but it has been able to deter Taiwan from independence or permanent separation. Taiwan has remained stymied from greater access to the international system, but it has been able to grow its economy, consolidate its democracy, provide individual liberties to its citizens, and expand the scope of its interactions with a growing number of countries. The United States has had to maintain a considerable force posture in the Western Pacific to sustain deterrence. At the same time, Washington has maintained considerable freedom of movement to deepen unofficial relations with Taiwan while at the same time benefitting materially from China's economic rise.

It is conceivable that all three sides could reach their own judgment that guarding against worst-case scenarios is preferable to courting conflict in pursuit of maximal outcomes. Beijing could lean in this direction if it feels it faces more proximate threats to regime legitimacy at home from decelerating economic growth, rising social inequality, worsening demographics, and flat productivity. Focusing on these proximate domestic challenges could increase the incentive for Beijing to seek to keep its periphery (including Taiwan) stable.

Beijing would maintain a posture of public confidence in its growing advantages in economic, military, and overall national power relative to Taiwan and continue to insist that time is on Beijing's side to achieve eventual unification. Beijing would remain quick to impose visible costs on Taiwan for any actions that are perceived to widen the separation between Taiwan and the mainland, in part to stay ahead of public sentiment at home by showing a "tough enough" attitude toward managing Taiwan affairs. Beijing would insist that the United States adhere to its "one-China policy," including maintaining only unofficial relations with Taipei. Beijing's over-riding focus would be on deterring erosion to its position on Taiwan, rather than compelling, coercing, or delivering unification in the near-term.

Taiwan would maintain a position of neither yielding to pressure nor testing the boundaries of permanent separation from the mainland, but rather focus on preserving Taiwan's autonomy and democratic way of life. It would work to fortify its polit-ical defenses against Beijing's unification ambitions, such as by strengthening Taiwan identity among its population, building internal consensus that Taiwan (or the ROC) is already sovereign and does not need to take further independence moves, and by developing a shared understanding across political parties that Taiwan's vot-ers will have final say over any significant changes to the relationship with Beijing. Taiwan's leaders would agree on a bipartisan basis that Taiwan's fate will never be negotiated above the heads of its people. To maintain continuing electability, the KMT would shift toward becoming a Taiwan-centric political party that responds to voter sentiment, which is turning away from unification under any timeline.

The United States would exercise prudence in its development of relations with Taiwan, maintaining limits on the visibility and level of its official contacts with Taiwan counterparts in keeping with its commitment to Beijing to maintain unofficial relations. Taiwan's president, vice president, premier, and vice premier would remain limited to transiting the United States and not making official visits. Washington similarly would retain limits on U.S. military activities with Taiwan, including by not conducting port calls in Taiwan, establishing bases or a perma-nent military presence on Taiwan, or reestablishing any commitments that could resemble mutual defense treaty obligations. Washington also would refrain from using Taiwan as a tool to impose strategic costs on Beijing.

For this scenario to have any realism, there would need to be a restoration of functionality in U.S.-China relations that would allow both sides to convey concerns over Taiwan directly and privately with the other side without having to resort to public condemnation or military signaling to register displeasure. This ability to privately register concerns and clarify the intentions of the other side's actions is a prerequisite for preservation of the status quo. This scenario also would require leaders in Beijing and Taipei to deal pragmatically with each other, including by engaging directly without preconditions. China's leaders would need to pursue a patient approach to narrowing cross-Strait differences, and leaders in Taiwan would need to be willing to buck demands from the fringes of the political spectrum and govern in a manner that reflects the status quo preferences of the population. All three sides would need to demonstrate through their restraint that they recognize the risks of challenging the other's bottom lines and remain willing to accept limits on their own freedom of maneuver in return for avoidance of crisis.

China Initiates Limited Military Action against Taiwan to Bolster Its "Red Lines"

If Beijing concludes that it must conduct a show of strength to prevent independence or permanent separation, but the PLA is not yet operationally ready for full-scale conflict, the PRC could take limited military action to seek to restore its "red lines." For example, a limited military action could include overflights of Taiwan by Chinese missiles, or regularized military or missile flights over Taiwan-controlled off-shore islands. The purpose would be to demonstrate a shock-and-awe show of force that would sober Taipei and Washington to the strength of China's concerns, but not seek to launch a full-scale conflict. Beijing would use such demonstrations of force to remind leaders in Taipei and Washington of its tolerance for risk and friction in upholding its "core interest" in territorial integrity and sovereignty. They also would seek to show their domestic audience their willingness to flex their growing military strength to protect their interests vis-à-vis Taiwan.

The purpose of such an operation likely would be to deter Taiwan from taking further steps away from the mainland or to induce caution in Washington against deepening ties with Taiwan. Chinese leaders could judge that such a crisis may be necessary to halt trends of deepening U.S.-Taiwan relations.

Such an action, particularly in the wake of Russia's invasion of Ukraine, would be a high-stakes gamble for the Chinese leadership. It would shine a bright international spotlight on China's external assertiveness. It would test China's capacity for escalation control. It also would heighten international focus on Taiwan's central role in the global economy, and thereby the global interest in preserving peace and stability in the Taiwan Strait.

On the other hand, Beijing may want to test the international response to a limited military operation against Taiwan to determine whether industrialized countries would respond as aggressively and cohesively against China in a Taiwan scenario as they did against Russia following its invasion of Ukraine. China's leaders may also convince themselves that they have no choice but to respond militarily to developments in U.S.-Taiwan relations, and to Taiwan's deepening relations with other major European and Asian powers, lest they lose the initiative to curb further expansion of Taiwan's international profile. Beijing's response to then-Speaker Pelosi's August 2022 visit to Taiwan reflected China's willingness to flex military power to reinforce the strength of its concerns over Taiwan.

Conflict Precipitated by Taiwan Declaration of *De Jure* Independence

Not since the Chen Shui-bian era (2000–2008) has Washington had to formulate policy for deterring movement by Taiwan in the direction of *de jure* independence. At that time, President Chen sought to harness nationalist sentiment for political advantage by proposing a public referendum on whether Taipei should pursue UN membership in the name of Taiwan. He saw such efforts as a useful mobilization strategy to rally support for his agenda. Washington viewed Chen's gambit as an attempt to unilaterally change the status quo and it made its opposition known privately and publicly.

Chen's two immediate successors, while different in temperament and in their agendas, have both sought to govern in a manner reflective of public sentiment on cross-Strait issues. When President Ma Ying-jeou went beyond what public sentiment would tolerate on cross-Strait relations, he faced the Sunflower movement, a student-led protest to block passage of the cross-Strait service in trade agreement that his administration had negotiated with Beijing. The Sunflower movement froze Ma's cross-Strait agenda for the rest of his term and laid the groundwork for power to flip to the DPP's standard-bearer, Tsai Ing-wen, in the 2016 presidential election.

President Tsai Ing-wen has managed cross-Strait relations through the maxim of not bowing to pressure from Beijing, but also not taking unnecessary risks because of support from the United States. She has pursued a cautious, predictable, and steady approach to cross-Strait relations. She has pinned responsibility on Beijing for the deterioration in cross-Strait relations and has used Beijing's obstreperousness as a rationale for Taiwan to intensify efforts to diversify its commercial and other interactions away from the mainland.

With President Tsai Ing-wen term-limited in office and set to retire in May 2024, there is yet again a possibility that Taiwan's next leader could revive Chen Shui-bian's political mobilization tactics by stirring the sentiments of the fringes of Taiwan's political spectrum in support of a unilateral change to the cross-Strait status quo. Such an effort would strain Taiwan's relations with both the United States and China. It also would challenge the long-standing consensus on Taiwan dating back to Chiang Kai-shek and repeated by Lee Teng-hui and other leaders that the Republic of China already is sovereign and there is no need for Taiwan to formally, officially, or legally declare independence.

A consistent body of public polling in Taiwan suggests that the people of Taiwan already are sober to the risks of pursing independence. Nevertheless, if Taiwan's leader caters to a fringe of the political spectrum and unilaterally declares *de jure* independence, there is a real possibility that Taiwan would face the consequences on its own. Beijing has clearly and consistently signaled that a formal declaration of Taiwan independence would mean war. Washington would not automatically intervene to help Taiwan if it judged that Taiwan's unilateral actions had stimulated the conflict.

PRC-Initiated Military Conflict in the Taiwan Strait

If, on the other hand, Beijing unilaterally initiated a military conflict to compel unification on its terms, there is a high likelihood of a robust American response. American passivity in the face of an unprovoked Chinese assault on Taiwan would break faith with the people of Taiwan, likely cause political fissures within the United States between the congressional and executive branches of government, and raise doubts at a global level about the credibility of American security commitments.

Even though the United States has no formal treaty obligation to come to Taiwan's defense, America's security support for Taiwan often is viewed as a bellwether of the strength of its security commitments worldwide. The credibility of American security commitments underpins America's global alliance network. This alliance network is foundational to America's position as the world's only superpower—a country with global political and economic interests and the ability to project force in every region of the world to protect those interests. Without its global alliance network and the dispersed basing arrangements it affords, the United States would no longer meet the definition of a superpower.

As discussed earlier, there are real reasons for concern about China embarking on a path leading to military confrontation in the Taiwan Strait. China's PLA forces now operate all around Taiwan. They conduct highly publicized dress rehearsals of assaults on Taiwan. They have steadily increased their incursions into Taiwan's ADIZ. China is investing considerably in military capabilities that could be employed in a Taiwan contingency, and also in capabilities—such as nuclear, space, and long-range strike—that would significantly raise the cost and risk to the United States of intervening in a cross-Strait contingency. There is a real risk that Beijing could overlearn a lesson from Russia's invasion of Ukraine that nuclear brinksmanship works—that is, China can freeze any American military involvement by threatening to employ nuclear force if American or other forces intervene in a cross-Strait conflict.

China's leaders also have employed sharp rhetoric on Taiwan issues. For example, President Xi Jinping reportedly warned President Joe Biden during a November 16, 2021, virtual meeting that supporting Taiwan independence or using Taiwan to contain China was tantamount to playing with fire, and "whoever plays with fire will get burnt."[7]

Even so, Beijing's calculations about whether to employ force almost certainly include factors beyond raw calculations of the balance of power in the Taiwan Strait. Beijing must factor in that it would have limited ability to control escalation or limit the geographic scope of conflict. The United States likely would intervene and target PRC vulnerabilities, though not necessarily at the direct point of attack. Also, the intensity and endurance of popular resistance in Taiwan to a PLA occupation is unknowable. Given the number of unknowable variables, Beijing could not be assured of absolute victory—unchallenged political control over Taiwan.

Beijing clearly is investing to make credible its threats to use military force to deter independence and eventually compel unification. That said, Beijing still has powerful reasons to look for options short of an unprovoked assault on Taiwan to achieve its political objective of unification of Taiwan with Mainland China.

***

The key point from this brief survey of future scenarios is that there is not a single preset path. There are a nearly limitless number of variables that could impact domestic conditions inside China, Taiwan, or the United States, as well as external relations between them. A series of decisions by leaders in all three capitals have brought cross-Strait relations to their present condition, and a series of decisions by these three leaders moving forward will determine the future direction of this consequential set of relationships.

There are specific signposts that, if reached, would almost certainly augur a shift in China's posture toward Taiwan. These include: if Taiwan formally declares independence; if the United States recognizes Taiwan as an independent state; if a growing number of countries recognize Taiwan as an independent state; if the United States reintroduces mutual security commitments into its relationship with Taiwan; or if the United States begins to use Taiwan as a platform for military operations and for force projection in the Western Pacific.

Any one of these events almost certainly would trigger a qualitative shift by China toward greater coercion and pressure on Taiwan, potentially including use of force. It also is conceivable that China's top leaders could embark on an aggressive campaign against Taiwan if their control over domestic developments begins to erode and they judge that a campaign to assert greater control over Taiwan could restore domestic cohesion. Such a "wag the dog" scenario is a low probability scenario, however, given that China's leaders since Mao generally have not responded to domestic turmoil by adding external challenges. That said, it cannot be ruled out as a possibility.

As much as Taiwan's leaders would like to insulate Taiwan's fate from U.S.-China relations, the reality is that it is not possible to fully divorce Taiwan from great power relations. This is not to suggest that the United States should make decisions in its relations with Taiwan based on its level of collegiality or confrontation with Beijing. Quite the contrary, in fact. America benefits from a steady, principled approach to managing cross-Strait relations, and is ill-served by uncoordinated or undisciplined actions that generate unpredictability or signal insecurity.

At the same time, it would be disingenuous to suggest that China does not factor into America's policy decisions toward Taiwan or vice versa. Given this reality, the survey of the various future scenarios suggests that the more adversarial U.S.-China relations become, the more pressure Taiwan will face to make alignment decisions between the United States and China. Beijing already regularly imposes costs on Taiwan for moving closer to Washington, for example, by conducting visible military operations near Taiwan when senior-level U.S. officials visit Taiwan, and by compelling one of Taiwan's few remaining diplomatic allies to switch recognition from Taipei to Beijing during Taiwan's participation in the United States-hosted Summit for Democracy. There is no basis to hope that this dynamic will abate in the foreseeable future.

Therefore, planners in Washington and Taipei must have clarity on the main risks to their interests and the most effective defenses against Beijing's efforts to pull cross-Strait relations in their preferred direction. Managing cross-Strait differences while preserving Taiwan's autonomy, political system, and way of life is the mark of success.

Given these dynamics, American interests are best served by dampening escalatory pressures, deterring unilateral changes by either side to the cross-Strait status quo, enhancing military deterrence to raise the price Beijing would pay for trying to seize Taiwan by force, and maintaining Taiwan's focus on preserving political autonomy and nonwar. The purpose of American policy is not to dictate any specific outcome to cross-Strait tensions. The limited aim of American strategy is to elongate the time horizon for leaders in Taipei and Beijing to explore peaceful, noncoerced solutions to cross-Strait challenges. If leaders in Taipei or Beijing abandon all hope of any peaceful solution to cross-Strait differences, then the risk will spike for one or both sides to take actions that could precipitate conflict. A war in the Taiwan Strait would constitute a failure of American statecraft.

THE TWIN THREATS TO TAIWAN'S SECURITY

Beijing presents two principal threats to security in the Taiwan Strait: one is military, the other is political. The objective of these parallel threats is the same—to compel the island's leaders and its public to capitulate and accept unification on Beijing's terms. The means Beijing employs in these parallel tracks are different, though.

The first threat militarily targets the island's armed forces and its territory. The second, more political threat targets the self-confidence of Taiwan's leaders and the public. It seeks to deepen a feeling of *wangguogan* (the feeling that the country is lost), but eschews violence that could trigger U.S. military intervention.[8] To achieve this psychological effect, Beijing uses various elements of national power in combination: diplomatic, information, cyber, United Front, military, and economic tools.

Properly diagnosing these twin, parallel challenges and developing effective counters to them will require intellectual dexterity. Leaders in Washington and Taipei cannot afford to fixate on one at the expense of the other. While it is not known when—if ever—Beijing might launch a military assault on Taiwan, it already is observable that Beijing is well underway in its political campaign of coercion without violence to pressure the Taiwan people into concluding that resistance is futile and that Taiwan's surest path to security and prosperity runs through Beijing.

We will next examine the nature of these threats and potential responses to each of them.

The Military Threat

Throughout the Cold War and for several years following it, China lacked the quantitative or qualitative edge in its ability to employ military capabilities to impose its will on Taiwan. The United States and Taiwan maintained a qualitative advantage in military capabilities that made any consideration by Beijing of employing force prohibitively risky in all but the most extreme circumstances.

Frustrated by these circumstances, Chinese strategic planners carefully studied America's conduct of warfare in the first Gulf War to ascertain America's military strengths and vulnerabilities.[9] They discovered, for example, that America's defenses against inexpensive sea mines are quite limited. China subsequently began developing capabilities that targeted America's military weaknesses.

Such efforts gained fresh impetus following Beijing's failed efforts to intimidate Taiwan's voters ahead of the island's first democratic election in 1996. Beijing's embarrassment at having to pull back its campaign of intimidation toward Taiwan in the face of America's overwhelming military force projection informed its decisions to pour resources into developing military capabilities for cross-Strait contingencies over the ensuing decades.

In the period since, China has accelerated its development of military capabilities—both quantitatively and qualitatively—with the apparent goals of seeking to overwhelm Taiwan's defenses and deter and deny American involvement in a cross-Strait contingency. During this same period, China's society has grown more nationalistic, fueled in part by a rising generation that has known nothing but China's rise.

The gap between Chinese and Taiwan military capabilities is likely to widen further in the coming decades. Taiwan's population will continue to age and there will be growing societal demands for scarce numbers of potential conscripts. The PLA likely will continue to enhance its military capabilities and do so faster than Taiwan can advance its own. China's economy will continue to grow in absolute terms in ways that will expand the gap in economic weight between both sides.

Former U.S. National Intelligence Officer for East Asia John Culver cautions, "At some point in the not-too-distant future, perhaps 2030 or 2035, the PLA probably will have the organizational and warfighting capacity for a Taiwan operation that it has always lacked. China will probably be the largest economy, and an even more dominant trading and advanced manufacturing powerhouse. Weakness could no longer be an excuse."[10] In other words, Beijing's previous operational obstacles to potential use of force against Taiwan may be receding.

These developments informed the findings of a Council on Foreign Relations Task Force on Taiwan in 2021, which warned, "China is now at a prewar tempo of political and military preparations. . . . Politically, it is preparing and conditioning its population for the possibility of armed conflict. Militarily, it is engaging now in a tempo of exercises and military preparations that are both sharpening and widening the readiness of its armed forces."[11]

These shifts have prompted American and Taiwan security experts to concentrate on three broad baskets of cross-Strait military contingencies. The first is an island seizure scenario, where Beijing begins taking offshore islands that are administered by Taipei and warns that it will continue moving closer to Taiwan's main island until or unless Taipei capitulates to Beijing's requirements. Such a scenario could begin with Beijing seizing Jinmen and Mazu, two militarily indefensible Taiwan-controlled islands off the coast of China, then moving toward the Pratas Islands, the Penghus, and eventually Taiwan. This scenario would be designed to intensify pressure on Taiwan's leaders to accommodate Beijing's conditions to avert bloodshed and massive destruction.

The second broad scenario would be for Beijing to impose a quarantine on Taiwan that seeks to coerce Taipei into some form of subjugation.[12] Beijing could insist that all inbound air and maritime traffic first be diverted to the mainland for inspection before traveling to Taiwan under PRC escort. Beijing could seek to justify such action by claiming that it is designed to screen for military hardware or contraband materials such as drugs destined for Taiwan. This scenario theoretically would limit physical violence against the people of Taiwan and would give Beijing the ability to calibrate the intrusiveness of its inspections depending upon circumstances. Beijing could pair a quarantine with a demand that Taiwan's authorities enter political negotiations on the future status of Taiwan or some other limited objective short of full occupation.

The third broad scenario would be an invasion of Taiwan, either by full-scale amphibious assault or by more surgical airborne assault and special operations to try to seize control of key nodes in Taiwan. Many defense planners worry that this scenario represents the fight Taiwan cannot afford to lose. Taiwan's elected leaders could face the loss of offshore islands or a blockade and still maintain political control, but they likely would struggle to sustain political control of Taiwan following military defeat and occupation by Chinese forces. A top concern of American military planners is a rapid Chinese invasion to establish a *fait accompli* on Taiwan before outside forces have an option of intervening to prevent Taiwan's seizure by force.

Anxieties over the near-term likelihood of a full-scale invasion should be leavened by the fact that China does not appear to be investing in capabilities that could be required for such an operation. According to the DoD's 2021 annual report to Congress on China's military capabilities, the PLA appears to be investing more in global expeditionary capabilities than in the "large number of landing ship transports and medium landing craft that would be necessary for a large-scale direct beach assault. There is no indication the PRC is significantly expanding its force of tank landing ships (LSTs) and medium sized landing craft at this time."[13]

As a further caution against uncritically adopting the evaluations of experts forecasting war, a group of RAND experts modeled the likely outcomes and consequences of a U.S.-China conflict. The authors concluded, "despite military trends that favor it, China could not win, and might lose, a severe war with the United States in 2025, especially if prolonged. Moreover, the economic costs and political dangers of such a war could imperil China's stability, end its development, and undermine the legitimacy of the state."[14] While this modeling provides a chastening conclusion for China's likelihood of annexing Taiwan by force, it is unknowable whether it is a conclusion that China's leaders accept. If China's leaders grow convinced that the PLA could prevail quickly and at low cost and risk, then the probability of an invasion scenario presumably would rise considerably.

A confluence of factors has made Taiwan scenarios a top-tier concern of American military planners. The first is China's increasing brazenness in its employment of military instruments around Taiwan, which Secretary of Defense Lloyd Austin has warned appear to be "rehearsals" for an invasion.[15] The second is the starkness of the potential implications for Taiwan, and potentially for America's global standing.

The third factor is the speed of China's military modernization, which persistently has outpaced U.S. government estimates and created consternation about America's military capacity to respond. The fourth is the planned retirement of U.S. air and naval platforms beginning in the mid-2020s, the surge of new PLA capabilities that will come online in a similar period, and the time gap before the DoD will be able to field new capabilities to backfill those being retired.

Such concerns have been exacerbated by Washington's diminishing confidence in its ability to read Beijing's intentions. Under Xi Jinping, China has shown greater tolerance for risk and friction in pursuit of its ambitions, such as in the South China Sea, with Hong Kong, and at the Sino-Indian border. As more power becomes concentrated around Xi Jinping, there is greater uncertainty over Washington's ability to anticipate China's moves on sensitive issues such as Taiwan and over the quality of advice Xi is receiving to inform his decisions.

At the same time, Taipei has demonstrated a disconcerting degree of complacency in addressing its own military shortcomings. Although the Tsai administration has increased military spending and sought to focus Taiwan's Ministry of National Defense on doctrinal reforms, progress has been uneven, there has not been bipartisan consensus around military reform, and there has not been an appreciable shift in Taiwan's hardware procurement priorities.

A final factor is the end of the Global War on Terror. Following America's August 2021 withdrawal from Afghanistan, Taiwan has been elevated to the hardest challenge confronting American military planners. China is now treated inside the Pentagon as the "pacing challenge," and a Taiwan contingency is viewed as "the pacing scenario."[16] Whereas the Biden administration preemptively ruled out direct U.S. military intervention in Ukraine, it has kept U.S. military intervention on the table for future Taiwan contingencies, with President Biden himself vowing publicly on multiple occasions that the United States would defend Taiwan.

Sharpening Deterrence Options

American responses to rising pressure on Taiwan's security will need to be informed by a focus on the goal of American strategy and policy—the preservation of peace and stability in the Taiwan Strait. There are some actions Washington could take that could bolster deterrence militarily, but that would have the inverse effect on Taiwan's overall security if they provoke the very Chinese military actions that America's strategy is designed to prevent. Permanently stationing U.S. forces on Taiwan or reconstituting some form of formal alliance commitments would fall into this category of actions that could make operational sense but would be strategically misguided. Such actions would unambiguously violate America's "one-China policy" and would likely activate a Chinese military response targeting Taiwan.

At a strategic level, it will be essential for the United States to establish with China that Taiwan is not a bilateral irritant that is cabined within the U.S.-China relationship. Rather, Taiwan's security is a matter of global consequence, particularly given Taiwan's role in supply chains for components such as semiconductors that are foundational technologies of the global economy. The United States will need to draw upon its regional and global network of allies to make this point real to Beijing. It will be vital for there to be visible coordination between Taiwan with Japan, within the Quadrilateral Security Dialogue, within the AUKUS alliance, within the G7, and with key Asian, European, and NATO allies.

There is deterrent value in Beijing learning that the United States and its partners are quietly and concertedly developing a package of nonmilitary response options that could target China's main vulnerabilities should it ever become necessary to do so. Such efforts would draw from the experiences of targeting Russia's financial weaknesses following its invasion of Ukraine. Given the scale of China's economy and its integration into the global economy, the United States and others would not be able to apply the same playbook used against Russia against China. A new set of tailored responses would be necessary to target China's pain points, such as its reliance on imports of semiconductors and fuel, and its lack of redundancies in its connections to the global internet. To have effect, Beijing would need to be made to conclude that the United States and others are prepared to accept major levels of economic pain in service of countering Chinese military moves against Taiwan, and that they are ready to move fast and hard against Chinese interests if the situation edges closer to conflict.

Beijing needs to be disabused of any hopes that it could prevail quickly and in an uncontested manner in a cross-Strait conflict that it initiates. It will be important for Beijing to hear from a variety of viewpoints that history offers little evidence that the United States would withdraw behind its borders if it receives a bloody nose in the initial phases of conflict. America's national history is one of complacency until provoked and then overwhelming response. A conflict involving the United States and China likely would inflict huge losses on both sides and would leave both powers weakened.

To limit risk of Beijing miscalculating American resolve, Washington will need to show tangibly that it is refocusing its military, diplomatic, and economic weight toward Asia to balance against China's expanding pursuit of its ambitions. Washington will need to demonstrate that it is not receding in its determination to preserve peace and stability in the Taiwan Strait. Making this point observable through actions will be essential to setting the predicate for dealing directly with Beijing to manage differences over Taiwan.

A serious effort at managing risks over Taiwan will require resumption of direct communication with Beijing, albeit in a manner consistent with the "six assurances." The purpose of such dialogue would not be to seek to negotiate above the heads of Taiwan's people or to seek to solve cross-Strait problems, but rather to communicate directly and authoritatively about U.S. concerns over Beijing's actions, to clarify the intentions of Beijing's actions, and to explore whether it is possible to create U.S.-China crisis management mechanisms to limit risk of unplanned incidents sparking unintended escalation.

U.S. officials could use this channel to reinforce that the United States does not seek conflict with China over Taiwan and remains committed to its longstanding policies on management of cross-Strait issues, but at the same time, it will not abandon Taiwan in service of smoother relations with Beijing. This channel also would allow U.S. officials to reinforce privately to their Chinese counterparts that Taiwan is a genuine democracy and that public attitudes there will be decisive to Taiwan's future. The burden is on Beijing to convince the Taiwan people that their future would be enhanced by accepting Beijing's vision for the future of cross-Strait relations. U.S. officials also could use direct diplomacy to urge Beijing to engage directly with Taiwan officials. Direct dialogue shrinks space for misjudgments and miscalculations.

As an element of these broader efforts to forestall conflict, the United States also will need to adapt its military doctrine and capabilities to sustain credible deterrence in the face of China's rapid advancements in military capabilities. This likely will require a shift away from large platforms and big facilities in the Western Pacific, which are easily targetable, to fielding large numbers of sensors and munitions that would be difficult for China to counter. The inescapable reality is that U.S. naval surface ships and air bases within China's missile envelope would have difficulty conducting high-tempo operations in the face of an anticipatable Chinese missile barrage.

As military analysts Michael O'Hanlon and Dave Ochmanek have argued, large numbers of small, unmanned aircraft and unmanned underwater vehicles could have far greater capacity to hold Chinese targets at risk. The United States could employ swarms of sensors to track Chinese ships and aircraft, loiter in the Western Pacific without easy detection, and launch missiles at targets or deploy sea mines in waters adjacent to Taiwan. The United States likely also would need to bolster its redundancy in space, including by diversifying its satellite fleet, to avoid overreliance on a small number of large satellites that could be targeted by China's space force at the onset of hostilities.[17] The U.S. military also could further disperse forces in the Pacific theater, hardening facilities, and building redundancies into America's regional force posture.[18] Taken together, these adjustments would not replace the role of legacy platforms in demonstrating presence and resolve, particularly during peacetime, nor the critical role of America's superior submarine fleet in any military contingency, but they would create a far harder challenge for China to counter.

Political-Military Campaign Planning

In addition to preparing for kinetic conflict, it also will be essential for the United States and its partners to develop a political and economic campaign plan to deter and, if necessary, respond to a PRC assault on Taiwan. In the event of war, China could be targeted with significant cyber operations. Its undersea fiber-optic internet cables could be cut, and its space-based assets likely would be targeted. There likely would be a coordinated international effort to deny China's access to war-critical commodities and technologies. U.S. naval vessels likely would be positioned to divert China-bound ships carrying oil and liquefied natural gas to neutral ports for impoundment until the cessation of hostilities. There also could be pressure placed on China's imports of foodstuffs, given China's resource scarcity.

The United States likely also would freeze all assets owned by the Chinese government or Chinese citizens in the United States. There would be active international efforts to limit trade and commercial transactions with China. The United States likely would suspend interest payments on U.S. Treasury bonds held by the Chinese government or Chinese citizens.[19] In other words, there would be traumatic disruption to the global economy; the United States and its allies would work to focus global anger on China for sparking such instability through its belligerence.

Bolstering Taiwan's Deterrence Capabilities

Another key element of preparation to counter any potential PRC-initiated military contingency is to support Taiwan's development of doctrine and capabilities that allow it to maximize its geographic advantages by targeting an invading force at its point of greatest vulnerability, in Taiwan's littoral. Washington will need to organize its four lines of security engagement with Taiwan to encourage movement in this direction. These lines of effort include: (1) working with Taiwan's leaders to craft a defense strategy; (2) making available weapons systems that support the agreed-upon strategy; (3) professional exchanges to provide tailored training for Taiwan's armed forces; and (4) steady, visible U.S. operations in Taiwan's vicinity to signal American support for Taiwan's security.

The United States likely will need to become more forceful in the coming period in encouraging Taiwan to move away from procuring large legacy platforms and instead focus on fielding large numbers of small, affordable, highly mobile units.[20] Senior U.S. officials will need to make clear to Taiwan counterparts that Washington will only support the transfer of weapons, platforms, and capabilities that align with an agreed-upon defense concept for Taiwan.[21] In other words, U.S. policymakers will need to learn to say "no" when Taiwan officials request big-ticket items such as M1 Abrams tanks or 66 F-16 aircraft at a price equal to roughly one-half of Taiwan's entire 2022 defense budget. Approving the sale of such items is net negative for Taiwan's defense, given tight budgetary constraints, the marginal role such equipment would have in an actual conflict, and the significant resource requirements for maintaining such equipment into the future.

The goal of American engagement with Taiwan on security issues is to push Taiwan to be capable of waging a prolonged denial campaign in the air, at sea, and on the ground that prevents China from quickly seizing control of Taiwan by force. This requires Taiwan to invest significantly in asymmetric capabilities such as sea mines, drones, anti-ship cruise missiles, and short-range mobile air defenses that enable Taiwan to field a mobile, survivable, innovative military.

Such a posture will require trade-offs. Taiwan likely will face diminished capacity to counter every gray zone intimidation by PLA forces around Taiwan. For example, Taiwan likely will confront constraints on its ability to launch sorties to intercept every PLA jet that briefly crosses into Taiwan's air defense identification zone. Taipei may not be able to respond visibly to every effort by the PLA to conduct maritime operations around Taiwan. This is the cost of constrained defense budgets.

Scarce resources will need to be used to strike a balance between checking gray zone challenges and problematizing for China the risk they would face if they launch a full-scale invasion. A steady American military presence near Taiwan should help mitigate the psychological impact of the PLA's gray zone intimidation efforts.

By intensifying focus on the fight Taiwan cannot afford to lose, defense of its homeland, Taiwan will improve its ability to hold Chinese platforms and lives at risk, should they ever attempt to launch an invasion of Taiwan. The objective is to inject uncertainty into the minds of Chinese leaders about the PLA's ability to achieve its political objectives through military means. The goal is to persuade China's leaders that there is not viable military solution at an acceptable cost and risk to the Taiwan challenge.

The Political Threat

Sustaining military deterrence is the minimum threshold, but not the measure of success. Beijing is not just investing in military capabilities. At the same time, it also is implementing an increasingly aggressive campaign of coercion without violence against Taiwan. This campaign operates below the threshold of conflict and is designed to foster a feeling inside Taiwan that resistance is futile, that Taiwan eventually will be absorbed by China, and that it would be wisest for the Taiwan people to sue for peace now rather than suffer societal harm by attempting to forestall the inevitable.

Beijing's efforts are aided by the deep partisan fissures that divide Taiwan society. Broadly speaking, the DPP believes that China is the adversary and that overreliance on China's economy gives Beijing leverage it will use to induce Taiwan's political capitulation. Leaders of the KMT believe that China's rise offers opportunity for Taiwan and that it is possible for Taiwan to profit from ties to the mainland without compromising its security, so long as cross-Strait relations are managed smoothly and in a manner that mitigates tensions. This juxtaposition between perceptions of China as an enemy or an opportunity creates openings for China to sow divisions. From Beijing's perspective, a divided Taiwan is less likely to move permanently away from China and is easier to manipulate than a unified Taiwan would be.

Military signaling is an element of China's psychological pressure toolbox. Through active and visible military operations in the waters and airspace surrounding Taiwan in all four directions, Beijing seeks to heighten Taiwan peoples' sense of vulnerability. Beijing often registers displeasure over Taiwan activities by conducting PLA air incursions into Taiwan's air defense identification zone as a form of retaliation. If cross-Strait relations deteriorate further in the future, the PLA could attempt to dial up its military intimidation by conducting incursions into Taiwan's twelve-nautical mile territorial air space, shooting missiles over Taiwan, or conducting military flights over Taiwan. It also could attempt to disrupt internet traffic into/out of Taiwan for a while to signal that Beijing controls Taiwan's links to the outside world. Each of these potential actions would amount to a high-stakes gamble for Beijing, given the risk of escalation, but they would be consistent with its "frog in the boiling pot" approach of steadily ratcheting up pressure on the people of Taiwan without firing the first shot.

Beijing also aims to intensify Taiwan's sense of international isolation. During President Tsai's tenure, Taiwan's diplomatic allies have dwindled from twenty-two to fourteen at the time of this writing. China's top diplomat, Wang Yi, has taunted Taipei by pronouncing publicly that Beijing could take Taiwan's diplomatic allies to zero whenever it wants. Beijing also has severely restricted Taiwan's access to international organizations, going so far as to insist that private Taiwan residents be blocked from entering UN buildings unless they have PRC-issued forms of identification. Beijing has stood in the way of Taiwan's participation in every international organization where it has a seat over the past six years.

China also uses economic coercion. One aspect of this approach has been its attempts to hollow-out Taiwan's talent pipeline by creating hefty incentives for Taiwan's innovators and experts to relocate to the mainland. One recent report suggests that as many as three thousand Taiwan semiconductor engineers have departed Taiwan for positions at Chinese rivals, a figure that—if accurate—would amount to nearly one-tenth of Taiwan's forty thousand engineers involved in semiconductor research and development.[22]

Another feature of Beijing's economic toolbox has been to penalize Taiwan businesses and businessmen operating in China who support Taiwan politicians Beijing opposes. As chapter 2 described, Beijing made a public example of the Far Eastern New Century conglomerate in November 2021 for its political donations to the DPP, even though the company also made contributions to the KMT during the same period.[23]

Beijing also employs united front tactics to try to create a more permissive environment in Taiwan for its objectives. This involves identifying, recruiting, and working with sympathetic elements within Taiwan. Beijing encourages its targets to use their own voices to undermine politicians and policies that Beijing opposes.

Chinese actors also carry out disinformation and cyber activities to discredit views they oppose and foment divisions within Taiwan. Cyber experts often point to Taiwan as a leading target of externally generated cyber intrusions and attacks. For example, the former United States representative in Taiwan, American Institute in Taiwan Director Brent Christensen, declared publicly at a September 2019 event in Taipei that mainland cyberattacks on Taiwan were seven times greater in 2018 than 2017 and that attacks in 2019 were projected to be another twenty times greater in 2020. Christensen reportedly said that malign actors use the openness of Taiwan's internet to sow division, create polarization, and spread outright falsehoods to begin to make people begin to lose faith in democratic institutions.[24] This anecdote offers a reminder that China's leaders find the presence of a high-functioning ethnic Chinese democratic society ninety miles off its coast as an intrinsically threatening model for its own people. Chinese leaders do not want Taiwan to present unflattering contrasts with their governance performance on the mainland.

Seen cumulatively, Beijing's various lines of effort to target the self-confidence of the Taiwan people carry fewer risks than war and could over time lead to the outcome Beijing wants—annexation of Taiwan without bloodshed. Beijing seeks to socialize the Taiwan public to the inevitability of unification and the undesirability of living in a domestically fractured, internationally isolated society. Unlike the risk of a potential future military conflict, these are not future hypothetical scenarios. Beijing's political campaign to annex Taiwan without bloodshed already is underway.

Policy Options for Responding to Coercion without Violence

The nature of China's gray-zone challenges does not correspond neatly to how the U.S. government is organized to respond to external threats. Unlike deterring the risk of conflict, which falls under the responsibilities of the DoD, there is no government agency responsible for countering China's multidimensional challenges against Taiwan. Instead, the American response will need to be diverse, agile, and structured around an easily understandable organizing principle—the more confident Taiwan becomes in its future, the less vulnerable to Chinese coercion it will be.

The task facing American policymakers will be to advance practical steps to support Taiwan's ability to enjoy dignity and respect on the world stage, remain at the cutting edge of innovation, feel secure in its economic competitiveness, and be capable of protecting the health of its people.

The United States has several unrealized options for expanding Taiwan's international space. Washington could initiate efforts to convene and host trilateral dialogues featuring Taiwan and key European, North American, and Asian counterparts. The more the United States normalizes such efforts, the less inhibited other countries would feel meeting below the leader level with Taiwan officials. In addition to the substantive value such exchanges would generate, they also would help focus other advanced industrialized countries on their interest in preserving peace and stability in the Taiwan Strait.

As chapter 2 discussed, recent trilateral collaborations through the GCTF provides a useful precedent for these types of issue-based exchanges. GCTF meetings provide venues for Taiwan to contribute to global challenges and benefit from the goodwill such efforts generate.

Washington also could establish a standard practice of consulting relevant Taiwan authorities on matters of public security and public health around multilateral meetings that exclude Taiwan. If, for example, Taiwan continues to be blocked from participating in meetings of the WHO and INTERPOL, then the United States could organize meetings with relevant Taiwan officials to share information Taiwan otherwise would not be able to access, including by sending U.S. officials to Taiwan for such conversations. These efforts would enhance safety and security for both sides. As another option, Washington could establish a standard practice of meeting publicly with Taiwan counterparts before and after multilateral events where Taiwan is excluded. This would allow U.S. officials to understand Taiwan's priorities and ensure they are represented in multilateral proceedings.[25]

Washington also could weigh in privately with Beijing to inform them that further diplomatic pressure tactics on Taiwan could activate compensatory American responses. Relevant American officials could emphasize to their Chinese counterparts that Washington has an interest in ensuring Taiwan is integrated into the international system in areas where statehood is not a requirement of membership. Taiwan has material contributions to provide for international challenges, and the health and safety of Taiwan's 23.5 million people is a matter of concern for the American people. Continued Chinese efforts to constrict Taiwan's international space could compel Washington to relax U.S. policy restrictions on senior Taiwan officials' transits of the United States, for example, or cause the United States to convene additional multilateral gatherings that include Taiwan. The goal of such private interventions with Chinese counterparts would not be to spark an escalatory cycle over Taiwan's international space, but rather to seek to influence China's cost-benefit calculus for squeezing Taiwan in ways that cause Beijing to conclude that its interests would be ill-served by ratcheting up pressure further. For such an approach to have impact, though, Beijing would need to have confidence that if it pulled back on its pressure, Washington would not exploit the gesture as a unidirectional concession, but rather would reciprocate in kind.

Another area requiring intensified American efforts to blunt Chinese pressure is trade and economic issues. An economically strong Taiwan is essential to reducing its vulnerability to coercion and is foundational to its security.[26] In recent decades, America's economic policy toward Taiwan has been divorced from its overall strategy; there have been no notable bilateral trade or investment agreements signed since 2001.

During this same period, Beijing has intensified efforts to marginalize Taiwan's economic competitiveness, including by keeping it outside of Asia's economic integration. Beijing also has limited Taiwan to concluding FTAs only with countries that already have FTAs with China and that Beijing consents to allow to establish FTAs with Taiwan. To date, the only two countries that have cleared this hurdle are New Zealand and Singapore. Both these agreements were reached during the Ma Ying-jeou era, when cross-Strait relations were marked by regular engagement and relatively greater flexibility on matters of Taiwan's international space and economic access. In other words, standing still on U.S.-Taiwan trade issues has resulted in Taiwan falling backward relative to its competitors, all of whom are members of Asian regional integration initiatives such as RCEP.

At the most ambitious end of the spectrum of policy options, the United States and Taiwan could negotiate a bilateral trade agreement. Such an effort could set a precedent and offer a blueprint for Taiwan's other trade partners to follow. If political winds in Washington remain averse to free trade agreements, both sides could negotiate chapters of an eventual trade agreement, taking a building block approach by establishing rules around emerging issues such as data privacy and cross-border data flows. Taiwan also would benefit from joining CPTPP, but since the United

States is outside of the agreement, Washington will have limited leverage in pushing for Taiwan's admission.

Washington and Taipei also should work to deepen supply chain and research-and-development integration around key technologies, including semiconductors. Taiwan Semiconductor Manufacturing Company's 2020 decision to build a $12 billion chip fabrication plant in Arizona is a promising step in this direction. Taiwan's investments in the United States generate jobs and goodwill among state-level officials, cultivating key constituencies supportive of deepening U.S.-Taiwan ties. Such investments in the United States also enable a more resilient and geographically balanced supply chain. They do not, however, diminish America's dependency on Taiwan for high-end semiconductor chips. As Intel CEO Pat Gelsinger has noted, there is no scenario whereby the United States will become independent of the need for chip manufacturing from Taiwan.[27] There is no other country in the world capable of becoming a substitute for semiconductor production from Taiwan. As a result, every other country that is integrated into the global economy has a stake in the preservation of cross-Strait stability.

The United States and Taiwan also would benefit from Taiwan becoming more integrated into international discussions on technology standards. The United States can play a facilitating role in bringing Taiwan into plurilateral discussions it already is holding with other partners, such as Australia, Japan, and the EU on harmonization of export controls and new regulations around cyber, the Internet-of-Things, driverless cars, and other emerging technologies. Taiwan's involvement in these discussions would allow it to contribute meaningfully to new regulations while at the same time giving impetus to leaders in Taiwan to adapt its policies to rapid industrial and technological changes.

The United States and Taiwan also would benefit from the formation of a leading group of policymakers, innovators, industry leaders, venture capitalists, and researchers to explore ways to deepen mutually beneficial collaboration that integrates Taiwan's hardware expertise with America's leading software breakthroughs.[28] The more that the United States and Taiwan lead the way in terms of developing public-private partnerships and establishing international standards and regulatory best practices around twenty-first-century trade issues such as data flows and privacy issues, the better positioned Taiwan will be to attract investment and talent.

Public health is another area where both sides would gain from deepened coordination. Taiwan is uniquely positioned to support a shift in medical supply chains away from China, given its cutting-edge medical manufacturing capabilities and its record of resilience in dealing with health crises such as SARS and COVID-19. The more plugged into global medical supply chains Taiwan becomes, the more aware it will become of emerging health situations around the world and best practices for responding to incipient health threats, even if China continues to block Taiwan's participation in the WHO.

A secondary benefit of U.S.-Taiwan coordination on diplomatic, economic, technological, and public health efforts—or some combination of them—would be to undercut Beijing's efforts to influence public perceptions in Taiwan. The surest way to pop Beijing's preferred narrative about Taiwan growing isolated and vulnerable is to demonstrate that Taiwan is thriving and deepening its relationships with the United States and others in the process.

To make such a narrative unassailable, Taiwan's leaders will need to take important steps on their own to build a durable political consensus around ways to strengthen Taiwan's society, its governance system, and its economic competitiveness. Three immediate steps stand out as rising above the rest.

First, Taiwan would benefit if its leaders reach a consensus on the need to generate more revenue to meet their responsibilities. Taiwan faces unique challenges, including the need for: a strong defense against a growing threat, enhanced care for a rapidly aging population, and expanded opportunities for rising generations to contribute to Taiwan's economic growth. At present, Taiwan authorities simply are not generating enough revenue to meet these dueling demands, nor are they making difficult choices to prioritize one over the others. The result is that Taiwan's leaders are providing half-solutions to problems that will only grow more acute with time. Tax revenues have remained relatively constant over the past decade at around 12.4 percent of gross domestic product (GDP) while Taiwan's GDP expanded by roughly one-third.[29] Looking forward, Taiwan's leaders will need to raise revenues to provide the care, security, and opportunity that Taiwan people expect.

Second, Taiwan would be strengthened if its leaders could forge a common view on what would be required to alter the relationship between Taipei and Beijing. They should be able to acknowledge as a matter of principle that any negotiated resolution of cross-Strait differences would need to be approved by a constitutional amendment. Such a shared understanding would remove political heat around cross-Strait issues by making clear that support from the people, not just elected officials, would be needed to ratify any adjustment in cross-Strait relations. Such a consensus would put the burden on Beijing to appeal to the interests of Taiwan's entire population if it wishes to make progress in pulling Taiwan closer to the mainland.

Third, and relatedly, Taiwan could put itself in a more durable position if its leaders could agree that Taiwan faces a real external threat and that bipartisan cooperation will be required to meet this threat. They will need to summon the spirit of President Truman and his political opponents at the outset of the Cold War, who agreed that "politics stops at the water's edge." In practical terms, leaders in Taiwan could translate this spirit into action by agreeing on a bipartisan basis to oppose external meddling in Taiwan's electoral processes. Given China's low approval ratings in Taiwan, KMT leaders should be guided by self-interest to recognize the reputational risks of being seen as in cahoots with Beijing. Whether justified or not, such impressions would harm KMT officials' electoral prospects, given the foul views of Taiwan voters toward Chinese meddling in their politics. Taiwan's democratic institutions would be strengthened by a bipartisan acknowledgment that the will of Taiwan's voters should be the sole basis for determining who leads Taiwan.

In sum, China's political campaign of coercion without violence is real, ongoing, and targeted at Taiwan's point of vulnerability, the confidence of Taiwan's people in their future. China's leaders are investing in this political campaign as they seek to compel Taiwan's capitulation without bloodshed. Washington and Taipei get a vote on whether Beijing's efforts to induce psychological pressure generate results. There are ample opportunities available to fortify the confidence of the people of Taiwan in their future and to ensure that their voices are determinative of Taiwan's future.

Policymakers in Washington and Taipei should expect that Beijing will continue to advance its political coercion campaign, given the relatively low costs and risks associated with it. The outstanding question is whether leaders in Washington and Taipei will summon the determination and political will to act upon the illustrative opportunities that this brief chapter has identified.

RECALLING AMERICA'S ROLE IN PRESERVING CROSS-STRAIT PEACE AND STABILITY

In the wake of America's ignominious exit from Afghanistan, against the backdrop of Russia's invasion of Ukraine, amidst its domestic political turmoil, and in the face of China's rapid military build-up, there is a palpably growing sense of urgency within America's policymaking community to "do something" to reverse trend-lines in the Taiwan Strait. There is a feeling that China is winning because it is eroding America's deterrent; if China is winning, then America must be losing. And if America is losing, then it must make major changes to its policy and posture.

Such sentiments, while understandable, are not a basis for sound strategy and policy. The inescapable reality is that not all problems in the world are conducive to an American solution. Taiwan provides a stark reminder.

The purpose of American policy and strategy on Taiwan is not to "win" against China. The 23.5 million people of Taiwan are not chess pieces in a great power competition to determine mastery of Asia in the twenty-first century. They are friends of the United States who share similar ideals and aspirations with the American people.

The maintenance of peace and stability in the Taiwan Strait and the prevention of conflict have been the consistent objective of U.S. policy since World War II. American policy is designed to preserve Taiwan's political autonomy, its cultural and economic dynamism, and the credibility of America's security commitments, without triggering conflict. Successful American policy means creating conditions for Taiwan to serve as an example of a thriving democratic success story while at the same time protecting time and space for an eventual peaceful solution to emerge that is acceptable to Taiwan's people.

As the late Alan Romberg wisely advised:

> The basic decisions regarding cross-Strait relations rest in the hands of those most directly involved: Taipei and Beijing. But the U.S. role is crucial. And while any [American] President has the right to change policy, (s)he has an obligation to do so only in light of considered understanding of what it is (s)he is changing and what the long-term effects are likely to be. In the case of policy toward Taiwan, and its impact on overall U.S. relations with the PRC, this requires a dedicated effort to grasp clearly not just the broad outlines of the normalization undertakings, but the detail and nuance—and the

essential ambiguities—that give them effect. To do less would be irresponsible and could take us all over the brink of the precipice.[30]

It is not America's job to solve the Taiwan challenge. There is no mediation role for the United States between Beijing and Taipei. Neither party currently seeks American intervention in cross-Strait deliberations.

It also is not the role of the United States to negotiate with Beijing about America's relationship with Taiwan over the heads of Taiwan's leaders, who are elected to represent the popular will of the people. There is historical precedent for American leaders taking these actions, including President Franklin Delano Roosevelt's decision to return Taiwan to China after the end of World War II, Richard Nixon's private statements to Chinese leaders in 1971–1972 that he viewed Taiwan as a part of China, and Jimmy Carter's decision to normalize relations with Beijing and de-recognize Taipei in 1979. Since Taiwan's transition to democracy in 1986, U.S. officials generally have consulted in advance with Taiwan's leaders on changes to U.S. policy that would affect Taiwan's security.[31] They should continue to do so. Taiwan's leaders are the best judges of how U.S. decisions will impact Taiwan's interests.

The United States traditionally has not taken a position on the substance of any potential solution to cross-Strait differences, whether it be unification of Taiwan with China, a federation, or any other scenario. But Washington has been consistent in not supporting Taiwan independence, and it has remained steadfast in opposing any unilateral change to the status quo, by either side.

A little over a decade ago, this required the United States to publicly oppose attempts by Taiwan's President, Chen Shui-bian, to push a referendum to apply to join the United Nations under the name Taiwan. Now, America's policy focus is more squarely centered on deterring China militarily and challenging China's relentless coercion against Taiwan. It remains to be seen whether future events may compel America to shift its focus. Whether in 2024, 2028, or later, there always is the risk of a firebrand leader emerging in Taiwan who is willing to pursue policies that are at odds with America's fundamental interests. Whatever the case, the United States will be best positioned to respond to any scenario that emerges by preserving its policy of dual deterrence—deterring any attempts by Beijing to annex Taiwan by force, as well as any efforts by Taiwan to pursue *de jure* independence. America's abiding interest in peace and stability in the Taiwan Strait requires it to stand in the way of these two paths to conflict.

American policy on Taiwan is most effective when it is seen as principled, balanced, confident, and purposeful. Recent American insecurities about its eroding position in the Taiwan Strait have generated impulses for activism that have led to departures from America's long-standing policy posture. Many of these recent policy experiments have been ill-advised and have generated more harm than benefit for America's long-term objectives.

For example, linking support for Taiwan to anger about events in Hong Kong, as Secretary of State Mike Pompeo did, fed an unhealthy narrative that Washington views Taiwan as a pawn instead of a partner.[32] Publicizing private consultations between senior U.S. and Taiwan officials, as then-National Security Advisor John Bolton did following talks with his Taiwan counterpart, compelled Beijing to take visible cost-imposition measures against Taiwan that it otherwise would not have taken had the consultations remained out of view, as had been the case for years prior. Referring to Taiwan as a "country" in official U.S. government documents and statements, as both the Trump and Biden administrations have done, lends an impression that Taiwan policy is being handled either by amateurs who lack an understanding of the history of U.S. policy or by activists who wish to instrumentalize Taiwan to bludgeon China or weaken U.S.-China relations. Neither of these poses reflects well on perceptions of the competence of senior U.S. officials.

Congressional virtue signaling in support of Taiwan also creates complications for American policy. Such nonbinding resolutions have negligible impact on the conduct of U.S. policy, which falls constitutionally within the purview of the executive branch. Such resolutions do raise expectations in Taiwan of U.S. support, though. They also elevate cross-Strait tensions, in part because Beijing does not have the most sophisticated understanding of how to interpret non-binding legislation, given its absence of experience with the division of power among co-equal branches of government. In other words, such legislation—viewed through a foreign policy prism—generates costs and risks without meaningful offsetting benefits.

There also has been a strand of thought in defense planning circles recently that the United States needs to foreclose the possibility of Taiwan falling into Beijing's hands. According to this logic, which is reflected in Elbridge Colby's book, *The Strategy of Denial*, among other places, if Taiwan ever did unify with China—peacefully or otherwise—then China would be able to use Taiwan to project power, flank Japan and the Philippines, and set off a domino effect leading toward an exclusive Chinese sphere of influence in Asia at America's expense. In other words, Taiwan is the cork in a bottle preventing the unwinding of American leadership on the world stage. While Colby and others have intensified projections of American anxiety and insecurity relative to previous periods, their concerns are fundamentally derivative of the views of General Douglas MacArthur in the early 1950s, who argued that Taiwan was a strategic asset that must be kept on America's side as "an unsinkable aircraft carrier." Much has changed in terms of power projection, the distribution of power in the international system, and the sources of national power since the 1950s. So, too, must understandings of American interests vis-à-vis Taiwan.

Washington would be wise not to steal hypothetical problems from the future by preemptively opposing any peaceful resolution of cross-Strait differences. American opposition to unification under any circumstances likely would set the United States and China on an inalterable collision course. It would send the signal that U.S. support for Taiwan is driven by a strategic logic that is indifferent to the views of the Taiwan people. And it would generate needless antagonisms, given that the political barriers in Taiwan to a peacefully negotiated resolution of cross-Strait differences already are prohibitively high. American opposition to peaceful resolution of cross-Strait differences is not needed or net beneficial to America's abiding interest in preserving peace and stability in the Taiwan Strait.

The present circumstances in the Taiwan Strait call for American resoluteness and steadiness, not alarm. There is a real risk of conflict. Washington, Taipei, and others must strengthen their capacity to resist China's forceful annexation of Taiwan. But they also must keep an eye on the bigger strategic picture.

Conflict is not preordained. Any such conflict in the Taiwan Strait would be devastating to all involved. If China initiated aggression against Taiwan, it could not be sure the United States would stand aside. If the United States intervenes, as is likely, it would be next to impossible for Beijing to control escalation or the geographic scope of conflict.

Beijing has its incentives to avoid war. Beijing could not be assured of absolute victory in current circumstances, and anything short of quick and absolute unification would risk undermining CCP legitimacy at home. The longer the conflict prolonged, the more losses and suffering the Chinese people would endure. Beijing would need to mortgage its long-term national ambitions for its goal of unifying Taiwan.

American policymakers must remain clear in their thinking that cross-Strait tensions are not simply a military contest. They also are not a test of great power wills. They are not a future hypothetical. China already is underway in its political campaign to wear down the will of Taiwan's people. This is currently the center of gravity in the contest for the future of Taiwan.

If American policymakers want to support Taiwan, they will need to do more than fixate on the military threat. Shoring up defenses against Chinese invasion is the start, not the end, of the work that needs to be done. American officials also will need to pursue efforts to strengthen Taiwan's international standing, its economic competitiveness, its public health, and its confidence in its capacity to continue serving as a model of a dynamic, democratic polity in the heart of Asia.

Focusing American efforts in support of these goals falls well within the bounds of longstanding strategy and policy. It also is consistent with the overriding focus of America's activities in the Taiwan Strait—to keep space open for Taipei and Beijing to find a peaceful solution to cross-Strait differences that is acceptable to Taiwan's people. This task may take years, decades, or longer. America's role is not to solve these problems, it is to keep open a path for these problems to be solved.

NOTES

1. See Richard C. Bush, "Conference on the Risks to the Asian Peace: Avoiding Paths to Great Power War," Brookings Institution, June 25, 2019, www.brookings.edu/on-the-record/conference-on-the-risks-to-the-asian-peace-avoiding-paths-to-great-power-war/.

2. Thomas Christensen, "A Strong and Moderate Taiwan," U.S. Department of State (archived, 2001–2009), September 11, 2007, https://2001-2009.state.gov/p/eap/rls/rm/2007/91979.htm.

3. David C. Gompert, Astrid Stuth Cevallos, and Cristina L. Garafola, *War with China: Thinking Through the Unthinkable*, RAND Corporation, 2016, www.rand.org/pubs/research_reports/RR1140.html.

4. Robert D. Blackwill and Philip Zelikow, *The United States, China, and Taiwan: A Strategy to Prevent War*, Council on Foreign Relations, February 2021, www.cfr.org/report/united-states-china-and-taiwan-strategy-prevent-war, p. 64.

5. Yimou Lee, Norihiko Shirouzu, and David Lague, "T-Day: The Battle for Taiwan," *Reuters*, December 27, 2021, https://www.reuters.com/investigates/special-report/taiwan-china-chips/.

6. John Culver and Ryan Hass, "Understanding Beijing's Motives Regarding Taiwan, and America's Role: A 35-Year CIA Officer's View," Brookings Institution, March 30, 2021, www.brookings.edu/on-the-record/understanding-beijings-motives-regarding-taiwan-and-americas-role/.

7. "President Xi Jinping Had a Virtual Meeting with US President Joe Biden," Ministry of Foreign Affairs of the People's Republic of China, November 16, 2021, www.fmprc.gov.cn/mfa_eng/zxxx_662805/202111/t20211116_10448843.html.

8. Richard C. Bush, *Difficult Choices: Taiwan's Quest for Security and the Good Life* (Washington, D.C.: Brookings Institution Press, 2021), 230.

9. Rush Doshi, *The Long Game: China's Grand Strategy to Displace American Order* (Oxford University Press, 2021).

10. Culver and Hass, "Understanding Beijing's Motives."

11. Blackwill and Zelikow, "The United States, China, and Taiwan."

12. Blackwill and Zelikow, "The United States, China, and Taiwan."

13. Office of the Secretary of Defense, *Military and Security Developments Involving the People's Republic of China*, U.S. Department of Defense, 2021, https://media.defense.gov/2021/Nov/03/2002885874/-1/-1/0/2021-CMPR-FINAL.PDF.

14. Gombert et al., "War with China."

15. Rebecca Kheel, "As US and China Warily Eye Each Other, Taiwan Could Be the Flashpoint," *Military*, December 13, 2021, www.military.com/daily-news/2021/12/13/us-and-china-warily-eye-each-other-taiwan-could-be-flashpoint.html.

16. Ely Ratner, "Statement by Dr. Ely Ratner Assistant Secretary of Defense for Indo-Pacific Security Affairs," Testimony before the Senate Committee on Foreign Relations, 117th Cong., 1st sess., December 8, 2021, www.foreign.senate.gov/imo/media/doc/120821_Ratner_Testimony1.pdf.

17. David Ochmanek and Michael O'Hanlon, "Here's the Strategy to Prevent China from Taking Taiwan," *The Hill*, December 8, 2021, https://thehill.com/opinion/national-security/584370-heres-the-strategy-to-prevent-china-from-taking-taiwan.

18. Michael J. Green and Evan S. Medeiros, "Can America Rebuild Its Power in Asia?" *Foreign Affairs*, January 31, 2022, https://www.foreignaffairs.com/articles/asia/2022-01-31/can-america-rebuild-its-power-asia.

19. Blackwill and Zelikow, "The United States, China, and Taiwan."

20. Drew Thompson, Winning the Fight Taiwan Cannot Afford to Lose, National Defense University, November 4, 2021, www.ndu.edu/News/Article-View/Article/2833332/winning-the-fight-taiwan-cannot-afford-to-lose/.

21. Michael A. Hunzeker, "Taiwan's Defense Plans Are Going off the Rails," *War on the Rocks*, November 18, 2021, https://warontherocks.com/2021/11/taiwans-defense-plans-are-going-off-the-rails/.

22. Evan A. Feigenbaum, *Assuring Taiwan's Innovation Future*, Carnegie Endowment for International Peace, January 29, 2020, https://carnegieendowment.org/2020/01/29/assuring-taiwan-s-innovation-future-pub-80920.

23. Yang Sheng, Wang Qi, and Chi Jingyi, "Chinese Mainland Punishes Pro-Secessionist Taiwan Companies 'For Better Cross-Straits Economic Ties, to Push Reunification,'" *Global Times*, November 23, 2021, www.globaltimes.cn/page/202111/1239752.shtml.

24. Bush, *Difficult Choices*, 244.

25. Bonnie Glaser, Richard Bush, and Michael J. Green, *Toward a Stronger U.S.-Taiwan Relationship*, CSIS, October 2020, www.csis.org/analysis/toward-stronger-us-taiwan-relationship.

26. Glaser et al., *Toward a Stronger U.S.-Taiwan Relationship*, 30.

27. "Intel CEO Pat Gelsinger: The U.S. Needs More Geographically Balanced Supply Chains," CNBC, May 23, 2022, https://www.cnbc.com/video/2022/05/23/intel-ceo-pat-gelsinger-the-u-s-needs-more-balanced-geographic-supply-chains.html.

28. Blackwill and Zelikow, "The United States, China, and Taiwan."

29. Bush, *Difficult Choices*, 322.

30. Alan D. Romberg, *Rein in at the Brink of the Precipice: American Policy toward Taiwan and U.S.-PRC Relations* (Washington, D.C.: Henry L. Stimson Center, 2003), 231.

31. Richard C. Bush, *One-China Policy Primer*, Brookings Institution, March 2017, www.brookings.edu/wp-content/uploads/2017/03/one-china-policy-primer.pdf.

32. Michael R. Pompeo, "On the Mass Arrests of Democracy Advocates in Hong Kong," U.S. Department of State (archived, 2017–2021), January 6, 2021, https://2017-2021.state.gov/on-the-mass-arrests-of-democracy-advocates-in-hong-kong/index.html.

Further Reading

There is extensive English-language literature concerning Taiwan in both single- and multi-author volumes, created by both Taiwan-based scholars and Western Taiwan specialists. Each new scholarly cohort has brought its own, valuable perspective to what we know. Here, we provide only a sampling of what is available for further study, and these books themselves provide leads to other works.

Two multi-author volumes trace how Taiwan has changed over time and examine various aspects of the island's society. The first, edited by Murray A. Rubenstein, is *Taiwan: A New History* (Armonk, NY: M. E. Sharpe, 1999), which covers every historical period from prehistory to the end of the twentieth century. The second—*The Routledge Handbook of Contemporary Taiwan* (New York: Routledge, 2016)—was edited by German scholar Gunter Shubert and focuses more on Taiwan history and society from the late 1940s on. *Taiwan: A Political History*, by Denny Roy (Cornell University Press, 2003), offers a good, one-volume history of who ruled Taiwan over time and how.

John Robert Shepherd's *Statecraft and Political Economy on the Taiwan Frontier, 1600–1800* (Stanford University Press, 1993) provides an in-depth account of the settlement and development of Taiwan by ethnic Chinese. Three useful books on the Japanese colonial period are Chih-ming Ka, *Japanese Colonialism in Taiwan: Land Tenure, Development and Dependency* (Taipei, Taiwan: SMC Publishing, 1995); George H. Kerr, *Formosa: Licensed Revolution and the Home Rule Movement, 1895–1945* (University of Hawaii Press, 1974); and Leo T. S. Ching, *Becoming "Japanese": Colonial Taiwan and the Politics of Identity Formation* (University of California Press, 2001).

For the KMT takeover of Taiwan, see Steven E. Phillips, *Between Assimilation and Independence: The Taiwanese Encounter with Nationalist China, 1945–1950* (Stanford University Press, 2003); George H. Kerr and Jonathan Benda, *Formosa Betrayed* (Manchester, United Kingdom: Camphor Press Ltd., 2018); and Lai Tse-han, Ramon H. Myers, and Wei Wou, *A Tragic Beginning: The Taiwan Uprising of*

February 28, 1947 (Stanford University Press, 1991). Sheena Chestnut Greitens' *Dictators and Their Secret Police* (Cambridge University Press, 2016) carries forward the story of repression under the KMT Party-State.

Two biographies by retired diplomat Jay Taylor provide the story of Taiwan from the perspective of Chiang Kai-shek and his son Chiang Ching-kuo, who ruled Taiwan from the late 1940s to the late 1980s: *The Generalissimo's Son: Chiang Kai-shek and the Struggle for Modern China* (Harvard University Press, 2000) and *The Generalissimo's Son: Chiang Ching-kuo and the Revolutions in China and Taiwan* (Harvard University Press, 2000). Issue 15 of *The China Quarterly* (July–September 1963) provides a snapshot of Taiwan society in the early 1960s. Issue 99 (September 1984) does the same for the early 1980s.

Several works discuss Taiwan's transition to democracy, from the late 1980s to the early 1990s. Linda Chao and Ramon H. Myers, *The First Chinese Democracy: Political Life in the Republic of China on Taiwan* (Johns Hopkins University Press, 1998) is a general account. Shelley Rigger's *Politics in Taiwan: Voting for Democracy* (New York: Routledge, 1999) describes how local-level elections prepared Taiwan voters to participate in a fully competitive system. In *Taiwan: National Identity and Democratization* (Armonk, NY: M. E. Sharpe, 1994), Alan Wachman describes the emergence of a Taiwanese identity, which has remained strong until this day. For interesting detail on President Lee Teng-hui, who presided over the democratic transition, see Richard C. Kagan, *Taiwan's Statesman: Lee Teng-hui and Democracy in Asia* (Naval Institute Press, 2007). Shelley Rigger analyzes the rise of the DPP as a credible alternative to the Kuomintang in *From Opposition to Power: Taiwan's Democratic Progressive Party* (Boulder, CO: Lynne Rienner Publishers, 2001).

Dafydd Fell's *Government and Politics in Taiwan* (New York: Routledge, 2012) is a good primer on the various elements of the political system. *Dynamics of Democracy in Taiwan: The Ma Ying-jeou Years*, edited by Kharis Templeman, Yun-han Chu, and Larry Diamond (Boulder, CO: Lynne Reinner Publishers, 2020) covers the Ma Ying-jeou administration from a variety of perspectives. Dafydd Fell, editor, *Taiwan's Social Movements under Ma Ying-jeou: From the Wild Strawberries to the Sunflowers* (New York: Routledge, 2017) addresses a key development in recent Taiwan politics.

Regarding Taiwan's relations with the United States, Nancy Bernkopf Tucker's *Taiwan, Hong Kong, and the United States, 1945–1992: Uncertain Friendships* (New York: Twayne Publishers, 1994) provides a good baseline. David Finkelstein's *Washington's Taiwan Dilemma, 1949–1950: From Abandonment to Salvation* (Naval Institute Press, 2014) describes a pivotal point in the story. John Garver provides a detailed account of the U.S.-ROC alliance from the time the KMT regime relocated to Taiwan to the termination of U.S.-ROC relations in his *The Sino-American Alliance: Nationalist China and American Cold War Strategy in Asia* (Armonk, NY: M. E. Sharpe, 1997). In *At Cross Purposes: U.S.-Taiwan Relations since 1942* (Armonk, NY: M.E. Sharpe, 2004), Richard C. Bush examines key issues on the bilateral relationship. Nancy Bernkopf Tucker's *Strait Talk: United States-Taiwan Relations and the Crisis with China* (Harvard

University Press, 2009) is an up-to-date analysis of U.S.-Taiwan ties from the late 1960s through the Chen Shui-bian administration. Alan D. Romberg's *Rein in at the Brink of the Precipice: American Policy toward Taiwan and U.S.-PRC Relations* (Henry L. Stimson Center, 2003) is essential reading on the formulation and articulation of U.S. policy. In her *Why Taiwan Matters: Small Island, Global Powerhouse* (Lanham, MD: Rowman & Littlefield, 2013), Shelley Rigger lays out why the U.S. government, the American public, and others should care about Taiwan's survival and well-being.

The evolution of cross-Strait relations has generated an enormous literature. For the broad strategic context, see Alan Wachman, *Why Taiwan?: Geostrategic Rationales for China's Territorial Integrity* (Stanford University Press, 2007). For a solid introduction to developments from the beginning of the Cold War to the twenty-first century, see Steven M. Goldstein, *China and Taiwan* (Malden, MA: Polity Press, 2015). Richard C. Bush describes the political and security complexities of the cross-Strait dispute in *Untying the Knot: Making Peace in the Taiwan Strait* (Brookings Institution Press, 2005). Shelley Rigger details the economic dimension in *The Tiger Leading the Dragon: How Taiwan Propelled China's Economic Rise* (Lanham, MD: Rowman & Littlefield, 2021).

Robert L. Suettinger describes the evolution of the Taiwan-U.S.-China triangle in *Beyond Tiananmen* (Brookings Institution Press, 2003). Nancy Tucker does the same for the Chen Shui-bian administration in her edited volume, *Dangerous Strait: The U.S.-Taiwan-China Crisis* (Columbia University Press, 2005). In *Taiwan's Relations with Mainland China: A Tail Wagging Two Dogs* (New York: Routledge, 2008), Su Chi provides an account of both the Lee and Chen administrations. Richard C. Bush covers most of the Ma Ying-jeou administration in *Uncharted Strait: The Future of China-Taiwan Relations* (Brookings Institution Press, 2013) and examines the dilemmas that faced Taiwan during the Tsai Ing-wen administration in *Difficult Choices: Taiwan's Quest for Security and the Good Life* (Brookings Institution Press, 2021). He analyzes how the one country, two systems formula, which was originally devised for Taiwan, ran into difficulties in Hong Kong in *Hong Kong in the Shadow of China: Living with the Leviathan* (Brookings Institution Press, 2016). Elbridge Colby provides a provocative approach to securing Taiwan's security going forward in his *Strategy of Denial* (Yale University Press, 2021).

Books aside, several organizations produce shorter monographs and briefing papers concerning Taiwan and U.S. policy. Among these publications are:

- Richard C. Bush, *One-China Policy Primer*, Brookings Institution, March 2017, https://www.brookings.edu/research/a-one-china-policy-primer/.
- Congressional Research Service, "China/Taiwan: Evolution of the "One China" Policy—Key Statements from Washington, Beijing, and Taipei," last updated January 5, 2015, www.everycrsreport.com/reports/RL30341.html.
- Bonnie Glaser, Richard Bush, and Michael J. Green, *Toward a Stronger U.S.-Taiwan Relationship*, CSIS, October 2020, www.csis.org/analysis/toward-stronger-us-taiwan-relationship.

- Robert D. Blackwill and Philip Zelikow, *The United States, China, and Taiwan: A Strategy to Prevent War*, Council on Foreign Relations, February 2021, www .cfr.org/report/united-states-china-and-taiwan-strategy-prevent-war.
- Richard C. Bush and Ryan Hass, *Taiwan's Democracy and the China Challenge*, Brookings Institution, February 2019, www.brookings.edu/research/taiwans -democracy-and-the-china-challenge/.
- Office of the Secretary of Defense, *Military and Security Developments Involving the People's Republic of China*, U.S. Department of Defense, 2021, https:// media.defense.gov/2021/Nov/03/2002885874/-1/-1/0/2021-CMPR-FINAL .PDF.
- Drew Thompson, *Winning the Fight Taiwan Cannot Afford to Lose*, National Defense University, November 4, 2021, www.ndu.edu/News/Article-View/ Article/2833332/winning-the-fight-taiwan-cannot-afford-to-lose/.
- Bonnie Glaser, *Taiwan's Quest for Greater Participation in the International Community*, CSIS, November 21, 2013, www.csis.org/analysis/taiwan%E2 %80%99s-quest-greater-participation-international-community.

Finally, there are two sources of periodic, up-to-date information. The first is "Comparative Connections," which is produced by Pacific Forum. Every quarter it disseminates reports on recent developments in an array of bilateral relationships in East Asia (accessible at https://cc.pacforum.org/). One of the reports is on cross-Strait relations. Second is *Taiwan Business Topics*, the monthly magazine of the American Chamber of Commerce in Taiwan (accessible at https://topics.amcham .com.tw/). It is the best, ready source of information on the Taiwan economy and cross-Strait economic interactions.

Appendix A

Joint Communiqué of the United States of America and the People's Republic of China (Shanghai Communiqué)

February 27, 1972

JOINT COMMUNIQUÉ
February 28, 1972
Shanghai, People's Republic of China

President Richard Nixon of the United States of America visited the People's Republic of China at the invitation of Premier Chou En-lai of the People's Republic of China from February 21 to February 28, 1972. Accompanying the President were Mrs. Nixon, US Secretary of State William Rogers, Assistant to the President Dr. Henry Kissinger, and other American officials.

President Nixon met with Chairman Mao Tse-tung of the Communist Party of China on February 21. The two leaders had a serious and frank exchange of views on Sino-US relations and world affairs.

During the visit, extensive, earnest and frank discussions were held between President Nixon and Premier Chou En-lai on the normalization of relations between the United States of America and the People's Republic of China, as well as on other matters of interest to both sides. In addition, Secretary of State William Rogers and Foreign Minister Chi Peng-fei held talks in the same spirit.

President Nixon and his party visited Peking and viewed cultural, industrial and agricultural sites, and they also toured Hangchow and Shanghai where, continuing discussions with Chinese leaders, they viewed similar places of interest.

The leaders of the People's Republic of China and the United States of America found it beneficial to have this opportunity, after so many years without contact, to present candidly to one another their views on a variety of issues. They reviewed the international situation in which important changes and great upheavals are taking place and expounded their respective positions and attitudes.

The Chinese side stated: Wherever there is oppression, there is resistance. Countries want independence, nations want liberation and the people want revolution—this has become the irresistible trend of history. All nations, big or small, should be equal: big nations should not bully the small and strong nations should not bully the weak. China will never be a superpower and it opposes hegemony and power politics of any kind. The Chinese side stated that it firmly supports the struggles of all the oppressed people and nations for freedom and liberation and that the people of all countries have the right to choose their social systems according their own wishes and the right to safeguard the independence, sovereignty and territorial integrity of their own countries and oppose foreign aggression, interference, control and subversion. All foreign troops should be withdrawn to their own countries. The Chinese side expressed its firm support to the peoples of Viet Nam, Laos and Cambodia in their efforts for the attainment of their goal and its firm support to the seven-point proposal of the Provisional Revolutionary Government of the Republic of South Viet Nam and the elaboration of February this year on the two key problems in the proposal, and to the Joint Declaration of the Summit Conference of the Indochinese Peoples. It firmly supports the eight-point program for the peaceful unification of Korea put forward by the Government of the Democratic People's Republic of Korea on April 12, 1971, and the stand for the abolition of the "UN Commission for the Unification and Rehabilitation of Korea". It firmly opposes the revival and outward expansion of Japanese militarism and firmly supports the Japanese people's desire to build an independent, democratic, peaceful and neutral Japan. It firmly maintains that India and Pakistan should, in accordance with the United Nations resolutions on the Indo-Pakistan question, immediately withdraw all their forces to their respective territories and to their own sides of the ceasefire line in Jammu and Kashmir and firmly supports the Pakistan Government and people in their struggle to preserve their independence and sovereignty and the people of Jammu and Kashmir in their struggle for the right of self-determination.

The US side stated: Peace in Asia and peace in the world requires efforts both to reduce immediate tensions and to eliminate the basic causes of conflict. The United States will work for a just and secure peace: just, because it fulfills the aspirations of peoples and nations for freedom and progress; secure, because it removes the danger of foreign aggression. The United States supports individual freedom and social progress for all the peoples of the world, free of outside pressure or intervention. The United States believes that the effort to reduce tensions is served by improving communication between countries that have different ideologies so as to lessen the risks of confrontation through accident, miscalculation or misunderstanding. Countries should treat each other with mutual respect and be willing to compete peacefully, letting performance be the ultimate judge. No country should claim infallibility and each country should be prepared to reexamine its own attitudes for the common good. The United States stressed that the peoples of Indochina should be allowed to determine their destiny without outside intervention; its constant primary objective has been a negotiated solution; the eight-point proposal put forward by the Republic of Viet Nam and the United States on January 27, 1972 represents a basis for the attainment of that objective; in the absence of a negotiated settlement the United States envisages the ultimate withdrawal of all US forces from the region consistent with the aim of self-determination for each country of Indochina. The United States will maintain its close ties with and support for the Republic of Korea; the United States will support efforts of the Republic of Korea to seek a relaxation of tension and increased communication in the Korean peninsula. The United States places the highest value on its friendly relations with Japan; it will continue to develop the existing close bonds. Consistent with the United Nations Security Council Resolution of December 21, 1971, the United States favors the continuation of the ceasefire between India and Pakistan and the withdrawal of all military forces to within their own territories and to their own sides of the ceasefire line in Jammu and Kashmir; the United States supports the right of the peoples of South Asia to shape their own future in peace, free of military threat, and without having the area become the subject of great power rivalry.

There are essential differences between China and the United States in their social systems and foreign policies. However, the two sides agreed that countries, regardless of their social systems, should conduct their relations on the principles of respect for the sovereignty and territorial integrity of all states, non-aggression against other states, non-interference in the internal affairs of other states, equality and mutual benefit, and peaceful coexistence. International disputes should be settled on this basis, without resorting to the use or threat of force. The United States and the People's Republic of China are prepared to apply these principles to their mutual relations.

With these principles of international relations in mind the two sides stated that:

— progress toward the normalization of relations between China and the United States is in the interests of all countries
— both wish to reduce the danger of international military conflict
— neither should seek hegemony in the Asia-Pacific region and each is opposed to efforts by any other country or group of countries to establish such hegemony
— neither is prepared to negotiate on behalf of any third party or to enter into agreements or understandings with the other directed at other states.

Both sides are of the view that it would be against the interests of the peoples of the world for any major country to collude with another against other countries, or for major countries to divide up the world into spheres of interest.

The two sides reviewed the long-standing serious disputes between China and the United States. The Chinese side reaffirmed its position: the Taiwan question is the crucial question obstructing the normalization of relations between China and the United States; the Government of the People's Republic of China is the sole legal government of China; Taiwan is a province of China which has long been returned to the motherland; the liberation of Taiwan is China's internal affair in which no other country has the right to interfere; and all US forces and military installations must be withdrawn from Taiwan. The Chinese Government firmly opposes any activities which aim at the creation of "one China, one Taiwan", "one China, two governments", "two Chinas", an "independent Taiwan" or advocate that "the status of Taiwan remains to be determined".

The US side declared: The United States acknowledges that all Chinese on either side of the Taiwan Strait maintain there is but one China and that Taiwan is a part of China. The United States Government does not challenge that position. It reaffirms its interest in a peaceful settlement of the Taiwan question by the Chinese themselves. With this prospect in mind, it affirms the ultimate objective of the withdrawal of all US forces and military installations from Taiwan. In the meantime, it will progressively reduce its forces and military installations on Taiwan as the tension in the area diminishes. The two sides agreed that it is desirable to broaden the understanding between the two peoples. To this end, they discussed specific areas in such fields as science, technology, culture, sports and journalism, in which people-to-people contacts and exchanges would be mutually beneficial. Each side undertakes to facilitate the further development of such contacts and exchanges.

Both sides view bilateral trade as another area from which mutual benefit can be derived, and agreed that economic relations based on equality and mutual benefit are in the interest of the peoples of the two countries. They agree to facilitate the progressive development of trade between their two countries.

The two sides agreed that they will stay in contact through various channels, including the sending of a senior US representative to Peking from time to time for concrete consultations to further the normalization of relations between the two countries and continue to exchange views on issues of common interest.

The two sides expressed the hope that the gains achieved during this visit would open up new prospects for the relations between the two countries. They believe that the normalization of relations between the two countries is not only in the interest of the Chinese and American peoples but also contributes to the relaxation of tension in Asia and the world.

President Nixon, Mrs. Nixon and the American party expressed their appreciation for the gracious hospitality shown them by the Government and people of the People's Republic of China.

Source: Public Papers: Nixon, 1972, pp. 376–79.

JOINT COMMUNIQUÉ ON THE ESTABLISHMENT OF DIPLOMATIC RELATIONS BETWEEN THE UNITED STATES OF AMERICA AND THE PEOPLE'S REPUBLIC OF CHINA

Beijing, People's Republic of China
January 1, 1979

The United States of America and the People's Republic of China have agreed to recognize each other and to establish diplomatic relations as of January 1, 1979.

The United States of America recognizes the Government of the People's Republic of China as the sole legal Government of China. Within this context, the people of the United States will maintain cultural, commercial, and other unofficial relations with the people of Taiwan.

The United States of America and the People's Republic of China reaffirm the principles agreed on by the two sides in the Shanghai Communique and emphasize once again that:

—Both wish to reduce the danger of international military conflict.

—Neither should seek hegemony in the Asia-Pacific region or in any other region of the world and each is opposed to efforts by any other country or group of countries to establish such hegemony.

—Neither is prepared to negotiate on behalf of any third party or to enter into agreements or understandings with the other directed at other states.

—The Government of the United States of America acknowledges the Chinese position that there is but one China and Taiwan is part of China.

—Both believe that normalization of Sino-American relations is not only in the interest of the Chinese and American peoples but also contributes to the cause of peace in Asia and the world.

The United States of America and the People's Republic of China will exchange Ambassadors and establish Embassies on March 1, 1979.

Source: Public Papers: Carter, 1978, Book II, pp. 2264–2265.

JOINT COMMUNIQUÉ ISSUED BY THE GOVERNMENTS OF THE UNITED STATES AND THE PEOPLE'S REPUBLIC OF CHINA (AUGUST 17, 1982)

1. In the Joint Communique on the Establishment of Diplomatic Relations on January 1, 1979, issued by the Government of the United States of America and the Government of the People's Republic of China, the United States of America recognized the Government of the People's Republic of China as the sole legal government of China, and it acknowledged the Chinese position that there is but one China and Taiwan is part of China. Within that context, the two sides agreed that the people of the United States would continue to maintain cultural, commercial, and other unofficial relations with the people of Taiwan. On this basis, relations between the United States and China were normalized.

2. The question of United States arms sales to Taiwan was not settled in the course of negotiations between the two countries on establishing diplomatic relations. The two sides held differing positions, and the Chinese side stated that it would raise the issue again following normalization. Recognizing that this issue would seriously hamper the development of United States–China relations, they have held further discussions on it, during and since the meetings between President Ronald Reagan and Premier Zhao Ziyang and between Secretary of State Alexander M. Haig, Jr., and Vice Premier and Foreign Minister Huang Hua in October 1981.

3. Respect for each other's sovereignty and territorial integrity and non-interference each other's internal affairs constitute the fundamental principles guiding United States–China relations. These principles were confirmed in the Shanghai Communique of February 28, 1972 and reaffirmed in the Joint Communique on the Establishment of Diplomatic Relations which came into effect on January 1, 1979. Both sides emphatically state that these principles continue to govern all aspects of their relations.

4. The Chinese government reiterates that the question of Taiwan is China's internal affair. The Message to the Compatriots in Taiwan issued by China on January 1, 1979, promulgated a fundamental policy of striving for Peaceful reunification of the Motherland. The Nine-Point Proposal put forward by China on September 30, 1981 represented a Further major effort under this fundamental policy to strive for a peaceful solution to the Taiwan question.

5. The United States Government attaches great importance to its relations with China, and reiterates that it has no intention of infringing on Chinese sovereignty and territorial integrity, or interfering in China's internal affairs, or pursuing a policy of "two Chinas" or "one China, one Taiwan." The United States Government understands and appreciates the Chinese policy of striving for a peaceful resolution of the Taiwan question as indicated in China's

Message to Compatriots in Taiwan issued on January 1, 1979 and the Nine-Point Proposal put forward by China on September 30, 1981. The new situation which has emerged with regard to the Taiwan question also provides favorable conditions for the settlement of United States–China differences over the question of United States arms sales to Taiwan.

6. Having in mind the foregoing statements of both sides, the United States Government states that it does not seek to carry out a long-term policy of arms sales to Taiwan, that its arms sales to Taiwan will not exceed, either in qualitative or in quantitative terms, the level of those supplied in recent years since the establishment of diplomatic relations between the United States and China, and that it intends to reduce gradually its sales of arms to Taiwan, leading over a period of time to a final resolution. In so stating, the United States acknowledges China's consistent position regarding the thorough settlement of this issue.

7. In order to bring about, over a period of time, a final settlement of the question of United States arms sales to Taiwan, which is an issue rooted in history, the two governments will make every effort to adopt measures and create conditions conducive to the thorough settlement of this issue.

8. The development of United States–China relations is not only in the interest of the two peoples but also conducive to peace and stability in the world. The two sides are determined, on the principle of equality and mutual benefit, to strengthen their ties to the economic, cultural, educational, scientific, technological and other fields and make strong joint efforts for the continued development of relations between the governments and peoples of the United States and China.

9. In order to bring about the healthy development of United States China relations, maintain world peace and oppose aggression and expansion, the two governments reaffirm the principles agreed on by the two sides in the Shanghai Communique and the Joint Communique on the Establishment of Diplomatic Relations. The two sides will maintain contact and hold appropriate consultations on bilateral and international issues of common interest.

Source: Department of State, *American Foreign Policy: Current Documents, 1982* (Washington, DC: Government Printing Office, 1985), p. 1038.

Appendix B

Taiwan Relations Act

Public Law 96-8
96th Congress

An Act

To help maintain peace, security, and stability in the Western Pacific and to promote the foreign policy of the United States by authorizing the continuation of commercial, cultural, and other relations between the people of the United States and the people on Taiwan, and for other purposes.

Be it enacted by the Senate and House of Representatives of the United States of America in Congress assembled,

SHORT TITLE

SECTION 1. This Act may be cited as the "Taiwan Relations Act".

FINDINGS AND DECLARATION OF POLICY

SEC. 2. (a) The President—having terminated governmental relations between the United States and the governing authorities on Taiwan recognized by the United States as the Republic of China prior to January 1, 1979, the Congress finds that the enactment of this Act is necessary—

(1) to help maintain peace, security, and stability in the Western Pacific; and
(2) to promote the foreign policy of the United States by authorizing the continuation of commercial, cultural, and other relations between the people of the United States and the people on Taiwan.

145

(b) It is the policy of the United States—

(1) to preserve and promote extensive, close, and friendly commercial, cultural, and other relations between the people of the United States and the people on Taiwan, as well as the people on the China mainland and all other peoples of the Western Pacific area;

(2) to declare that peace and stability in the area are in the political, security, and economic interests of the United States, and are matters of international concern;

(3) to make clear that the United States decision to establish diplomatic relations with the People's Republic of China rests upon the expectation that the future of Taiwan will be determined by peaceful means;

(4) to consider any effort to determine the future of Taiwan by other than peaceful means, including by boycotts or embargoes, a threat to the peace and security of the Western Pacific area and of grave concern to the United States;

(5) to provide Taiwan with arms of a defensive character; and

(6) to maintain the capacity of the United States to resist any resort to force or other forms of coercion that would jeopardize the security, or the social or economic system, of the people on Taiwan.

(c) Nothing contained in this Act shall contravene the interest of the United States in human rights, especially with respect to the human rights of all the approximately eighteen million inhabitants of Taiwan. The preservation and enhancement of the human rights of all the people on Taiwan are hereby reaffirmed as objectives of the United States.

IMPLEMENTATION OF UNITED STATES POLICY WITH REGARD TO TAIWAN

SEC. 3. (a) In furtherance of the policy set forth in section 2 of this Act, the United States will make available to Taiwan such defense articles and defense services in such quantity as may be necessary to enable Taiwan to maintain a sufficient self-defense capability.

(b) The President and the Congress shall determine the nature and quantity of such defense articles and services based solely upon their judgment of the needs of Taiwan, in accordance with procedures established by law. Such determination of Taiwan's defense needs shall include review by United States military authorities in connection with recommendations to the President and the Congress.

(c) The President is directed to inform the Congress promptly of any threat to the security or the social or economic system of the people on Taiwan and any danger to the interests of the United States arising therefrom. The President and the Congress shall determine, in accordance with constitutional processes, appropriate action by the United States in response to any such danger.

APPLICATION OF LAWS;
INTERNATIONAL AGREEMENTS

SEC. 4. (a) The absence of diplomatic relations or recognition shall not affect the application of the laws of the United States with respect to Taiwan, and the laws of the United States shall apply with respect to Taiwan in the manner that the laws of the United States applied with respect to Taiwan prior to January 1, 1979.

(b) The application of subsection (a) of this section shall include, but shall not be limited to, the following:

(1) Whenever the laws of the United States refer or relate to foreign countries, nations, states, governments, or similar entities, such terms shall include and such laws shall apply with such respect to Taiwan.

(2) Whenever authorized by or pursuant to the laws of the United States to conduct or carry out programs, transactions, or other relations with respect to foreign countries, nations, states, governments, or similar entities, the President or any agency of the United States Government is authorized to conduct and carry out, in accordance with section 6 of this Act, such programs, transactions, and other relations with respect to Taiwan (including, but not limited to, the performance of services for the United States through contracts with commercial entities on Taiwan), in accordance with the applicable laws of the United States.

(3)(A) The absence of diplomatic relations and recognition with respect to Taiwan shall not abrogate, infringe, modify, deny, or otherwise affect in any way any rights or obligations (including but not limited to those involving contracts, debts, or property interests of any kind) under the laws of the United States heretofore or hereafter acquired by or with respect to Taiwan.

(B) For all purposes under the laws of the United States, including actions in any court in the United States, recognition of the People's Republic of China shall not affect in any way the ownership of or other rights or interests in properties, tangible and intangible, and other things of value, owned or held on or prior to December 31, 1978, or thereafter acquired or earned by the governing authorities on Taiwan.

(4) Whenever the application of the laws of the United States depends upon the law that is or was applicable on Taiwan or compliance therewith, the law applied by the people on Taiwan shall be considered the applicable law for that purpose.

(5) Nothing in this Act, nor the facts of the President's action in extending diplomatic recognition to the People's Republic of China, the absence of diplomatic relations between the people on Taiwan and the United States, or the lack of recognition by the United States, and attendant circumstances thereto, shall be construed in any administrative or judicial proceeding as a basis for any United States Government agency, commission, or department to make a finding of fact or determination of law, under the Atomic Energy Act of 1954 and the Nuclear Non-Proliferation Act of 1978, to deny an export license application or to revoke an existing export license for nuclear exports to Taiwan.

(6) For purposes of the Immigration and Nationality Act, Taiwan may be treated in the manner specified in the first sentence of section 202(b) of that Act.

(7) The capacity of Taiwan to sue and be sued in courts in the United States, in accordance with the laws of the United States, shall not be abrogated, infringed, modified, denied, or otherwise affected in any way by the absence of diplomatic relations or recognition.

(8) No requirement, whether expressed or implied, under the laws of the United States with respect to maintenance of diplomatic relations or recognition shall be applicable with respect to Taiwan.

(c) For all purposes, including actions in any court in the United States, the Congress approves the continuation in force of all treaties and other international agreements, including multilateral conventions, entered into by the United States and the governing authorities on Taiwan recognized by the United States as the Republic of China prior to January 1, 1979, and in force between them on December 31, 1978, unless and until terminated in accordance with law.

(d) Nothing in this Act may be construed as a basis for supporting the exclusion or expulsion of Taiwan from continued membership in any international financial institution or any other international organization.

OVERSEAS PRIVATE INVESTMENT CORPORATION

SEC. 5. (a) During the three-year period beginning on the date of enactment of this Act, the $1,000 per capita income restriction in insurance, clause (2) of the second undesignated paragraph of section 231 of the reinsurance, Foreign Assistance Act of 1961 shall not restrict the activities of the Overseas Private Investment Corporation in determining whether to provide any insurance, reinsurance, loans, or guaranties with respect to investment projects on Taiwan.

(b) Except as provided in subsection (a) of this section, in issuing insurance, reinsurance, loans, or guaranties with respect to investment projects on Taiwan, the Overseas Private Insurance Corporation shall apply the same criteria as those applicable in other parts of the world.

THE AMERICAN INSTITUTE OF TAIWAN

SEC. 6. (a) Programs, transactions, and other relations conducted or carried out by the President or any agency of the United States Government with respect to Taiwan shall, in the manner and to the extent directed by the President, be conducted and carried out by or through–

(1) The American Institute in Taiwan, a nonprofit corporation incorporated under the laws of the District of Columbia, or

(2) such comparable successor nongovernmental entity as the President may designate, (hereafter in this Act referred to as the "Institute").

(b) Whenever the President or any agency of the United States Government is authorized or required by or pursuant to the laws of the United States to enter into, perform, enforce, or have in force an agreement or transaction relative to Taiwan, such agreement or transaction shall be entered into, performed, and enforced, in the manner and to the extent directed by the President, by or through the Institute.

(c) To the extent that any law, rule, regulation, or ordinance of the District of Columbia, or of any State or political subdivision thereof in which the Institute is incorporated or doing business, impedes or otherwise interferes with the performance of the functions of the Institute pursuant to this Act; such law, rule, regulation, or ordinance shall be deemed to be preempted by this Act.

SERVICES BY THE INSTITUTE TO UNITED STATES CITIZENS ON TAIWAN

SEC. 7. (a) The Institute may authorize any of its employees on Taiwan–

(1) to administer to or take from any person an oath, affirmation, affidavit, or deposition, and to perform any notarial act which any notary public is required or authorized by law to perform within the United States;

(2) To act as provisional conservator of the personal estates of deceased United States citizens; and

(3) to assist and protect the interests of United States persons by performing other acts such as are authorized to be performed outside the United States for consular purposes by such laws of the United States as the President may specify.

(b) Acts performed by authorized employees of the Institute under this section shall be valid, and of like force and effect within the United States, as if performed by any other person authorized under the laws of the United States to perform such acts.

TAX EXEMPT STATUS OF THE INSTITUTE

SEC. 8. (a) The Institute, its property, and its income are exempt from all taxation now or hereafter imposed by the United States (except to the extent that section 11(a)(3) of this Act requires the imposition of taxes imposed under chapter 21 of the Internal Revenue Code of 1954, relating to the Federal Insurance Contributions Act) or by State or local taxing authority of the United States.

(b) For purposes of the Internal Revenue Code of 1954, the Institute shall be treated as an organization described in sections 170(b)(1)(A), 170(c), 2055(a), 2106(a)(2)(A), 2522(a), and 2522(b).

FURNISHING PROPERTY AND SERVICES TO AND OBTAINING SERVICES FROM THE INSTITUTE

SEC. 9. (a) Any agency of the United States Government is authorized to sell, loan, or lease property (including interests therein) to, and to perform administrative and technical support functions and services for the operations of, the Institute upon such terms and conditions as the President may direct. Reimbursements to agencies under this subsection shall be credited to the current applicable appropriation of the agency concerned.

(b) Any agency of the United States Government is authorized to acquire and accept services from the Institute upon such terms and conditions as the President may direct. Whenever the President determines it to be in furtherance of the purposes of this Act, the procurement of services by such agencies from the Institute may be effected without regard to such laws of the United States normally applicable to the acquisition of services by such agencies as the President may specify by Executive order.

(c) Any agency of the United States Government making funds available to the Institute in accordance with this Act shall make arrangements with the Institute for the Comptroller General of the United States to have access to the books and records of the Institute and the opportunity to audit the operations of the Institute.

TAIWAN INSTRUMENTALITY

SEC. 10. (a) Whenever the President or any agency of the United States Government is authorized or required by or pursuant to the laws of the United States to render or provide to or to receive or accept from Taiwan, any performance, communication, assurance, undertaking, or other action, such action shall, in the manner and to the extent directed by the President, be rendered or provided to, or received or accepted from, an instrumentality established by Taiwan which the President determines has the necessary authority under the laws applied by the people on Taiwan to provide assurances and take other actions on behalf of Taiwan in accordance with this Act.

(b) The President is requested to extend to the instrumentality established by Taiwan the same number of offices and complement of personnel as were previously operated in the United States by the governing authorities on Taiwan recognized as the Republic of China prior to January 1, 1979.

(c) Upon the granting by Taiwan of comparable privileges and immunities with respect to the Institute and its appropriate personnel, the President is authorized to extend with respect to the Taiwan instrumentality and its appropriate personnel, such privileges and immunities (subject to appropriate conditions and obligations) as may be necessary for the effective performance of their functions.

SEPARATION OF GOVERNMENT PERSONNEL
FOR EMPLOYMENT WITH THE INSTITUTE

SEC. 11. (a)(1) Under such terms and conditions as the President may direct, any agency of the United States Government may separate from Government service for a specified period any officer or employee of that agency who accepts employment with the Institute.

(2) An officer or employee separated by an agency under paragraph (1) of this subsection for employment with the Institute shall be entitled upon termination of such employment to reemployment or reinstatement with such agency (or a successor agency) in an appropriate position with the attendant rights, privileges, and benefits the officer or employee would have had or acquired had he or she not been so separated, subject to such time period and other conditions as the President may prescribe.

(3) An officer or employee entitled to reemployment or reinstatement rights under paragraph (2) of this subsection shall, while continuously employed by the Institute with no break in continuity of service, continue to participate in any benefit program in which such officer or employee was participating prior to employment by the Institute, including programs for compensation for job-related death, injury, or illness; programs for health and life insurance; programs for annual, sick, and other statutory leave; and programs for retirement under any system established by the laws of the United States; except that employment with the Institute shall be the basis for participation in such programs only to the extent that employee deductions and employer contributions, as required, in payment for such participation for the period of employment with the Institute, are currently deposited in the program's or system's fund or depository. Death or retirement of any such officer or employee during approved service with the Institute and prior to reemployment or reinstatement shall be considered a death in or retirement from Government service for purposes of any employee or survivor benefits acquired by reason of service with an agency of the United States Government.

(4) Any officer or employee of an agency of the United States Government who entered into service with the Institute on approved leave of absence without pay prior to the enactment of this Act shall receive the benefits of this section for the period of such service.

(b) Any agency of the United States Government employing alien personnel on Taiwan may transfer such personnel, with accrued allowances, benefits, and rights, to the Institute without a break in service for purposes of retirement and other benefits, including continued participation in any system established by the laws of the United States for the retirement of employees in which the alien was participating prior to the transfer to the Institute, except that employment with the Institute shall be creditable for retirement purposes only to the extent that employee deductions and employer contributions as required, in payment for such participation for the period of employment with the Institute, are currently deposited in the system's fund or depository.

(c) Employees of the Institute shall not be employees of the United States and, in representing the Institute, shall be exempt from section 207 of title 18, United States Code.

(d)(1) For purposes of sections 911 and 913 of the Internal Revenue Code of 1954, amounts paid by the Institute to its employees shall not be treated as earned income. Amounts received by employees of the Institute shall not be included in gross income, and shall be exempt from taxation, to the extent that they are equivalent to amounts received by civilian officers and employees of the Government of the United States as allowances and benefits which are exempt from taxation under section 912 of such Code.

(2) Except to the extent required by subsection (a)(3) of this section, service performed in the employ of the Institute shall not constitute employment for purposes of chapter 21 of such Code and title II of the Social Security Act.

REPORTING REQUIREMENT

SEC. 12. (a) The Secretary of State shall transmit to the Congress the text of any agreement to which the Institute is a party. However, any such agreement the immediate public disclosure of which would, in the opinion of the President, be prejudicial to the national security of the United States shall not be so transmitted to the Congress but shall be transmitted to the Committee on Foreign Relations of the Senate and the Committee on Foreign Affairs of the House of Representatives under an appropriate injunction of secrecy to be removed only upon due notice from the President.

(b) For purposes of subsection (a), the term "agreement" includes-

(1) any agreement entered into between the Institute and the governing authorities on Taiwan or the instrumentality established by Taiwan; and
(2) any agreement entered into between the Institute and an agency of the United States Government.

(c) Agreements and transactions made or to be made by or through the Institute shall be subject to the same congressional notification, review, and approval requirements and procedures as if such agreements and transactions were made by or through the agency of the United States Government on behalf of which the Institute is acting.

(d) During the two-year period beginning on the effective date of this Act, the Secretary of State shall transmit to the Speaker of the House and Senate House of Representatives and the Committee on Foreign Relations of the Senate, every six months, a report describing and reviewing economic relations between the United States and Taiwan, noting any interference with normal commercial relations.

RULES AND REGULATIONS

SEC. 13. The President is authorized to prescribe such rules and regulations as he may deem appropriate to carry out the purposes of this Act. During the three-year period beginning on the effective date of this Act, such rules and regulations shall be transmitted promptly to the Speaker of the House of Representatives and to the Committee on Foreign Relations of the Senate. Such action shall not, however, relieve the Institute of the responsibilities placed upon it by this Act.

CONGRESSIONAL OVERSIGHT

SEC. 14. (a) The Committee on Foreign Affairs of the House of Representatives, the Committee on Foreign Relations of the Senate, and other appropriate committees of the Congress shall monitor-

(1) the implementation of the provisions of this Act;
(2) the operation and procedures of the Institute;
(3) the legal and technical aspects of the continuing relationship between the United States and Taiwan; and
(4) the implementation of the policies of the United States concerning security and cooperation in East Asia.

(b) Such committees shall report, as appropriate, to their respective Houses on the results of their monitoring.

DEFINITIONS

SEC. 15. For purposes of this Act-

(1) the term "laws of the United States" includes any statute, rule, regulation, ordinance, order, or judicial rule of decision of the United States or any political subdivision thereof; and

(2) the term "Taiwan" includes, as the context may require, the islands of Taiwan and the Pescadores, the people on those islands, corporations and other entities and associations created or organized under the laws applied on those islands, and the governing authorities on Taiwan recognized by the United States as the Republic of China prior to January 1, 1979, and any successor governing authorities (including political subdivisions, agencies, and instrumentalities thereof).

AUTHORIZATION OF APPROPRIATIONS

SEC. 16. In addition to funds otherwise available to carry out the provisions of this Act, there are authorized to be appropriated to the Secretary of State for the fiscal year 1980 such funds as may be necessary to carry out such provisions. Such funds are authorized to remain available until expended.

SEVERABILITY OF PROVISIONS

SEC. 17. If any provision of this Act or the application thereof to any person or circumstance is held invalid, the remainder of the Act and the application of such provision to any other person or circumstance shall not be affected thereby.

EFFECTIVE DATE

SEC. 18. This Act shall be effective as of January 1, 1979.

Approved April 10, 1979.

Source: United States. Congress. Conference Committees 1979. Taiwan Relations Act: Conference Report to Accompany H.R. 2479. (Washington, DC: U.S. Government Printing Office), 1979.

Appendix C

The Text of the Six Assurances from the U.S. to Taiwan (1982)

Cable: Assurances for Taiwan
Drafted August 17, 1982
From: Secretary of State George Shultz
To: American Institute of Taiwan Director James Lilley

Concerning Taiwan's request to make public President Reagan's assurances,

—You should urge Chien
—to say in their public statement that, based on information received through appropriate channels, it is their understanding that the U.S. side:
—Has not agreed to set a date for ending arms sales to Taiwan
—Has not agreed to consult with the PRC on arms sales to Taiwan
—Will not play mediation role between Taipei and Beijing
—Has not agreed to revise the Taiwan Relations Act
—Has not altered its position regarding sovereignty over Taiwan. FYI: If asked why we have modified the statement on sovereignty, you should explain that we have consistently used this terminology in our public statements.
—Will not exert pressure on Taiwan to enter into negotiations with the PRC.

In their statement, there should of course be no linkage to President Reagan.
  You should tell Chien that we will also make these points in John Holdridge's public testimony tomorrow (Tuesday) before the SFRC.

Source: Declassified Cables: Taiwan Arms Sales & Six Assurances (1982), American Institute in Taiwan

Appendix D

Taiwan Trade with U.S. and PRC (2000–2021)

Taiwan Total Trade with the US and China (Goods)

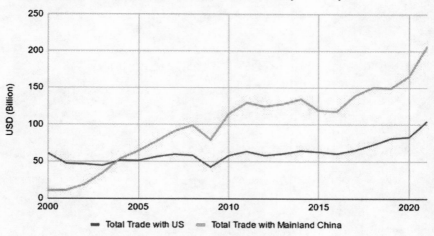

Figure D.1 *Source:* Ministry of Finance of the Republic of China.

Taiwan Exports to the US and China (Goods)

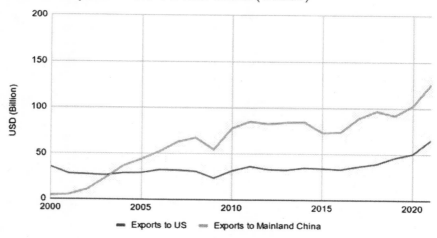

Figure D.2   *Source:* Ministry of Finance of the Republic of China.

Taiwan Imports from the US and China (Goods)

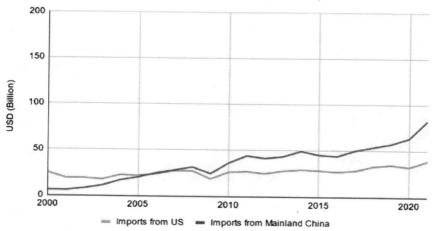

Figure D.3   *Source:* Ministry of Finance of the Republic of China.

Appendix E

GCTF Workshops

Date	Program Name
August 12–14, 2015	Workshop on Molecular Diagnosis of MERS-CoV
December 7–8, 2015	International Conference on Dengue Prevention and Control
March 11, 2016	Workshop on Enhancing Prosperity and Opportunity for Women in Asia-Pacific Region
April 13–15, 2016	Workshop on Laboratory Diagnosis for Zika
June 16–17, 2016	Conference on Energy Efficiency in Asia
October 5–11, 2016	Workshop on E-Commerce Facilitation
April 25–28, 2017	Workshop on Laboratory Diagnosis for Mosquito-borne Viral Diseases (Dengue, Zika, and Chikungunya)
July 5–7, 2017	Workshop on Humanitarian Assistance and Disaster Relief
November 14–16, 2017	Workshop on Building a Bright Future for Women Entrepreneurs in Tech
December 4–8, 2017	Workshop on Enhancing Broadband Penetration and Bridging the Digital Divide in the Asia-Pacific
April 23–26, 2018	Workshop on Laboratory Diagnosis of Enteroviruses
August 14–15, 2018	Workshop on Combating Transnational Crime and Forensic Science
October 18–19, 2018	Workshop on Defending Democracy Through Media Literacy
December 10–12, 2018	Workshop on Achieving 50-50: Empowering Women Leaders in the Indo-Pacific Region
December 14, 2018	Workshop on Humanitarian Assistance and Disaster Relief

(Continued)

March 26–28, 2019	Workshop on Anti-Corruption in the Public and Private Sectors (co-hosted with Japan)
April 16–18, 2019	Workshop on Women's Economic Empowerment (co-hosted with Japan)
April 30–May 4, 2019	Workshop on the Programmatic Management of Drug-Resistant Tuberculosis (co-hosted with Japan)
May 28–31, 2019	Workshop on Network Security and Emerging Technologies (co-hosted with Japan)
September 10–11, 2019	Workshop on Defending Democracy Through Media Literacy II (co-hosted with Japan and Sweden)
September 29–October 2, 2019	International Austronesian Languages Revitalization Forum* (co-hosted with Japan)
November 20–22, 2019	Workshop on Good Energy Governance in the Indo-Pacific (co-hosted with Japan and Australia)
April 29, 2020	Online Workshop on Combating COVID-19 Disinformation and Strengthening Media Literacy in the Indo-Pacific (co-hosted with Japan)
June 24, 2020	Online Workshop on Preparing for a Potential Second Wave of Coronavirus (co-hosted with Japan)
September 9, 2020	Online Workshop on Helping Countries Deploy Digital Tools to Respond to COVID-19 in the Western Hemisphere (co-hosted with Japan and Guatemala)
September 29, 2020	Virtual GCTF on Advancing International Development through Public Partnership
October 15–16, 2020	Workshop on Trade Secrets and Digital Piracy Prevention
October 28, 2020	Online Workshop Combatting COVID-19 related Crimes (co-hosted with Japan and Australia)
November 3–10, 2020	Online Workshop on Sustainable Material Management – Solution to Marine Debris (co-hosted with Japan and The Netherlands)
December 15, 2020	Joint Statement on the 2020 Global Cooperation and Training Framework (GCTF) Joint Committee (co-hosted with Japan)
March 10, 2021	Building the Resilience of Nations and Communities to Disasters (co-hosted with Japan and the UK)
April 14, 2021	Supply chain restructuring and SME financing (co-hosted with Japan and the EU)
May 18, 2021	Online Workshop COVID-19 Vaccine Roll-out: Experiences and Challenges (co-hosted with Japan, the UK, and Australia)
May 26, 2021	Online Workshop GCTF Workshop on Anti-Money Laundering (co-hosted with Japan and Australia)
June 17–18, 2021	Online Workshop New Developments in IP Protection and Combating Digital Infringement
August 12, 2021	Online Workshop GCTF Virtual Conference—Green Energy: A Way to a Clean and Sustainable Earth
September 9–10, 2021	Online Workshop the Future of Work in a Post COVID-19 Economic Recovery
September 24, 2021	Online Workshop Building Disaster Resilience at Global and National Levels (co-hosted with Japan, Australia, and the UK)

(Continued)

September 29, 2021	Online Workshop GCTF on Building Resilience and Accelerating the SDGs through Technology
October 6, 2021	Online Workshop Combating Cybercrime through International Law Enforcement Collaboration
October 27, 2021	Online Workshop 2021 GCTF Virtual Conference on Road to Parity: Women's Participation in Public Life (co-host Japan, Australia, and Canada)
November 4–5, 2021	Online Workshop GCTF Virtual Conference on the Rights of Persons with Disabilities (co-hosted with Japan, Australia, and Israel)
November 9–10, 2021	Online Workshop 2021 Global Cooperation and Training Framework (GCTF) Virtual Conference on Defending Democracy Through Media Literacy III (co-hosted with Japan, the UK, and Slovakia)
November 19, 2021	Taiwan, the United States, and St. Kitts and Nevis staged the First GCTF-Affiliated Workshop on "Climate-Smart Agriculture: Building Sustainability and Resilience of Agriculture" in the Caribbean
December 3, 2021	GCTF Virtual Conference on Women's Empowerment (co-hosted with the U.S. Embassy in the Kingdom of Eswatini)
December 17, 2021	2021 GCTF Joint Committee Meeting (co-hosted with the U.S., Japan, and Australia)
February 25, 2022	GCTF Hybrid Workshop on Collaboration on Digital Healthcare; the first GCTF event held in the Indian Subcontinent (co-hosted with U.S. Embassy and Consulates in India and Indian thinktank Voice of Healthcare)
March 22, 2022	GCTF Online Workshop on Combating Digital Crimes (co-hosted with Ministry of Foreign Affairs, Ministry of Justice Investigation Bureau, American Institute in Taiwan, Japan-Taiwan Exchange Association, Australia Office, and Slovak Economic and Cultural Office in Taipei)
May 24–25, 2022	GCTF Hybrid Workshop on Ending Gender-based Violence (co-hosted with Executive Yuan [Department of Gender Equality], Ministry of Foreign Affairs, American Institute in Taiwan, Japan-Taiwan Exchange Association, Australian Office in Taipei, British Office Taipei, Canadian Trade Office in Taipei, European Economic and Trade Office, and Israel Economic and Cultural Office in Taipei.)
June 17, 2022	GCTF Online Workshop on Efforts and Development on Eliminating Hepatitis C (co-host American Institute in Taiwan, Ministry of Foreign Affairs, Ministry of Health and Welfare, Japan-Taiwan Exchange Association, and Australia Office Taipei)
August 26, 2022	GCTF-Affiliated Event – Pursuing Inclusive and Gender-Equal Recovery: Empowering Women in the Post-Pandemic Era (co-hosted with the U.S. and Saint Lucia)
September 27–28, 2022	GCTF Hybrid Workshop on the Challenges and Strategies for the Industrialization of Smart Agriculture (co-hosted with Ministry of Foreign Affairs, American Institute in Taiwan, Japan-Taiwan Exchange Association, Australia Office Taipei, Israel Economic and Cultural Office, and Netherlands Office Taipei)

(Continued)

September 29, 2022	GCTF Hybrid Workshop on Finding Transformative Solutions through Innovative Partnership Mechanisms (co-hosted with Ministry of Foreign Affairs, American Institute in Taiwan, Japan-Taiwan Exchange Association, and Australian Office in Taipei)
September 30, 2022	GCTF Hybrid Seminar on Building a Sustainable Aviation System: Safe and Green. On the sidelines of the 41st ICAO assembly in Montreal, Canada.
October 26, 2022	GCTF Hybrid Workshop on Sustainable Oceans Based on the Rule of Law (co-hosted with American Institute in Taiwan, Ministry of Foreign Affairs, Ocean Affairs Council, Japan-Taiwan Exchange Association, and Australian Office Taipei)
November 21, 2022	GCTF Workshop on Opportunities and Outlooks Under the Trend of Digital Economy

Source: "Global Cooperation and Training Framework (GCTF) Programs," American Institute in Taiwan, https://www.ait.org.tw/our-relationship/global-cooperation-and-training-framework-programs-gctf/. Information current as of December 19, 2022.

Appendix F

A List of U.S. Arms Sales to Taiwan (2008–2022)

Date	Description of Arms Package	US$ Billions
10/03/2008	• (330) Patriot Advanced Capability (PAC)-3 missile defense missiles • (32) UGM-84L sub-launched Harpoon anti-ship missiles • Spare parts for F-5E/F, C-130H, F-16A/B, and IDF aircraft • (182) Javelin anti-armor missiles • Upgrade of (4) E-2T aircraft (Hawkeye 2000 configuration) • (30) AH-64D Apache Longbow attack helicopters	$6.4
01/29/2010	• (114) PAC-3 missile defense missiles • (60) UH-60M Black Hawk utility helicopters • (12) Harpoon Block II anti-ship telemetry (training) missiles • (60) MIDS (follow-on technical support for Po Sheng C4 systems) • (2) Osprey-class mine hunting ships	$6.4
09/21/2011	• Retrofit of (145) F-16A/B fighters, with 176 AESA radars, JDAMs, etc. • Continuation of training of F-16 pilots at Luke Air Force Base • Spare parts for F-16A/B, F-5E/F, C-130H, and IDF aircraft	$5.9
12/16/2015	• (208) Javelin Guided Missiles • (36) Assault Amphibious Vehicles (AAVs) • Taiwan Advanced Tactical Data Link System (TATDLS) and Link-11 Integration • Follow-on life-cycle support to maintain the Multifunctional Information Distribution Systems Low Volume Terminals (MIDS/LVT-1) and Joint Tactical—Information Distribution Systems (JTIDS) previously procured	

(Continued)

Date	Description of Arms Package	US$ Billions
	• Sale, refurbishment, and upgrade of (2) Oliver Hazard Perry-class Frigates (FFG-7) and associated weapons systems • (13) MK 15 Phalanx Block 1B Baseline 2 Close-in Weapons System (CIWS) Guns, upgrade kits, ammunition, and support • (769) TOW 2B Aero, Radio Frequency (RF) Missiles (BGM-71FSeries) • (250) Block I-92F MANPAD Stinger Missiles	$1.7
06/29/2017	• Surveillance Radar Program (SRP) Operations and Maintenance support • (50) AGM-88B High-Speed Anti-Radiation Missiles (HARMs) and (10) AGM88B Training HARMs • (16) Standard Missile-2 (SM-2) Block IIIA All-Up Rounds (AUR) and components • (46) MK 48 Mod 6AT Heavyweight Torpedoes (HWT) and support • (168) MK 54 Lightweight Torpedo (LWT) Conversion Kits • (56) AGM-154C Joint-Standoff JSOW Air-to-Ground Missiles • AN/SLQ-32(V)3 Electronic Warfare Systems in support of four (4) ex-KIDD Class (now KEELUNG Class) destroyers	$1.4
09/24/2018	• Blanket order requisitions for stock replenishment supply of standard spare parts, repair/replace of spare parts in support of the F-16, C-130, F-5, IDF, and all other aircraft systems and subsystems	$0.3
04/15/2019	• Continuation of a pilot training program and maintenance/logistics support for F-16 aircraft	$0.5
07/08/2019	• (108) M1A2T Abrams Tanks and related equipment and support • (250) Block I-92F MANPAD Stinger missiles, (4) Block I-92F MANPAD Stinger Fly-to-Buy missiles, and related equipment and support	$2.2
08/20/2019	• (66) F-16C/D Block 70 aircraft and related equipment	$8.0
05/20/2020	• (18) MK-48 Mod6 Advanced Technology (AT) Heavyweight Torpedoes (HWT) and related equipment	$0.2
07/09/2020	• Recertification of Patriot Advanced Capability-3 (PAC-3) missiles	$0.6
10/21/2020	• (11) High Mobility Artillery Rocket Systems (HIMARS) M142 Launchers • (64) Army Tactical Missile Systems (ATACMS) M57 Unitary Missiles • (7) M1152AI High Mobility Multipurpose Wheeled Vehicles (HMMWVs)	

(Continued)

Date	Description of Arms Package	US$ Billions
	• (11) M240B Machine Guns, 7.62MM	$0.4
	• (17) International Field Artillery Tactical Data Systems (IFATDS)	
10/21/2020	• (135) AGM-84H Standoff Land Attack Missile Expanded Response (SLAM-ER) Missiles	$1.0
	• (4) ATM-84H SLAM-ER Telemetry Missiles	
	• (12) CATM-84H Captive Air Training Missiles (CATM)	
10/21/2020	• (6) MS-110 Recce Pods and related equipment	$0.4
	• (3) Transportable Ground Stations	
	• (1) Fixed Ground station	
10/26/2020	• (100) Harpoon Coastal Defense Systems (HCDS) consisting of up to (400) RGM-84L-4 Harpoon Block II Surface Launched Missiles and related equipment	$2.4
	• (4) RTM-84L-4 Harpoon Block II Exercise Missiles	
11/03/2020	• (4) Weapons-Ready MQ-9B Remotely Piloted Aircraft	$0.6
	• (2) Fixed Ground Control Stations	
	• (2) Mobile Ground Control Stations	
	• (14) Embedded Global Positioning System/Inertial Navigations Systems (EGI) with Selective Availability Anti-Spoofing Module (SAASM)	
12/07/2020	• Field Information Communications System (FICS)	$0.3
08/04/2021	• (40) 155mm M109A6 Medium Self-Propelled Howitzer Systems	$0.8
	• (20) M992A2 Field Artillery Ammunition Support Vehicles (FAASV)	
	• (1) Advanced Field Artillery Tactical Data System (AFATDS)	
	• (5) M88A2 Hercules vehicles	
	• (5) M2 Chrysler Mount .50 caliber machine guns	
	• (1,698) multi-option, Precision Guidance Kits (PGK)	
02/07/2022	• (40) 155mm M109A6 Paladin Medium Self-Propelled Howitzer System	$0.1
	• (20) M992A2 Field Artillery Ammunition Support Vehicles (FAASV)	
	• (1) Advanced Field Artillery Tactical Data System (AFATDS)	
	• (5) M88A2 Hercules vehicles	
	• (5) M2 Chrysler Mount	
04/05/2022	• Patriot International Engineering Services Program and Field Surveillance Program	$0.1
06/08/2022	• Patriot Contractor Technical Assistance	$0.1
07/15/2022	• Contractor Technical Assistance Support	$0.1
09/02/2022	• Contract Logistics Support for the Surveillance Radar Program	
	• (60) AGM-84L-1 Harpoon Block II missiles	
	• (4) ATM-84L-1 Harpoon Block II exercise missiles	

(Continued)

Date	Description of Arms Package	US$ Billions
	• (100) AIM-9X Block II Sidewinder tactical missiles • (4) AIM-9X Block II tactical Guidance Units	$1.1
12/06/2022	• Stock replenishment supply of standard spare parts, consumables, and accessories, and repair and replacement support for the F-16, C-130, Indigenous Defense Fighter (IDF), and all other aircraft and systems or subsystems of U.S. origin	$0.3
12/06/2022	• Stock replenishment supply of aircraft non-standard spare parts and related equipment	$0.1
12/06/2022	• (100) Patriot PAC-3 Missile Segment Enhancement (MSE) missiles • Radar and support equipment	$0.9
12/28/2022	• Volcano (vehicle-launched) anti-tank munition-laying systems; M977A4 HEMTT 10-Ton cargo trucks; M87A1 Anti-Tank (AT) munitions; M88 canister training munitions (practice dummy ammunition rounds); M89 training munitions (test ammunition rounds); organic U.S. Army Depot build of Volcano system permanently mounted on M977A4 HEMTT truck; logistics support packages to include spare parts, spare secondary assemblies, tool kits and test equipment; technical manuals; organic depot production, integration and testing; Operator and Maintenance Training; logistics and fielding support; USG technical assistance CONUS and OCONUS to include engineering services, program management, site surveys, facility, logistics and maintenance evaluations; quality assurance and de-processing team; field service representative(s); Repair and Return services; any transportation charges to execute the program; and related elements of logistical and program support	$0.2

Source: "Major Arms Sales," Defense Security Cooperation Agency, https://www.dsca.mil/press-media/major-arms-sales?page=2; and Shirley Kan, "Taiwan: Major U.S. Arms Sales Since 1990, CRS Report No. RL30957" (Washington, D.C.: Congressional Research Service, 2014), https://fas.org/sgp/crs/weapons/RL30957.pdf. Information current as of December 31, 2022.

Appendix G

Map of Taiwan and China

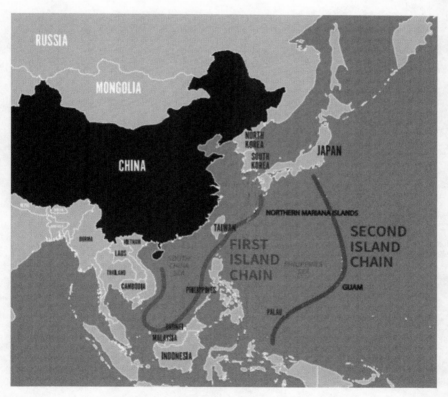

Figure G.1 Map of Taiwan's positioning in Asia's First Island Chain. *Source:* Bonnie S. Glaser, Richard C. Bush, and Michael J. Green, "Toward a Stronger US-Taiwan Relationship." Washington, D.C.: Center for Strategic and International Studies (2020).

Index

About the Authors

Ryan Hass is the Chen-Fu and Cecilia Yen Koo Chair in Taiwan Studies and the Michael H. Armacost Chair in Foreign Policy Studies at the Brookings Institution.

Bonnie Glaser is managing director of the Indo Pacific Program at the German Marshall Fund of the United States.

Richard Bush is author of seven books, including most recently, *Difficult Choices: Taiwan's Quest for Security and the Good Life* (Brookings Press, 2021).